Foreigners In France

Triumphs & Disasters

edited by
Joe & Kerry Laredo

SURVIVAL BOOKS • LONDON • ENGLAND

First published 2004

Survival Books Limited, 1st Floor,
60 St James's Street, London SW1A 1ZN, United Kingdom
☎ +44 (0)20-7493 4244, ▤ +44 (0)20-7491 0605
✉ info@survivalbooks.net
🖳 www.survivalbooks.net
To order books, please refer to page 278.

British Library Cataloguing in Publication Data.
A CIP record for this book is available
from the British Library.
ISBN 1 901130 38 X

Printed and bound in Finland by WS Bookwell Ltd

ACKNOWLEDGEMENTS

Our sincere thanks to all the people whose stories are included in this book as well as to the many others who submitted information for which we unfortunately couldn't find space. Special thanks and our condolences go to Madeleine Keyte, whose husband, Michael, was to have contributed his own story but sadly died before he could write it. We're grateful to Graeme Chesters for his input at the planning stage. A big thank-you is also due to Jim Watson for his superb cartoons and cover design.

TITLES BY SURVIVAL BOOKS

The Alien's Guide To Britain;
The Alien's Guide To France;
The Best Places To Live
In France; The Best Places To
Live In Spain; Buying, Selling &
Letting Property;
Foreigners In France: Triumphs
& Disasters; Foreigners In Spain:
Triumphs & Disasters;
How To Avoid Holiday &
Travel Disasters;
Costa del Sol Lifeline;
Dordogne/Lot Lifeline;
Poitou-Charentes Lifeline;
Renovating & Maintaining Your
French Home; Retiring Abroad;
Rioja And Its Wines;
The Wines Of Spain

Living And Working Series

Abroad; America; Australia;
Britain; Canada; The European
Union; The Far East; France;
Germany; The Gulf States &
Saudi Arabia; Holland, Belgium
& Luxembourg; Ireland; Italy;
London; New Zealand; Spain;
Switzerland

Buying A Home Series

Abroad; Florida;
France; Greece & Cyprus;
Ireland; Italy;
Portugal; Spain

Order forms are on page 278.

ABOUT THE EDITORS

Joe Laredo began working for Survival Books in 1997, having spent the previous decade in the marine industry. He has written and compiled four Survival Books – *The Best Places to Buy a Home in France, Buying a Home in Ireland, Living and Working in Ireland* and *Renovating & Maintaining Your French Home* – and has edited numerous others. He is also responsible for upating *Buying a Home in France* and *Living and Working in France*.

Kerry Laredo joined Survival Books in 2000 to take on the design and layout of the books and has since proofread several Survival titles.

Having moved from England to France in 2001, Kerry and Joe can identify with many of the experiences related in this book, although their own story hasn't been included.

'On n'emporte pas sa patrie à la semelle de ses souliers.'

French proverb

'Wherever you may travel, your shoes will go with you but not your country.'

CONTENTS

STORIES

EDITORS' NOTES

- British English is used throughout, even for those stories which have been told by Americans.
- French words are italicised and an English translation has been given where appropriate.
- The following symbols are used in this book: ☎ (telephone), ▤ (fax), 🖥 (Internet) and ✉ (e-mail).

IMPORTANT NOTE

The stories in this book have been written by the people they relate to and haven't been changed in any material way or factual detail. Only minor amendments have been made in the interest of clarity and readability. Where names are given, these are actual names; where the authors have asked to remain anonymous, this request has been respected.

From the many stories submitted to us for consideration, we chose those that we thought would be the most interesting and instructive to readers and have attempted to include as wide as possible a variety of nationalities, situations and geographical locations. We haven't selected contributors on the basis of any prejudice or bias as to nationality, opinions or any other criteria. Nor has any attempt been made to paint a rosy (or any other kind of) picture of France; there are positive and negative opinions, with which the editors and publisher don't necessarily agree.

Any information or advice offered by contributors has been provided in good faith, but it shouldn't be used as the basis of any major decisions or irrevocable action. For authoritative and unbiased information, you're recommended to obtain the latest edition of a book such as Survival Books' *The Best Places to Buy a Home in France, Buying a Home in France* or *Living and Working in France* (see page 278). **Nevertheless, you shouldn't believe everything you read, and all information should be checked with an independent and reliable source.**

INTRODUCTION

Moving to a foreign country can be traumatic, but it can also be an exciting and life-enhancing experience. The people who have told their stories in this book have had successes as well as failures and offer advice to others contemplating life as an expatriate.

As several of them have said, living in France isn't always the idyllic dream that's conjured up in television programmes and travelogue books. France – and the French – can be challenging, difficult and even downright *impossible*. "Life has its ups and downs, no matter where you are," as one contributor puts it. Nevertheless, the majority of people who have made the move are glad they did and, given a second chance, would do so again.

If you're thinking of going to live in France, you will need to obtain the latest edition of an authoritative book such as Survival Books' *Living and Working in France, Buying a Home in France* and *The Best Places to Buy a Home in France* (see page 278) for the essential information that will help you avoid pitfalls and prevent your dream turning into a nightmare. *Foreigners in France: Triumphs & Disasters* is a vital companion to those volumes, giving personal and emotional accounts of life in France, which will instruct, amuse, surprise, shock and – hopefully – inspire you.

Of course, people's experiences are unique, and generalisations aren't always valid. If you move to France, you will no doubt have different experiences, but these stories may help you to anticipate and overcome the obstacles and set-backs you encounter. 'A problem shared is a problem halved' goes the saying; when you realise that your difficulties have been faced by others, you will find them easier to cope with.

The French don't wish people 'luck', they wish them 'courage', which is a far more positive attribute with which to approach a life-changing experience.

Bon courage!

Joe & Kerry Laredo
July 2004

In Search Of Comfort

Roger and Julia Moss moved from rural England
to rural France and found the transition relatively
straightforward. Setting up a business, however, was
more complicated and costly than they had imagined.

Although we were both born in the UK, our lives had for some years been focused on France, not only on a professional level but also as a means of spending time in what had come to feel like a more comfortable environment. Whilst we had never actually lived in France, the more time we spent here the more it had come to feel like home. Eventually, after years of living in a small moorland village in Cornwall and reaching what is considered to be middle age, we sensed that it was time for a change.

We already had a good knowledge of France and began looking in the Poitou-Charentes region because of its sunny climate, good communications (road, rail, air), affordable property and southern architectural style. Property prices and distance from the UK meant that, for now at least, our first love – Provence – wasn't an option.

The Ideal Home

We found just the home we had hoped for during autumn 1999 and moved here permanently in November 2002. Visiting another country is one thing, but actually buying a chunk of it feels like putting down roots and so changes everything. In any case, the house was always intended to be a permanent home rather than simply a base for holidays. But first we had a small mountain of DIY to climb just to make it habitable.

So began a surreal period of juggling day-to-day commitments in the UK while sneaking back to the house whenever possible for DIY blitzes. Somehow we always achieved less than planned, but each attempt brought us a step closer to our dream, plus a gradual familiarity with our new surroundings.

The village itself, little more than a cosy huddle of farmhouses, cottages and stone barns set amid fields and forests, retains the air of a modest farming community. It is also currently home to a dozen or so families. On our arrival we were the only British owners, although the figure has since risen to four (two being resident). We were all preceded, perhaps unsurprisingly, by a Dutch couple, who have had a second home here for many years.

The community turned out to be all we could have wished for. When we first set eyes on the village, we sensed an atmosphere of well-being – relaxed but far from comatose. Our previous rural lifestyle had taught us that it takes people to make a healthy community, and all the vital signs here were encouraging. Our instincts proved well founded, and our neighbours are friendly and helpful, welcoming and supportive. They are also avid gardeners, evidenced by the blaze of summer colour around the village and the bundles of vegetables which appear frequently and unexpectedly on top of our garden walls; around here people still like to share the good things in life.

Not that everything revolves solely around the rural idyll. For an occasional much-needed energy boost in dramatically more vibrant surroundings we have Poitiers as our nearest city, another plus factor when we chose our location.

> *the customs officials at either end merely waved the van through without so much as a glance at the contents*

If regular visits before severing ties with the UK enabled us to get to know our neighbours and new surroundings without undue pressure, the move itself was not entirely stress-free. We had booked a box van, driver and helper well in advance to arrive on the morning of departure day, allowing us plenty of time to make an 11.15pm ferry from Plymouth. In theory.

However, an unforeseen hitch meant that the van didn't arrive until after lunch, by which time the calm, sunny morning had given way to storms. As a result, what remained of the contents of our tiny cottage and distant garden shed were loaded into the van while being lashed by moorland rain and gales.

After cramming in the final items in near-total darkness, we enjoyed a relaxing meal with friends nearby, finally rolling out of the village without a backward glance; we were relieved to know that we were finally ending our unsettling double-life in France and the UK, the latter having long ceased to feel like home. We followed the van in our car, laden with more valuable and breakable items plus Jessie, our aged Springer spaniel. Blind and almost deaf, she slept peacefully on the back seat throughout the overnight journey, blissfully unaware that she was also embarking upon a new adventure. She eventually roused herself, briefly, in Roscoff, then settled down once again for more doggy dreams.

The formalities of her emigration had been simple: her microchip was scanned and the export licence verified at the ferry check-in. Our possessions entered France even more smoothly. Despite the detailed inventory we had put together, the customs officials at either end merely waved the van through without so much as a glance at the contents.

After an uneventful run down from the ferry port, we arrived at our new home and began unloading all our worldly goods, manageable items being passed through a large window which opened onto a little-used lane. The hired help was invaluable, not least since it removed from us the chore of driving the van back to the UK. Our substantial four-bedroom traditional farmhouse swallowed the contents of our two-up, two-down Cornish cottage with ease, as well as the items which we had previously brought across by car or purchased here. Had it not done so, we had our pick of four stone-built barns for further storage. Life had certainly changed.

Destruction & Restoration

Buying the house had been pretty straightforward, thanks to our agents having translated all documents and attended the final signing with us at the *notaire's* office. However, between payment of the deposit and completion, two of our outbuildings were damaged by the unprecedented gales which hit France as the millennium was dawning.

Two large doors were torn from one barn and smashed, while almost the entire roof was ripped from another. It was at this point that we learned that the vendor's property insurance had lapsed. As it turned out, the agents calmly appointed a contractor to repair the damage, the *notaire* then deducting the cost of repairs from the proceeds of the sale. The agent also arranged for both water and electricity services to be connected from the day of completion.

While the electricity suppliers' efficient team scaled a tall pole to connect the power with a flash-looking cherry-picker, the water company had sent a large man on a small moped to turn on the water. Finding the meter corroded beyond redemption, he promised to return the following day with a replacement, asking slightly sheepishly if we were planning to spend the night at the house. Our reply of *"Oui – en principe . . ."* produced a firm handshake and a sympathetic smile.

you are almost certain to have a long wait for French specialists with glowing reputations

So far the only minor (and not entirely unforeseen) setback has been having to completely re-roof another of our outbuildings after the aged timbers had begun to disintegrate, eating into funds we had set aside for working on our home. The previous owners of the house had done all the major work, including re-roofing, re-plumbing, installing a septic tank and dividing the former *grenier* area upstairs into individual rooms. What remained was all the finishing off, installing a fitted kitchen, and replacing ground-floor windows, front doors and shutters. The exterior rendering and stonework was in poor condition and currently awaits the attentions of a local mason.

While we have tackled all interior finishing and decorating ourselves, we have resolved to use registered French artisans, wherever possible, to tackle any work requiring traditional skills and experience in working with local architectural styles.

For example, the passage of time and a long period of neglect meant that some doors and windows were providing an all-too-easy way in for both rain and draughts. Their successors, in solid French oak, were made and fitted by a joiner from the next village, replicating the style and proportions of the originals. The cost was comparable to that of made-to-measure factory units, and they help maintain the all-important original character of the house.

For much the same reason, we have recuperated cut stone from a ruined building behind the main house for our mason to use in some restoration work for us (he will also be applying traditional lime mortar to two tired-looking facades).

Another factor in the choice of artisans is the personal recommendation of our French neighbours, who can show us the high standard of similar work already carried out nearby. The only downside is that you are almost certain to have a long wait for French specialists with glowing reputations. We waited almost a year for our windows – around half the delay so far experienced by one of our French neighbours. If you too can wait, though, you will eventually get a job well done, backed by a meaningful guarantee.

Language & Red Tape

Discussing building work can be a challenge for anyone unfamiliar with the arcane vocabulary of the building trade. No surprises there, perhaps, just as long as you are *au fait* with local dialects (there are times when a basic grounding in *patois* wouldn't go amiss).

Our French was passable when we moved over and doubtless continues to improve, although the more you learn, the more you sense your own shortcomings. This is the tough bit. Repetition in everyday situations helps a lot, but you can still run out of steam in more formal or technical situations. We haven't taken lessons here, but French friends, local and national TV and radio programmes, plus listening to everyday conversations all keep us learning.

Embarrassing misunderstandings have so far been harmless, e.g. the time when sloppy pronunciation thwarted my attempt to say that what I lacked most was grammar (*grammaire*). Once we had both realised that I was not, in fact, missing my French grandmother (*grand-mère*), my interlocutor responded with an amused smile, followed by a sympathetic shrug. It is easily done.

Understanding and being understood are important to us. We began working together well before relocating to France, but the work was already focused here. (Roger is a travel writer and photographer specialising in France, and Julia does the research and looks after the administration side of things.) We were both self-employed and naïvely intended to do much the same here in France while enjoying the obvious geographical advantages of being on the spot. In practice it wouldn't be that simple, thanks to the impenetrable wall of bureaucracy which greeted our attempts to slot into the French system.

In the UK, you can be self-employed in several allied activities, whereas in France, your professional activity determines the relevant organisations with whom you must register for your health cover, pension contributions, etc. You can register with only one type of profession. Since photography and journalism fell unexpectedly into quite different categories, we had no choice but to create a limited company (*Société à Responsabilité Limitée* or *SARL*) with clearly specified activities, and for one of us to work for that company.

Even our English-speaking French accountant couldn't believe the complexity of all this. And we aren't there yet. Social payments are so much higher here than in the UK that it has proved prohibitively costly for both of us to be employed and making contributions. Until we are more established Julia must remain, reluctantly, non-employed.

The eventual costs of winding up tax affairs in the UK and establishing the *SARL* were impossible to foresee. In order to establish the new company we were required to deposit a minimum of €6,500 of working capital, some of which was in the form of fixed assets. The remainder, however, was a substantial sum deposited in a new business bank account, which was then frozen until the company's registration was completed. Legal announcements and accountant's fees totalled a further €2,000.

More bizarrely, Roger couldn't apply for his *carte de séjour* until he had formal proof of his employment status, yet he couldn't be the manager of the company and resident in France without possessing one . . . Eventually we had to agree to our previous UK address appearing on the official documents, while waiting for the vital *carte de séjour* (no longer required for EU citizens) to arrive. It hasn't yet. We hope that such needlessly obstructive bureaucracy is now mostly behind us, and that we will be able to continue and diversify our work. While we maintain our UK clients, we have begun building new relationships here in France, using our expertise in the UK tourism marketplace and our expanding picture library.

Running the business from home is a convenient and flexible way of working, although the *bureau* (being no longer a bedroom) is now taxed separately from the rest of the house. How much this amounts to remains to be seen. Our plans include launching a website and producing a series of illustrated books on French themes. Since this is in addition to our magazine work, we have our hands pretty full.

Now that we are finally in the system, health and retirement payments (*cotisations*) are a formidable ongoing expense, with obligatory regular payments to three organisations: URSSAF (social security), AVA (Assurances Vieillesse des Artisans) for retirement provision, and RAM (Réunion des Assureurs Maladie), which provides health cover for professional non-salaried workers. RAM issues the all-important *carte vitale*, which entitles the holder to reimbursement of sixty to seventy per cent of the cost of most medical care (being officially non-employed, Julia had to provide proof of marriage and residence to get her *carte vitale*, which is currently funded by Roger's contributions).

> *with time genuine friendships do develop, regardless of nationality*

Although we were surprised, like other working friends, at the levels of pension and health costs, we remain convinced that the system is ultimately fair and performs well, not least through being adequately funded.

French Life

We get on well with our neighbours, some of whom have become valued friends, and we have made many other friends in France (not least through our work), although doing so from scratch in rural surroundings involves making an effort – entertaining at home, for example.

French villages don't have a lively local pub to provide a social hub for meeting people, as might be the case in the UK. Rural French bars (assuming you have one nearby) are often quiet and can be rather basic in the comfort department, so the atmosphere is entirely different from the friendly British pub. Initially, we spent time with English-speaking people with whom we otherwise had little in common, but with time genuine friendships do develop, regardless of nationality.

Social occasions organised by the commune have given us relaxed ways of getting to know other local people, who have been welcoming and often go out of their way to break the ice and introduce themselves. The commune seems pleased to have received more and more newcomers and is genuinely flattered that they have chosen to make their home here. Increased revenue from local taxation has also benefited the community and everyone is pleased to see improvements to long-neglected buildings bringing villages back to life.

We travel frequently throughout the country, combining business with pleasure. In our free time we enjoy cycling, skiing, gardening and music

(Roger is a guitarist), plus times spent with friends. We have certainly found the better quality of life we sought. We enjoy a much better climate and a less crowded environment, and live in a less materialistic and more educated society. We have also come to value the inbuilt respect for the rights of every citizen which still underpins French society. Finally, we have a home the like of which we couldn't have hoped to own in the UK – and with no mortgage. That is a dream come true in itself.

> *all things considered, if we could go back in time, knowing what we know now, we would still move to France*

Minus points? Not too many, really. We have already mentioned bureaucracy (but once more won't do any harm). And then there is language, of course: few conversations, however successful in practical terms, are without a pang of frustration at knowing that speaking a second language means reducing to basics everything we say – and, to an even greater extent, write. Without subtlety and nuance, it is so much harder to get across the little things which reveal our true personalities.

On a more mundane note, we loathe the inflexible midday shutdown, which still brings each working day grinding to a two-hour halt. And near-vegetarians (fortunately we do eat fish) aren't exactly overwhelmed by choices, whether in a restaurant or at the supermarket. Finally, after a long-term involvement in running a lively performance venue in Cornwall, we miss the nearby presence of something similar, and the creative contacts (particularly in music) which go with it. But, all things considered, if we could go back in time, knowing what we know now, we would still move to France. We simply can't imagine going back.

Our advice to others planning a similar move centres on language, communication being the key to everything. Oh, and aim to live a French lifestyle and contribute to the society which welcomes you.

The Rough With The Smooth

Americans Bruce and Rachael Epstein had never
thought of moving to another country but found
themselves leaving rural USA for the Paris suburbs —
with no choice as to where they were to live.

Although we were always mobile and open to new vistas, we never set out specifically to live in France. Yet here we are, having now spent a longer period in Orsay (nine and a half years and counting) than at any other address in our adult lives.

Back in 1994, we were living in Townsend, Massachusetts, a small semi-rural town (8,000 people) fifty miles (80km) outside Boston, on the New Hampshire border. Bruce's position at a local high-tech company was eliminated, so we found ourselves free to explore our options. We knew what was important to us in terms of quality of life, education for our daughter, and types of work for Bruce. We were definitely open to new possibilities geographically, and we set out to find our ideal location. However, we must admit that the thought of moving to another country never even crossed our minds.

A Dream Job

Then, one day, Bruce saw the 'job of his dreams' advertised. It just happened to be located in France, near Paris. Bruce had previously been to Europe five times on business, Rachael accompanying him once. One of Bruce's solo trips had taken him to the Côte d'Azur for a week (in mid-winter), but neither of us had ever seen Paris before landing there in October 1994 for our final employment contract negotiations.

After convincing the hiring manager (who happened to be German) that the cost of living in France was significantly higher than in the US (fifty per cent higher at the time, according to the company's own International Mobility Manager), not to mention the fact that we would have to totally equip our new house, we were able to come to agreement on an acceptable salary and relocation package.

Thus began our adventure.

All in all, we are quite happy with the town where we live. Orsay, a university town of 16,000 inhabitants twenty-five kilometers (15 miles) southwest of Paris in the midst of a scientifically rich area, is quite cosmopolitan – although there are no official statistics, we believe that there are at least 50 nationalities present in the surrounding area. The Relocation Manager at Bruce's company had initially suggested Orsay not only because of its proximity to the company, but also for its location along the main north-south train line with direct service to both of Paris's main airports (Charles de Gaulle and Orly). We were open to her suggestion, since we were looking to avoid isolating ourselves in an 'American enclave'. Our attitude was that, if we were going to live in France, we wanted to experience it fully, which we have done.

We left a rural area in the USA to come to the Paris suburbs. This contrast was overwhelming and significantly more challenging than any other aspect of the transition (though there were certainly other challenges as well!).

Rachael is a country kid (born on a dairy farm) and had never lived in a large metropolitan area. For her, coping included learning how to use public transport for the first time in her life; the fact that it was in a new language and culture made it more challenging. Bruce had grown up closer to New York and had already been to other large cities like Tokyo and London, so negotiating a transport system was second nature for him.

Unlike all the places we had lived in the US, there were no neighbors available to help with the transition when we arrived (several houses in the neighborhood were empty). Rachael learned to cope initially with the help of our French tutor, who became more of a friend than teacher; she accompanied Rachael in her daily struggles with the administration, market, making contact with associations, etc. It helped that she had also lived through the experience of raising a family abroad, so she could empathize with the situation of an expat mother.

Moving In

Upon our arrival, we rented a semi-detached house on a piece of land barely larger than the house itself, located on the outer edge of the town of Orsay. For us, the process of house-hunting was an absolute nightmare! So much so, in fact, that despite our overwhelming dissatisfaction with the property, we have no inclination to even attempt to find another place to live.

it was quite disconcerting to see bare wires sticking out of the wall and ceiling where light sockets should have been

Rachael recounts the story:

"Perhaps it seemed much more difficult than it really was because of my expectations and previous experience with the house-hunting process in the US – I was shocked to discover that we didn't have any choice about where to live. Bruce had described some general criteria to the Relocation Manager of his employer about the type of place we would like to find, and she had arranged with an estate agent to show us exactly one such house. Granted, there were several identical units available in the same *résidence*, but the difference between them was negligible. When pressed to show us other available choices, the agent showed us a listing for another house at twice the price. It also dismayed me that we had less than 24 hours to decide and deliver our answer.

"I was also shocked to see the pitiful state of the house when I arrived (Bruce had completed the rental and move-in process on his own): huge cracks in ceilings and walls; building waste 'hidden' under the steps and mixed into the garden soil; floor tiles in disrepair, including the use of interior tiles on an exterior surface (and thus deteriorated by weather and use). In addition, a major shock for us as Americans was finding that the house was completely bare, in some cases even the wiring fixtures had been stripped. It was quite disconcerting to see bare wires sticking out of the wall and ceiling where light sockets should have been. It was also necessary to completely equip the kitchen.

> *the house had no electricity – we were shown it with just a small flashlight – and then given overnight to 'take it or leave it'*

"We have endured a constant struggle to maintain livable conditions – fighting to get the radiators replaced so that we could heat the house above 17°C (63°F) in the winter, for example, and at that the landlord only agreed to replace four of the eight radiators in the house. Getting any work done has been a constant struggle, requiring multiple phone calls/faxes to the landlord (who, incidentally, is a corporation and has changed ownership several times, so our dossier was constantly being shuttled from person to person, just to keep it interesting)."

Bruce is rather more phlegmatic about the move:

"It is difficult to evaluate our experience. After all, from the perspective of the French, it was an ideal situation: the Relocation Manager did the research, set up the appointment with the agency that had a house available to rent, in the desired area, at a reasonable price. What more could we possibly have wanted? What right did we have to expect to have a choice or be satisfied?

"Of course, the fact that the house had no electricity – we were shown it with just a small flashlight – and then given overnight to 'take it or leave it' didn't help. Then, for the *état des lieux* (inventory), again, it was a rush through (under the pretext that the agency was overloaded with work), in the dark, without a translator, so of course none of the many minor problems were noted. It turned out that the landlord has sued the builder for *malfaçon* – that's how badly built the place is.

"The condition of the house is more remarkable because we are not dealing with an antique home; this is a relatively new building, less than twenty years old and we are only the second family to inhabit it."

The actual move was relatively uneventful, with the exception of an administrative snag that delayed the final delivery, but perhaps that can be attributed to the quality of the removal company that Bruce's employer engaged. Of course, most of our belongings were left in storage in the US, since our bedroom furniture was too large for the new house, appliances were useless due to the difference in voltage, etc.

We should note that at Rachael's insistence, in order to maintain as much 'normalcy' for our family life while Bruce traveled for his job, we even brought our two ten-year-old cats. Before leaving the US, they had to undergo an 'approved' veterinary exam (analogous to their human counterparts), but otherwise there was no problem bringing them into the country – no quarantine or other formalities. They adjusted reasonably well, loving the year-round milder climate in their new territory, although they have both passed away in recent years. The French vets that we found in our local town were quite understanding and patient with us over the years, even when facing difficult choices.

Once we had taken possession of the house and recovered from the shock of finding a completely bare kitchen containing nothing but a sink, we set out to equip the house. This was relatively straightforward, though expensive, despite the occasional cultural gaps between US-style appliances and European ones. For example, the built-in timer in our American microwave oven was available even when not cooking, but this is not the case here. When we tried to explain what we wanted (first in French, then even in English), the appliance salesperson finally understood and answered: "But why would anyone want to do that?" He offered to sell us a separate cooking timer! In order to furnish the kitchen, the bedrooms, and so on, it seemed that every weekend of our first year in the country followed the pattern of Saturday shopping at Ikea and Sunday furniture assembly. Not being particularly handy, we found this enough of a challenge; our kitchen cupboards are actually freestanding bookcases with doors so that we didn't have to deal with attaching items to the walls.

Faux Amis

It was quite an advantage that both of us spoke at least some French when we arrived; Rachael is now fluent and Bruce virtually bilingual (despite his noticeable accent). We each found it fairly easy to learn, by a combination of methods. As part of the relocation package, Bruce's employer provided a private tutor to each of us for three hours a week for the first year. In addition, Rachael had the good fortune to participate in French conversation groups offered by the local chapter of the AVF (Accueil des Villes Françaises).

> **" I couldn't for the life of me figure out what books had to do with the half-kilo of cherries I wanted to buy "**

It definitely helped to have studied French back in school, as well as other languages (we have each studied two others at different points of our lives). Plus, living in an international area, many of the local people were patient and helpful during our period of struggling (Rachael adds: "which is still often the case, even after almost ten years.")

Rachael describes her linguistic experiences:

"At first I received numerous compliments from the French people I met on 'how well I spoke French', even though I knew I was far from fluent. After a while I realized that these compliments were due to the fact that my accent was less pronounced than other Anglophone French-speakers (I was usually mistaken for a Continental European, often Belgian or German) and thus didn't 'hurt their ears'.

"One particularly embarrassing moment occurred at the local market when I couldn't for the life of me figure out what books had to do with the half-kilo of cherries I wanted to buy (only later did I understand that the merchant was asking if I wanted "*une livre*" and not *un livre*). I still get stumped occasionally by problems due to gender and subtleties."

Bruce experienced an interesting reaction from his French colleagues. As he says, "they refused to speak French to me because 'it was too hard to speak slowly, not use contractions or idioms, and avoid cultural references' yet when speaking English (the official office language), the native English speakers were expected to 'speak slowly, not use contractions or idioms, and avoid cultural references'. My colleagues never seemed to see the irony there.

"I also have a fond memory of a meeting between French and German colleagues, when, although they were all speaking 'English', I ended up having to translate so that everyone could understand each other. Watching them try to spell difficult words (like their names, acronyms, etc.) was hilarious – apparently none of them had ever learned the letters of the alphabet in any language but their own.

"Another time, I watched two French colleagues get into a heated debate because they didn't realize that they understood two different meanings for the same English word (and neither of them was the 'normal' meaning). In response, I compiled a list of dangerous *faux amis* (between English and French).

"I too have made some memorable French errors, for example using the word *baiser* (a vernacular term for 'copulate') when I meant *baisser* (to lower) in the midst of one of my early business presentations delivered exclusively in French.

"My favorite 'nightmare' story, however, is the time I couldn't get a taxi dispatcher at Orly airport to understand where I wanted to go simply because I used the wrong preposition: I said "*à l'Essonne*" when it should have been *en Essonne*. Of course, when I recounted the story to any French people, I got no sympathy at all: I was supposed to know which *départements* were masculine and which were feminine!

"After ten years, I have become sufficiently proficient in French to proofread my colleagues' work (which annoys them no end!)."

Contracts & Cards

"Speaking of work, I am currently employed by a small French high-tech company as Director of R&D. This is my fourth employer in France. The first and fourth I found through advertisements (the first in the newspaper while still in the US, the most recent via the French national employment agency, ANPE). The other two I found through personal relations. I have recently spent fourteen months unemployed (after my third employer, an American company, completely shut down its French subsidiary); until then I had never had any problem finding work. I suspect that the difficulty this time was partially due to the fact that I had now passed the 'magical' age barrier of forty-five.

"In general, I have gotten along very well with my French counterparts. However, I did have one horrendous experience with my second employer, the French division of a German company. Basically, the strategic direction that my boss was following directly contradicted his (German) boss's orders. When my boss scolded me for "not being French enough" (meaning that I was implementing the German strategy instead of the French one), I realized that my future there was severely limited.

"In fact, this was soon followed by my being *placardisé* (literally, 'put in the closet'). Since it is difficult to fire someone in France, the usual technique in large organizations is to shuffle 'undesirables' into meaningless positions organizationally and physically (away from the all-important 'corner office').

"Otherwise, I have become well respected by my colleagues on both sides of the Atlantic as well as in other continents for my ability to transcend the differences and serve, not just as language interpreter, but also as cultural interpreter. Of course, when one is leading a project with collaborators on three continents, it becomes indispensable!"

On the other hand, we never have become accustomed to the bureaucracy. If there's one area that continues to annoy us, this is it. Our very first financial experience in this country was getting a bank account – it took all day! At least when we were done, we had our account; another American family going through the process with us had to wait two weeks until they finally discovered that the bank's computer rejected the wife's last name – different from the husband's, and French-looking – because "her first name wasn't permitted for her birth date". (Until 1966, only a limited number of names could be given to French children by law.)

We were shocked to see that the bank's books were indeed still physical books! Then, even though we had no cash to deposit, the bank officer gave us a checkbook and instructions on writing the checks; further, he helped us write the deposit check for renting the house. His response was : "Don't worry, we know that the company will be depositing money soon; in the meantime, we'll just hold any checks that come in." In the US, knowingly writing a check without sufficient funds to cover it is a felony.

Bruce managed to get his *carte de séjour* without any difficulty, but it took several months longer than necessary for Rachael to obtain her first *carte.*

"After accomplishing my pre-visa medical visit, I packed the pink paper (the *convocation* instructing me to submit to this exam) with our other important papers and household goods, since the medical report should have been sufficient as proof of the visit. When I presented myself at the *préfecture*, their first question was: "Where's the pink *convocation*?" I don't even remember how many times I needed to go back to the *préfecture* to renew the application, yet still without the pink paper due to an unfortunate delay in the delivery of our household goods.

"Our household goods were held up for a very long time without notice from either the authorities or the removal company. Then, one day, we happened to learn almost incidentally that the problem was the import duties being requested for our box marked 'computer parts' (i.e. the keyboard, mouse, etc. for our old personal computer). Once we explained what was in that box, we received our belongings very quickly, and *voilà*, there was the pink paper. When I finally went back to the *préfecture* with the long-requested pink *convocation*, the agent didn't even look at it!

"But at last I received my *carte de séjour*."

On the bright side of this experience, we did get to know our local immigration official quite well. Over the years of having to renew our *cartes de séjour* annually, the procedure became more and more informal, until one year when he suggested that it was time to apply for *cartes de résident* (which are valid for ten years), explaining thoroughly what we needed to do. It is probably no coincidence that our application was approved quite quickly without a hitch.

> *we had to practically beg the customs agent to stamp our passports for proof of entry into the country*

After being in France for eighteen months on an international contract, we were offered the chance to stay permanently. However, we knew we were in for bureaucratic trouble when the HR manager asked for our US address for the new application for the working papers and *cartes de séjour*, starting the entire process again from scratch, including medical visits (and another set of famous pink slips, which we scrupulously saved with our passports this time).

Apparently it is not possible to request a change in visa status while living in France, it is assumed that re-entry will be requested from the originating country. We no longer had a US address, having sold our house, but fortunately Bruce's parents live near Washington DC, so we used their address, and his father was able to visit the Embassy periodically in person to check on the progress of the paperwork (the Embassy didn't answer phone calls or faxes). Then, when returning to France, we had to practically beg the customs agent to stamp our passports for proof of entry into the country (we had already been warned about needing this to get our new *cartes de séjour*)!

Once on a French *CDI* (*contrat de durée indéterminée* – a permanent work contract), we had to apply for acceptance into Sécurité Sociale. What a nightmare! To begin with, an interminable list of documents to supply (duly translated into French, of course). Then, each time the dossier was submitted, instead of reviewing all the documents and indicating, for example, that documents numbered 3, 5, and 9 were unacceptable, they rejected it at the first document that didn't meet the – unwritten – standards; so we had to submit four times before finally receiving our official Sécurité Sociale number.

In the meantime Rachael was diagnosed with a serious illness, and each time we went to the hospital the admissions officer took it upon herself to give us a lecture about the importance of getting our definitive Sécu number. Finally, when Bruce couldn't take it any more, he showed her the stack of rejections and asked if we should go to the Sécu office and not come back until we had the number. She finally relented, and admitted that getting Rachael's condition treated was more important than a silly number; afterward, though, the clerks had to make one up for the computer file! (It was all straightened out when the number finally arrived.)

Seven years later, the Sécu asked for a new translation of Rachael's birth certificate! Why they took so long to decide that they didn't like the first one, or why they objected to only that one document out of the dozen or so translated documents that we originally submitted, we will never know.

the headmistress was somewhat miffed when our daughter received higher scores on her French tests than the native students

We have also had our share of hilarious situations with the tax people, including one year where our *taxe d'habitation* (residential tax) was accidentally paid twice. We had signed up for the payment to be automatically withdrawn from our checking account, which is a common practice here, but we never received any confirmation of this. So, when the deadline drew near, we sent a check as well. The next day, we finally received our automatic payment confirmation, so we asked the bank to stop payment on the check. However, it was already too late. The tax department credited our account twice, and issued a reimbursement, but then noticed that the check had been blocked. So we got a notice – the same day as the reimbursement – indicating that we had not paid and therefore owed not only the tax, but also the penalties. Fortunately, Bruce found an understanding *fonctionnaire* at the tax office who straightened this out for us.

Marks Out Of Ten

One important aspect of French administration that we have been quite pleased with is the school system. For the most part, we have been delighted with the education our daughter has received, but mostly because we have found extraordinary schools. When we first arrived, it was mid-year, she was seven years old (*CE1*) and spoke no French at all. The local state primary school resisted taking such a student (perhaps understandably, as it was overcrowded and understaffed and thus unable to manage 'exceptions'), but fortunately the local Catholic school was more than happy to accept her (even though we aren't Catholic). She received a wonderful education there, although the headmistress was somewhat miffed when our daughter received higher scores on her French tests at *CM2* than the native students (a feat she repeated throughout *collège*)!

For *collège*, it happened that a local state school (Martin Luther King, in Buc) was opening a bilingual section just the September when our daughter entered *6ème*. Her four years there were fantastic, and she added a solid mastery of German to her linguistic repertoire (plus beginning Spanish in *4ème*).

Then began the nightmare called *lycée* (she is currently in *1ère* at Lycée Hoche in Versailles). It seemed as if the focus had transformed overnight from learning for its own sake to having to receive high marks on the *Bac*. The pressure is inappropriate (in our opinion) and our daughter is now suffering tremendously. In fact, she is now so turned off by the French higher education system that she isn't even considering staying in the country for her university studies.

Rachael adds some personal notes:

"It was surprising at first how frequently there was no school – after arriving in France at the end of March, between April's school holidays and May and June's national holidays, I don't think there were two consecutive full weeks of school the remainder of that year. That was, in fact, an important respite for us, since for much of those first few months our daughter came home from school in tears, not understanding what was happening in school, since, after all, they were all speaking French. We did insist that she stay at school for lunch (incidentally, the school had an excellent *cantine*) to facilitate the immersion process and avoid the temptation to revert to English during the day.

"I had one particularly harrowing experience one day during the early years when I arrived late to collect my daughter from elementary school and she wasn't there. Nobody had seen her leave, and the headmistress, who supposedly spoke fluent English, refused to do so even though I was obviously flustered and incapable of managing in French at that moment. It turned out that our daughter had gone home with a friend, and the school's reaction was simply '*mais bien sûr*, no reason to have been so worried'."

Another generally positive administrative aspect is the national health system. Bruce has been fortunate not to have had any serious health problems, although Rachael did suffer a serious illness which was quite efficiently handled – as she reports:

"The health system gets two marks: 'good' for the physical care I received during my serious illness; 'bad' for the lack of bedside manner and impersonal treatment, although as a foreigner (with a certain amount of medical background) I expect and demand a greater quantity of information than the healthcare providers are accustomed to giving. I expect to be an active participant in the decision-making regarding my care, not just a piece of sick meat that needs to be treated. One technician, trying to 'lighten up', said: "Sometimes we need to bear pain to be beautiful" rather than attending to the fact that my body was cramping due to the awkward position I had to maintain for that particular treatment.

"On the positive side, I applaud the fact that I was admitted to the hospital without any delay (despite the administrative hurdles recounted earlier). I must also acknowledge that I trusted the French system completely and never considered seeking care in any of the private hospitals (e.g. American Hospital of Paris).

"It was also a pleasant surprise that we never had to pay a *centime* for this care: surgery, hospitalization, treatments, follow-up check-ups. Further, I am impressed that I will be covered at a hundred per cent reimbursement for any treatment related to my illness, for the remainder of my life or as long as I stay in France – although I did have to request several annual extensions via my physician before it was finally resolved permanently."

Quality Of Life

We are generally quite pleased with the quality of life in France, with its emphasis on family and leisure time. Rachael takes full advantage of our local municipal swimming pool, far more than at any time since university days (twenty-five years ago). The highlight of her other leisure activities is the international focus, be it AVF or other associations. As mentioned above, we specifically did not seek to live in an 'American ghetto' and neither of us belongs to any exclusively American associations. The local AVF chapter is very diverse (reputedly the most international chapter in the country) and satisfies Rachael's desires to interact with and sample other cultures while supporting others who have recently arrived, without having to travel to Paris. In addition, Rachael helped to establish the Paris chapter of an International Women's Club.

Before coming to France, we were quite active in adult team sports, especially volleyball and softball. We didn't expect to find softball (although we did find an informal group who have been playing every Sunday in the Bois de Vincennes for the past twenty years), but by the time we finally found volleyball, Rachael's arthritis had gotten too severe, and Bruce can no longer keep up with the twenty-somethings who come to play.

One hurdle we have had to overcome is the fact that activities don't start until after 8.30pm, but it is easier now that our daughter is old enough to leave alone at home in the evening. Even at that, our only evening activity is the community choir in which we sing together, a local chapter of the national choir association, A Coeur Joie (which is a pun on *coeur* – heart – and *choeur* – choir – pronounced identically).

Our final major leisure activity is traveling as a family, which we have taken full advantage of during our presence in Europe. In fact, when our daughter was studying the EU in geography, she was surprised to realize that she had already visited more than half the capital cities of the fifteen (at the time) EU countries. Although we hardly know our neighbors, we have made many friends in France. It would be difficult to imagine finding, in our country of origin, a circle of friends as diverse and cosmopolitan as we have here. However, the only neighbors (with the exception of one French family) who ever became friends were other foreigners, this despite living in the same house for more than nine years. Many of these friends have since continued on their respective journeys. Making friends has been difficult for Bruce, while for Rachael it is much easier. Part of that is due to our personalities, Rachael being much more gregarious than Bruce, but another major factor is that the French tend not to see their co-workers as potential friends. Rachael explains:

"We are very spoiled to live in such a diverse region; the other members of the AVF find it as enriching as I do to have foreigners in their midst. I find that the French are taking more and more advantage of the presence of Anglophones as a way to improve their level of English mastery – and their children's – without having to resort to *séjours linguistiques*. With the other Anglophones, we lead English conversation groups to the French as a way to repay them for the support structure that they offer us, including the chance to improve our French."

we continue to hope that one day the concept of 'customer service' will exist in French society

What we have found is that as long as a foreigner makes an honest attempt to integrate himself into French society, he will be more readily accepted than one who tries to maintain his former national identity at all costs. In any case, that's the approach we took; although the town we live in is international in flavor, it is definitely not one of the well known American enclaves, and we associate with other Americans as little as necessary. As a result, we feel that the French have accepted us more easily into their midst.

Some of the other aspects of French life that we appreciate are the accessibility to all our daily needs and the availability of inexpensive, reliable public transport;

the balance between work and the other, more important, aspects of life such as family and friends; freedom of speech/opinion truly respected and encouraged.

On the other hand: pollution is awful and environmental awareness is poor (e.g. recycling has just been introduced in our town, whereas we had it in the US back in the eighties). It has been difficult to adjust to the idea that laws are generally considered to be only suggestions (e.g. traffic and no-smoking laws). The national right to go on strike whenever and wherever and the 'Latin' method of promising whatever is necessary to avoid confrontation without any intention to follow through, also annoy us.

We continue to hope that one day the concept of 'customer service' will exist in French society (though it has gotten better since we learned how to insist by using constructive anger, but that is not always good for the blood pressure). Finally, the weather: seemingly always gray and damp (which the French claim is "English" and has never been our experience any of the times we have visited England), the summer heat wave of 2003 notwithstanding; this may end up chasing us away.

Overall, though, Paris is an incomparable city, it would be nearly impossible to live this close to the same range of cultural and social experiences in the US; even New York, Boston or San Francisco (the only US cities that compare) don't offer a similar quality of life.

Even if we could go back in time knowing what we know now, we would still both make the move to France. We came with very few expectations, and were willing to be flexible to make the most of our opportunity to live here. Rachael is someone who believes that people will find what they look for, and had no preconceived notions about France or the French and thus has experienced the best and worst of what they have to offer.

> *drop the habit of converting prices back into your home currency and accept the fact that life is more expensive here – it's worth it*

Would we ever move back 'home'? During our time in France, the US has experienced a major political and social shift (perhaps it had already started before we left), which would be difficult to tolerate should we ever try to live there again. In fact, we already feel like foreigners whenever we return for visits. What we miss most isn't the country itself, but certain key members of our family and circle of friends. However, if we did go back (which is possible but not inevitable), it would definitely have to be a cosmopolitan area; we would probably seek a French or Spanish-speaking area – after all, at this point, we find it incredibly boring to spend all day in a single language.

So, what advice can we offer others considering following in our footsteps? Come with no expectations, an open mind, a sense of humor, and a willingness to be very flexible (and patient!). Understand that you will be maladroit in French language and customs for a while. It will pass if you allow yourself to struggle through the awkward periods. Watch French TV, even if you don't understand it at first. Not only will it help you to learn the language, it will give you invaluable insight into the French psyche. As quickly as possible, convert your living rhythms and favorite foods to what the locals do. This will also help facilitate integration. Also, establish contact with other foreigners already in the area before moving, or at least find a welcoming organization or association in place. Two such organizations are the AVF and the annual program offered in Paris called Bloom Where You're Planted.

For sanity's sake, drop the habit of converting prices back into your home currency (even if you are unfortunate enough to still be paid in that currency), especially for US nationals. Accept the fact that life is more expensive here. It's worth it.

Finally, buy a copy of *Living and Working in France* [by David Hampshire, Survival Books] and read it cover to cover – we did. It helps enormously.

Bon courage!

Discovering Her Roots

Sonia Blaney moved from East Anglia to Normandy. Having dual French and British nationality, she thought the transition would be easy. Her problems began when she arrived with out-of-date money . . .

I came to France to discover my roots and be closer to my family. My parents moved to France ten years ago and now live in a town called Vernon in Eure. Dad promised to take Mum home one day. She wanted to be closer to her side of the family. Before moving here, I often came to France on holiday and really do like the country. I spent a lot of time with my grandparents, as a child, and know the area well. I also lived here in 1994 for a year. In 2000, I had just returned from an extended gap year in Italy and my parents had left the UK. Since I had no money and no roof, I decided that France wasn't such a bad option.

> *I still have a strong English accent and I just love the look on people's faces when I declare that I am French*

Louviers is a town of around 14,000 inhabitants and is a fairly central place to be. It is not too far from Paris and large towns such as Rouen and Evreux. The surrounding area is beautiful and, if you are interested, it is steeped in history. The ties between Britain and Normandy are strong and reach from the tenth century until the Second World War.

Physical & Cultural Transition

The actual move was fairly smooth. I sent all my furniture in advance (to my parents') and based myself with my parents until I found somewhere else to live. No problems here. I didn't have much and my father kindly came over to pick up my gear with a large van. I followed a couple of months later by plane.

The only unnerving thing that occurred was when I landed at Charles de Gaulle airport. For some unknown reason the flight wasn't announced when it landed and, since it was over an hour late, my father, who was picking me up, had come to the conclusion that I wasn't arriving that day and gone home. He did ask at the desk, only to be told there were no flights from Norwich!

One strong piece of advice I would give is remember to check, before leaving the country of departure, that the money you have from any previous trip isn't outdated. It saves a lot of grief when trying to pay for a phone card! Don't expect French newsagents at CDG airport to be understanding when you have the wrong money.

Having a British father and a French mother, I have the right to dual nationality, which made life easier in many ways – such as no need for a *carte de séjour*. The cultural transition has also been fairly smooth as I was used to being in a French atmosphere and I already spoke a certain amount of French (despite having a French mother, I wasn't brought up bilingual). I still have a strong English accent and I just love the look on people's faces when I declare that I am French.

I remember thinking that the way of life here was much more laid back and people took life at a leisurely pace. The French take time for lunch (an hour or more) and their weekends are very important to them. France still has a family orientated culture. Family comes first, holidays second, work last. For example, the month of August: most French people see this as the month to go on holiday. Three weeks is the average length of time taken to pack up and journey elsewhere to enjoy time out with the family. And this applies to the majority of the population – whole factories can close for August. This can make it hard, for the average Brit or American, to adapt to the work environment. A Frenchman won't take work with him and won't be contactable – even in an emergency.

There is also the 'bridging' concept. If a bank holiday (and there are many) happens to be on a Thursday, most people will take the Friday off to make it a nice long weekend, forgetting that the rest of the world is working.

I then bought an apartment . . . or tried to. At the first bank I went to, I was told quite openly to go and get married then come back

One other interesting fact is that the French prefer to stay within the borders of France for their holidays. I believe it is because you can find everything you want here. You have beaches, mountains, lakes, etc. and, guess what: everyone speaks French. Who can blame them? It is a beautiful country.

Renting & Buying

I originally rented a small apartment in the middle of town. This was fine, except you have to cough up three months' rent as a deposit. Prices are reasonable. I had a one-bedroom flat right in the centre of town (I paid 2,500 francs a month plus charges of 800 francs a year). Many young people rent while they save for a deposit on a house. However, leaving was a minor problem. You must give three months' notice – then clean the place. My landlord was particularly picky: "Don't forget to scrub behind ALL radiators and change the filter in the fan above the oven." Apart from having a few hundred francs knocked off for 'damage', I got my deposit back.

I then bought an apartment . . . or tried to.

As a single woman I found it quite difficult to buy. At the first bank I went to, I was told quite openly to go and get married then come back. This was a serious comment made by a youngish **female** bank clerk. I am sure that I am not the only single woman in France who has ever wanted to live by herself. I couldn't quite believe my ears. I was refused a loan because I was a single woman and didn't want to buy with anyone else. It was useless trying to compromise.

I went to another bank, who were a lot less sexist. However, I do believe that it helped that it was the same bank where my parents had a company account and I dealt directly with the bank manager. I expect it would be easier if you have a large deposit to place. It really is a different attitude from what I was used to. The banks are the opposite of British ones, i.e. they don't like to lend you money. It really helps to have connections or French friends who know how to work the system and help you, which I didn't. I still feel quite angry about the whole thing and frustrated that it can be that much harder because I am a woman.

Also, when buying a house there is a huge amount of paperwork to be signed. It would help to have a friendly solicitor who can go through it slowly with you. I was lucky in the fact that my solicitor was able to translate some of the technical jargon into English. I found the whole process quite stressful even with my level of French.

However, what a lovely feeling it is when everything has gone through and you have your own place. Then you think about decorating and see the price of paint! Buy it in England; the price is double over here. Seriously, though . . . the sense of achievement you have when you have managed to wade through all this French stress and come though the other end is wonderful; it is worth it.

Neighbours & Friends

I have had some problems with noisy neighbours. I live in a first floor apartment and my downstairs neighbours enjoy music that makes my floor vibrate. I tried explaining to them that neighbours should share but not that much. They didn't seem to understand what I was talking about – probably my accent again? Whatever, I tried to be nice and it didn't work. Action had to be taken, so I took it.

First step: I found out who the neighbours' landlord was and went directly to him to complain and I insisted that if the matter wasn't resolved I would take further action. After two such conversations action was taken (words were said). Nothing like an irate foreign woman turning up on your doorstep to get matters sorted. The problem seems to have been resolved. However, I did ask the municipal police what the procedure was if it got out of hand!

> *I have found people to be very welcoming and wanting me to join in and be part of the crowd*

You can call the police at any time of the day and they will come round. If you still have problems, you write a letter of complaint and send it recorded to the landlord and the police. It is also a good idea to check who the owners of the other apartments are.

I live in a house that has been divided into four apartments. For other issues, such as who pays for repairs to the outside walls and hall electricity, etc. I am in the process of setting up a proprietors' meeting so that they can be dealt with correctly. I am still not too sure of all the relevant French laws.

My French was average when I arrived and is now fluent. Being used to hearing French through family visits, I found it fairly easy to learn. I have used a variety of methods, including home study, work and talking to friends and family. I think being out and about helps. I joined different clubs, such as a rowing club, Jeet Kune Do (a martial art) and painting classes. I have found people to be very welcoming and wanting me to join in and be part of the crowd.

French people are really into their sports and keeping fit. September is when everybody sits down and makes a list of all the activities they are going to do during the year. Normally you can try out some classes once or twice before paying. If you go to the local town hall, they should be able to supply you with a list of the activities available in your town or village.

Also trying out what you know and not feeling intimidated by the language helps. A lot of people are scared of getting it wrong but nobody laughed at me; in fact they tried to understand what I was trying to say and help me learn. Don't be afraid to ask people to slow their speech down.

There is much more of a food and drink culture here than in the UK and most social activities centre around food and the table. French people don't drink to the extent that Brits do and they like to accompany their alcohol with food! Expect to be sat at the dinner table until the small hours of the morning. The French take great pleasure in eating slowly, drinking in the flavours. If you are a food fan, the restaurants are amazing here: reasonable prices and excellent food. I certainly eat out more than in the UK. However, I have gained the odd kilo!

Work & Paperwork

I work for a French company as a language trainer, mainly teaching business and technical English in multinational companies, where English is needed more and more. It still surprises me how much language training is needed. Younger people have a basic working knowledge of English but certainly not as strong as those in many other European countries such as Holland or Germany.

I was offered the job before I came to France as I knew the owner of the company. However, I do believe it is fairly easy to find work as a language trainer, as the need is there and is growing rapidly.

As for getting another job outside language training? I think you really need to speak the language to a high standard. You cannot get by on English alone in the industrial sector. However, most large companies will offer French tuition if you are moved over because of work.

I get on well with my French colleagues but there are cultural differences. The British are very punctual and organised people (on the whole). However, don't expect the French to be on time for an appointment or meeting or to be prepared. I have lost count of the number of times my students have arrived fifteen or twenty minutes late without an apology or good reason. It still drives me up the wall and I have problems excusing it.

I am sure the people working in the 'head office of French bureaucracy' have a great laugh seeing how many people they can push over the edge of insanity

Also the French attitude to jeans is very interesting. The 'denim look' is definitely still in. I still haven't quite got used to people wearing jeans to work. Give me another ten years and I shall probably be rolling up to work in faded flared jeans with nice fat turn-ups . . .

Here is something I am now fully qualified in: getting your papers sorted. ARRRRGHHHH! Beware! Be scared! If you want something done, be prepared to be faced with lots of obstacles.

I had had a French identity card for twenty-nine years. Last year it expired and I needed to get a new one by law. Easy: you take your old card to the town hall and exchange it for a new one . . .

It took me **six months** to renew a French ID card as I had to prove that I was French. For some stupid reason, I was of the understanding that my old **identification** card proved I was French, which was why I had it in the first place. Silly me. I had to prove that my great-grandparents were French, then obtain a certificate (from Nantes) proving that I existed in the first place. Then I could apply for French nationality. Head, brick wall – say no more.

To add insult to injury, I had it stolen two months later, which brings me straight into another fascinating area of French bureaucracy.

You are expected to carry round all your documents (ID card, driving licence, vehicle registration document, etc.). So when you get your handbag stolen (as I did recently) you have to go through the whole process of getting everything renewed and can't get them renewed because you haven't got proof of identity! You go round and round in circles. I am sure that the people working in the 'head office of French bureaucracy' have a great laugh seeing how many people they can push over the edge of insanity just by going in eternal circles with the paperwork.

I had to wait one month before I was allowed to apply for a new ID card (luckily I still had my certificate proving I existed); then I could get all my other papers in order, SLOWLY.

I now have photocopies of EVERYTHING and take those with me, as I have since found out you have only twenty-four hours to produce your originals.

Men & Health

I have experienced the French health system at first hand. My father was taken seriously ill and was in hospital for two months. There was no waiting. Everything went as quickly as you could hope and we were given answers quickly. All tests were done as quickly as humanly possible and we felt really looked after. In fact a lot of the junior doctors were here in France on training from other countries and spoke very good English.

I have a high opinion of the system here. You can see whichever doctor you like and be assured that you will be looked after. France has one of the best health systems in the world and I hope that it doesn't change. However, the government is proposing changes so I would advise checking out what the situation is before moving over. In any case, you are probably better off getting yourself complementary health insurance, which is a reasonable price.

As a young singleton I have been interested in finding out what French men are all about. This has been, and continues to be, a cultural and interesting experience. I can say I have learned a lot by my mistakes.

I would advise women not to be overly forward. Some Frenchmen will interpret "Would you like to go out for a drink some time?" as "Do you want to get married and have six children?" I have had a few "I'll call you some time"s using this approach!

Conclusion: men here in Normandy (I don't wish to speak for the rest of France; that would be unfair) are of the old-fashioned way. You flirt and wait and wait and wait until they invite you out to dinner. **Do not** make the first move. This is seen as over-keen and scares the hell out of them. **Do** try the maiden-in-distress act. This works (even if you aren't, which I am not). Frenchmen love to help out a 'poor, incapable' woman. For example, you can try asking some nice gentleman to help you change your plugs – and I am not talking about spark plugs. This worked very well for me and gives you a subject to talk about: 'differences between French and British electrics'. Erm?

The maiden-in-distress act works especially well when you are caught speeding. Start to let your eyes fill . . . If by some ill fortune you are stopped by a French policewoman, forget it and expect to be breathalysed and all your papers to be gone through with a fine-tooth comb.

An Enriching Experience

I do believe that most people can happily adapt to life here in France. I think that, if British people make an effort to understand the culture and way of doing things, it can be a very enriching experience – making contact with the local people and becoming part of life here.

despite all the moaning I do,
I love it here and feel at home.
I wouldn't go back to the
UK again

The quality of life is generally better. The attitude to life is more relaxed than in the UK. It is quieter and not so rushed. There is space on the roads to drive. I particularly like the idea of the country being big and having mountains, the sea, forests, etc. You can breathe. Accessibility is also to your advantage. You are on mainland Europe and the UK isn't far.

However, having said the roads have more space for driving, I must say that driving in France sometimes scares the hell out of me. French drivers can get 'a little stressed' on the roads and can drive like rhinos with an attitude problem. The government has recognised this and is taking measures to sort it out. There are more and more speed cameras and spot checks on the roads.

But despite all the moaning I do, I love it here and feel at home. I wouldn't go back to the UK again. I like to go back to visit but I feel that the UK has become too expensive and overcrowded. I also don't feel that I belong there any more.

My advice would be to spend as much time as you can here before making a decision to move. Even though I personally have adapted, the culture and way of life are very different in subtle ways and you must be prepared for that.

And also keep in mind that not everybody speaks English. In fact, only a minority speak English to conversational level. It might be a good idea to brush up on your French before throwing yourself in at the deep end.

From East To West

Dung Rahuel was born and brought up in Vietnam. She came to Paris first as a student, later to live with a Frenchman. Forty years after her first visit, she still finds certain aspects of French life amazing.

I was born in South Vietnam, near the Cambodian border, and my full name is Thi Dung (pronounced 'yung') Rahuel. Thi is just a sex indicator, which has become useless in a French environment, but I have kept it so as not to get into trouble with the authorities.

After graduating with distinction from high school, I was assigned a scholarship to attend college in France. My life in the astonishing Western world had begun!

Paris, 1960s

My first stay in France was as a student, and it was an adventure. Taking the underground was an adventure, attending lectures at the Sorbonne was an adventure, travelling in Europe was an adventure . . . I was shocked to see Parisians running here and there, in department stores, in the street, in underground corridors. They were packed like sardines in underground coaches at rush hours. They ran and ran, seeing no one on their way.

I felt miserable when I first got lost in the Sorbonne halls, and also when I had to wait in the corridor leading to such or such a lecture hall even when arriving on time for the class. I felt frustrated when having to queue up for hours to get a visa for travelling out of France. At that time, I had a Vietnamese passport and, for each journey, I needed at least two visas: an exit visa from France and an entry visa to the destination country; sometimes a transit visa was also required.

For my first journey in Europe, ill-advised, I didn't apply for a transit visa when going by train from Paris to Berlin. In Charleroi, the Belgian customs officers wouldn't let me go further. As a member of a cultural tour organised for students, I had a group ticket. There was no way I could return; I had to manage to get that transit visa by myself. I finally made it, and joined my group in Berlin the next day.

knowing the language is one thing; coping with daily life is another

During my first year at college, I studied Ancient History and languages, preparing for what was called a *Certificat d'Etudes Littéraires Générales*. My classmates told me it usually took two years to get it, i.e. no chance to get it right away. On the day the results of the exam were due to be published, an uncle of mine accompanied me to the university. Unfortunately, the list of successful candidates was first announced by candidate number, not by name.

So when I heard my number, I could hardly believe it. So I told my uncle, "I think that was my number."
He said, "Are you sure?"
"I don't know; there are so many digits, you know!"
As a matter of fact, it wasn't a question of memory: I could hardly believe that I had got it! Then they put up the list of names preceded by numbers.
"It **was** yours!" he said.

Such a procedure now seems quite irrational to me.

Knowing the language is one thing; coping with daily life is another. Although speaking French quite fluently, I found it hard to be a student in France, and even more difficult in Paris. Until then, I had lived with my parents, brothers and sisters in Saigon, in a traditional Asian environment with no other concern than study. But I was happy to acquire a broader knowledge of Western culture: literature, art, music. It was also interesting to discover other parts of France than Paris and to travel to other European countries.

Then I returned to Vietnam, where I stayed and worked for five and a half years before leaving the country again – this time as an adult, and in dramatic circumstances.

Saigon, 1970s

Even though I now earned my living, I was living at my parents' house. (It wasn't conceivable that a young unmarried girl live elsewhere than her parents' place.) As I had experienced an independent style of life in Europe, I suffered from some of the constraints of my former traditional life. I was in the situation of having '*le cul entre deux chaises*', according to a French expression.

One day, shortly after my arrival in Saigon, my parents told me we had to visit Mr and Mrs X. I asked them who these people were. In the end, it became obvious that my parents wished me to meet their friends' son. I refused to go with them; they were very upset. "What are we going to tell them?" they asked me.

"You arranged the meeting even before I returned home," I said. "I don't have any advice to give you." It was very disrespectful but they didn't give me any other choice.

Yet, however unpleasant it was to go back to this conservative way of life, it didn't disturb me tremendously. I was more at work than at home, being a teacher and a translator.

In the early seventies, the South Vietnamese regime was backed by the United States administration. For three years, I worked at the American Embassy. Therefore I had no alternative but to leave Vietnam in 1975, as North Vietnamese forces were determined to 'liberate' South Vietnam. I left Vietnam one week before Saigon collapsed.

There were no longer regular flights. I landed in the USA aboard a military plane like a few others and stayed one month there. I could have stayed and worked in the States, as a former employee of the Department of State. For personal reasons, I decided not to and flew to Paris.

The second part of my life in France began.

Promises, Promises

When I was a student in Paris, I had met many other students, French and foreign – among them the young Frenchman whom I later married. He had visited me in Vietnam twice when I returned there. That is one of the reasons I finally decided to settle in France.

I got married in Paris in December 1975. As I was determined to settle in France, it didn't make sense to keep my Vietnamese nationality. I would have liked to acquire dual nationality, but it didn't work out. My new nationality didn't make me a Frenchwoman, however.

We first rented an apartment in Paris. Renting is quite unpleasant in France, especially in Paris and its surroundings, as there are many more *demandes* than *offres*. When you rent, you have the feeling that your potential landlord or landlady is doing you a favour. Besides, you must provide quite a few documents: payroll, electricity bill, etc. You must earn at least three times the amount of money you are giving away to have a shelter. If this isn't the case, someone must certify that he will be responsible for you if you fail to pay. This person must naturally provide relevant documents defining his financial situation. Next, you must pay out a *caution* (deposit) amounting to twice the rent.

Your landlord or landlady may not let you have pets. He or she may not accept smokers. When you leave the apartment or the house you have rented, you must give three months' notice. However, you don't have to observe the three months' notice if you have found someone to replace you – someone fulfilling the above conditions, of course.

Some years later, we had our first son and the apartment in Paris became too small, so we began to search for an apartment to buy. In my opinion, it is easier to buy than to rent in France, or let us say in Paris, as I don't know much about how it is in provinces, depending perhaps on which provinces too.

> *they wanted ten thousand francs more ... they had found a younger couple whose parents were wealthy and could offer more*

As prices were high in Paris, and my husband was working in the southern suburbs, we decided to search there. Apartments are usually cheaper in the suburbs, depending also on which ones. In the western and southern areas, prices in general are higher than in other places. I had interrupted my career to raise my son. In fact, I was doing some translations at home, but these didn't keep me busy full time, so I had plenty of time for flat hunting.

I found a pleasant apartment without using an estate agency. The four of us met: my husband, who naturally wished to see the apartment, me and the owners – a husband and wife. We all agreed on the price, they agreed to sell, and we agreed to buy. An oral agreement. They offered us an *apéritif*. OK, fine.

Two days later, we got a call from them. They wanted ten thousand francs more, saying that we were trustworthy people but they had found a younger couple whose parents were wealthy and could offer more. My husband just said, "It's unfortunate, but OK, sell it to them then. We will find another one." The next day, another call: "In the end, we are ready to sell it to you."

Before signing the *promesse de vente* in Orsay, on which occasion we were to pay ten per cent of the total sum, the wife, who was sitting next to me, said, "We hope you will not think ill of us."

For the record, the husband was an engineer like my husband and the wife a teacher!

Before visiting this apartment, we had visited some others – among them, a two-storey apartment, which was quite attractive. But the landlord said he had promised to sell it to another couple, so we were second on the list. Then, some days later, he called to say that it hadn't worked out with the other couple, so we were now top of the list. We told him we were really very sorry as we had just made a commitment on another apartment; although it was an oral one, we could not go back on it.

Five years later, we bought our present house, old house of *pierre meulière* in Gif-sur-Yvette, Essonne (department 91). This time we referred to an agency, paying whatever was required not to have to deal with people like those from whom we had bought our apartment.

Gif-Sur-Yvette

Gif is a quiet, small town of 22,000 inhabitants, twenty-five kilometres from Paris. It houses the Centre National de Recherches Scientifiques (CNRS). In the neighbourhood, there are scientific and technical universities and colleges. The 'Paris' Agreements signed in the early seventies between the United States, represented by Kissinger, and North Vietnam, represented by Le duc Tho, actually took place in Gif, not in Paris. Both sides met to put an end to the Vietnam war. As a result, Kissinger and Tho were later awarded the Nobel Peace Prize.

The population in Gif is older than in the surrounding areas. There are a few *résidences* and many *maisons individuelles*. My neighbours on the left-hand side are a retired couple. The couple on the right-hand side passed away some years ago, leaving a daughter of around forty.

Parisians seem to be accustomed to expressing much of their ideas, little of their emotions

We have established formal and courteous relations with most of our neighbours: there has been neither improvement nor deterioration, which means no socialization of any kind for years!

Sometimes I have a chat with the lady across the street when we come across each other or when I give her a lift on her way back home from the station. She says my French is very good and talks a bit about her two children. That is all. As for us, we haven't made much more effort to get to know them either.

I certainly have quite a few good acquaintances, but they aren't close friends. The French are outgoing, but many individuals would rather live on their own, especially in large cities. For someone coming from a society where individualism isn't a usual practice, they are difficult to understand. Besides, Parisians seem to be accustomed to expressing much of their ideas, little of their emotions.

My French friends live in their own country. It is more difficult for foreigners, who have to get adjusted to daily life here and to the French mentality. I had experienced it myself. That is why I would rather mix with non-French people as often as I can.

Organisations such as the Association des Villes Françaises (AVF) and the International Women's Club (WIC) are good places for meeting people of various nationalities and for socialising. That is why I joined them.

Engineering Work

I work for a French company, doing technical writing and translation, and online documentation. Manuals are first produced in French, then some of them are translated into English. From the language standpoint, I am bilingual in Vietnamese and French. I am more fluent in French than English, because of my background.

This is the second French company I have worked for. Previously, I worked for the Matra group, where I gained experience in technical documentation. One day, my husband let me know that a section in the Matra group was looking for someone to produce documentation material.

"So what?" I said. "I'm not a technical person."
"You can try. Who knows?"

I applied reluctantly. In the end, as I was given an interview, I had to go. On the spot, the Technical Director welcomed me, introduced me to some of his engineers and showed me around with a brief description of their software. I didn't feel very comfortable. So I did my best to convince him that I wasn't the right person. I told him that what he needed was an American engineer.

He replied that he wasn't sure of that, in view of my CV. Besides, engineers were bad writers. "How about a test?" he said.
I didn't understand much – neither the technical material nor the commercial material I was asked to translate into English.

One week later, another appointment. This time he said he was pretty sure that I was the right person. "Your translations are very good," he said.
"Thank you," I replied, astounded. "In that case, why did you make all those corrections?"
"As you aren't working with us yet, you cannot know the product. You will be told how it works." He added I had the personality of the writer/translator he was looking for. So that was it. And I sweated for twelve years to produce CAD/CAM manuals . . .

Then, a former colleague of mine told me he knew a company that was looking for someone with my background. He had learnt that I was looking for another job to avoid being transferred to a remote place. I applied, was given an interview and was hired on a *CDI (contrat à durée indéterminée)*.

There are different ways of searching for a job here in France: through websites, newspapers, the Agence Nationale pour l'Emploi, etc. Those are official means. There are unofficial ways too. You may be introduced by X or Y, or you just learn that a position is available in such or such company and you apply for it. Anyway, you usually undergo two interviews before being hired: one conducted by the personnel department and the other one by your potential direct supervisor.

It is pleasant to work here, as many people are quite straightforward. Most of my colleagues are young engineers, between twenty-five and thirty-five. Younger people are more lively than older people. I have nothing much to say against them except that they are a bit too noisy. It isn't easy to concentrate your attention on your work in a noisy room. There are obviously cultural differences, and a generation gap, between us. Yet, in thirty years of living in France, I haven't met with great difficulties when dealing with the French in general.

Moods & Zones

Many French people think they are open-minded. Theoretically speaking, they may be so. Yet co-existence in a small group, be it a family or a social structure, will lead you to reflect on that openness. Foreigners are easier to deal with when they aren't on your doorstep. In general, my feeling is that it is better not to talk too much about differences. Even though the French might encourage you to talk about yourself and about your experience in France, they won't perceive you in a positive way if you are very different from them. I guess it is a reaction to an unknown world. Just give the impression of being almost like them, with some slight differences. This will make them feel comfortable and pleased, as you have enriched them with some exotic flavour while leaving them to their quiet life!

if we had lived on the other side of the street, our application would have been accepted

One day, when my elder son was about four and we were still living in Paris, we were waiting for the lift. A stout Frenchman was waiting for it too. As my husband had expressed some reluctance to growing fat, my kids were impressed by stout people. "*Bonjour, gros monsieur,*" Rémy greeted him. We had just had a nice walk in the Jardin des Plantes, the weather was fine and my son was in a very good mood. The *gros Monsieur* was not!

Fortunately, Asians are rather well regarded by the French in general. That isn't the case as far as some other communities are concerned.

Although relations with people in the street or with friends or colleagues aren't necessarily easy, they remain in some way under control. I wouldn't say the same about red tape, which is one of the points upon which the French and other nationalities would agree. (Yes, they do have something to agree upon – hurrah!)

As I have mentioned, after getting married I had been offered the alternative of keeping my Vietnamese nationality or acquiring French nationality, as my husband was French. What is remarkable about the procedure was that I didn't obtain French nationality by applying for it; I acquired it by certifying that I didn't wish to keep my former nationality. It had to be explained to me twice before I understood how it worked! It was my first – but not my last – experience of French bureaucracy.

Twelve years after we bought our present house, we wished to add a small room to it. There was plenty of space in the garden – seven hundred square metres – but we needed permission. We were aware of that. We also knew that the *Coefficient d'Occupation des Sols* (*COS*) had to be observed. This indicates the proportion of land that may be built on. The *COS* can vary from commune to commune; ours was 0.14, which was very low. What we didn't know about was the *Plan d'Occupation des Sols* (*POS*), a kind of 'zoning plan', which determines whether land may be built on at all.

Our application for a *permis de construire* was rejected because the house had to be at least four meters away from the next house, on each side. Gif-sur-Yvette is apparently a *site protégé*. If we had lived on the other side of the street, which is in the commune of Gometz-le-Chatel, our application would have been accepted. I thought France had a centralised administration!

Two years ago, my son Rémy had to renew his identity card. He went to the *mairie* in Gif to get the required forms for his file. He filled out these forms and provided some other records. His application was rejected by the *sous-préfecture* in Palaiseau, who said he should have gone to the *mairie* in Bures, as local administrations forward that kind of application to a higher level in the hierarchy.

But if Rémy had gone to Bures, he would have been told to go to the *mairie* in Gif, as we were Giffois. In fact, although we live in Gif-sur-Yvette, our post code is for Bures-sur-Yvette: our street is on the boundary separating Gif, Bures and Gometz-le-Chatel.

Eventually, he decided to go nowhere. "I don't care," he said. "I have a passport."

For many years, a French friend of mine had lived in South America, working as an anthropologist. Shortly after his return to France, his wife had a baby, whom he wanted to name Maya, after the Mayan civilisation. Impossible: the local authorities wouldn't let him give her such a crazy foreign name! In the end, he drove to Nantes to meet central registry officers and he was granted permission. There is now a French girl named Maya.

Strikes & Services

My children are now twenty-two and twenty-four. Both have been through the French education system: the younger one is currently studying applied arts; the elder one attended a business school. Each year, the personnel of the national education system – teachers, researchers, etc. – organise at least one strike with the aim of improving the school system and their own conditions. Nevertheless, I don't think that it is so bad here, compared to some other countries I either know or have heard of.

Higher education is generally less expensive in France than in some other countries, the States for example, although this depends on the subject students are studying. But the system is selective and not as democratic as it seems. In fact, it is so strict and so selective that it is hardly accessible to workers' and farmers' children. To my knowledge, fewer than ten per cent of them go to college.

As opposed to *facultés* (universities), there are schools called *Grandes Ecoles*, where admission isn't open to anyone: there are competitive exams and students' records are scrutinised. Business and engineering schools belong in that category.

Regarding secondary schools, there are so many sections nowadays that it is difficult to collect information about them. And students are usually quite young when they are offered these options. Depending on the section they choose, they may or may not have very heavy schedules, but in general, they have lots of subjects to learn about and lots of homework to do.

On the other hand, I have heard that teachers at primary schools are requested not to give homework in order to level inequalities generated by different social backgrounds.

There have recently been many strikes in the health service, too. In spite of that, the health system doesn't seem too bad in France, at least from the patient's point of view. Workers have to subscribe to a Social Security fund and many of them to a *mutuelle* – a complementary fund. Hospital fees are very high but they are eventually refunded to a large extent. However, you aren't refunded in the same way for all categories of treatment: eyes, teeth, general medicine.

The *carte vitale* issued a few years ago reduced the volume of red tape. But French people consume lots of medicine – much more than elsewhere, as the system allows it. This has created a big hole in the Social Security fund. Both left and right wing administrations have tried to solve this problem, without great success, so far.

Parisian Culture

I am happy with all the activities offered in and around Paris. Whatever your hobbies, you can always find something to your taste, in literature, in the arts or in music. There are so many museums and art galleries with permanent and exceptional exhibitions, as well as many concert halls and theatres. I could stay for days in the Louvre; one life isn't long enough to get to know the entire collection.

the French are a queer mixture of peoples. That may be the reason they are difficult to understand

I recently went to an exceptional exhibition on the seventeenth-century Chinese Emperor Kang Xi, which was held in the Château de Versailles. It was fascinating to discover that he opened his empire to Western scientists, including mathematicians and astronomers, and to many Chinese poets and painters.

I had never seen a painting twenty-five metres long in my life! It represented Kang Xi's trip to the southern provinces in great detail; it was gorgeous. I spent at least twenty minutes looking at it.

Life in France is very complex; I have always wondered why. What is paradoxical about it is that on the one hand the French are individualistic, especially Parisians, and on the other hand the French system is inclined to be social. The health service, for example, seems to be more social than in some other Western countries.

Although of Latin origin, the French are a queer mixture of peoples. That may be the reason they are difficult to understand. Admittedly, I have lived mostly in Paris and its surroundings. I have travelled around but had not stayed long enough in the provinces to know what life is like in smaller towns and in the countryside.

You don't perceive any feeling of belonging in large cities in the Western world. That disturbs me, as I come from a society where traditions are still very much alive, regardless of political regimes. It might be easier for a Brit or a German to settle in France, for example. For others who come from further away – Eastern Europe, the Middle East, Asia or Africa – the French way of life may seem quite surprising.

depending on what you are looking for and who you are, you may feel either happy or frustrated with life in Paris

Families are restricted to parents and children. Individuals are recognised mostly by their social status or their production. Beyond a certain age, many French people become foreigners in their own society! I have come across elderly people who have no one to rely on, no one who will care for them, no visitors.

I don't have any advice to give. Depending on what you are looking for and who you are, you may feel either happy or frustrated with life in Paris. I can't say I don't like life in Paris. Yet life there would be nicer with greater balance between rest and work, more courtesy by Parisians and closer relations between children, adults and the elderly. 'Age boxes' are just amazing.

Starting Again

Finding himself on the UK employment
scrap heap, Mr M got a job in Normandy but
discovered that life in France wasn't all it
was cracked up to be.

There are those who come to France with dreams of a more relaxed lifestyle, less stress; they have been on holiday, sampled the wine, the cheese and the cosy restaurants. There are those who come to escape the 'yob culture', the loss of civic responsibility, the aggression and the cluttered roads of the UK. There are those who come for the social one-upmanship or to follow fashion. There are those who come because their pensions have been swallowed up by the greed or bad management of others. There are those who come because there is little hope, no opportunities, no future at home.

I came because I couldn't find work in my own country. Dragging around a comprehensive CV with proven experience and capabilities, I was told I was too old at forty-two. When you don't 'fit the profile', you have nowhere to go. But you can at least go. You just have to decide where and when.

Oh, that life were so simple!

Re-Training

Sifting through papers, magazines and self-help books, I decided to use an old degree in French and Italian, re-train and become a TEFL teacher. Life choices are few for the desperate. Hopefully, with a full-time job and a regular salary, I could try to regain some self-respect and with any luck re-establish myself again.

After a brief career in car cleaning and insurance sales I had another diploma in my hand and a new direction. With my mother ailing and proximity to my daughter compulsory, destinations were limited. I made a lot of telephone calls, sent another pile of CVs and finally managed to secure a couple of interviews, both for jobs in France, but at opposite corners of the Hexagon. I accepted the nearer.

With two suitcases stuffed with anger and frustration, a briefcase full of bitterness, a heavy set of golf clubs and two hundred quid in my pocket, I embarked on the cheapest crossing I could find – Newhaven-Dieppe – on a chilly morning in September 1991.

For the first time in my life I left on a one-way ticket. If I hadn't felt like a man beaten senseless by the economic crisis and changing values, I might have experienced the trip as the Next Great Challenge. As it was, saying goodbye to family, to self-respect, to self-esteem and to self-confidence, it was a journey to Hell – a choppy crossing to oblivion.

In that frame of mind, on a misty, colourless morning, Dieppe wasn't a welcome sight. The old signs of adventure – the smell of Gauloises, fresh bread and coffee – had been switched off. Crumbling, shabby shore-front houses and hotels were shuttered and hostile. Down the gangplank and through an Art Nouveau terminus which had never made listed building status I dragged my exhausted body and baggage into a decidedly unromantic France.

Buying a single rail ticket, on an empty stomach, to a place you don't know, from a face which hasn't worn a smile since birth isn't what most people see as a warm welcome to a new life. I changed trains in Rouen – up one set of stairs, down another, up a third and down a fourth. People who use early trains consider contact with others as a socially transmitted disease. I asked several individuals if the train stopped at my destination. Were these blank looks better than the aggression and glib excuses I had left behind?

Perhaps my French wasn't well understood, because I didn't even raise a grunt. Finally a man in uniform confirmed that it was the train to Paris so I figured from the departure board that my station was somewhere along the line. I installed my cumbersome, ill-matched baggage near the doors, which didn't seem to please the few who had to walk past me.

Lesson 1: Never ask a French person to deviate from a daily routine.

My station had more stairs. It was cold and exposed with not a soul in sight. Even the ticket office hadn't yet opened for service. The station was of fairly modern construction, and outside stood a device for calling taxis. But how do you use a vandalised telephone system? In French? I had been hoping to escape all this. At least I had a written hotel confirmation. All I had to do was find the place. Walking with my baggage was out of the question so I pressed a button and spoke. Twice. And then a third time. *"Taxi. Gare. Formule 1."*

Too hungry, too thirsty and too exhausted to move, I sat on my cases and pulled my jacket around me. With so little money in my pocket a taxi was an extravagance but I didn't have the necessary language or motivation to negotiate.

> *the French haven't mastered the art of warm welcome. Or perhaps they have and have found it unprofitable*

I had visited France enough times before to know that the inhabitants would take the opportunity to take advantage given the slightest chance. Here weakness goes unpardoned.

A Renault Laguna with a taxi sign arrived. The driver opened his window without a smile. I understood *"Bonjour"* but the rest went over my head. I gave him a piece of paper with the hotel address and he got out, reluctantly, to open the boot. From somewhere the strength came and I lifted my bags over the number plate. He offered no help but seemed overly concerned that I didn't scratch his car.

The route he took didn't seem to be false and wasn't long but he made it plain that conversation was an extra. I didn't want to break into his reverie and he wanted another fare.

I unloaded the boot, paid the fare but gave no tip. You pay for service. I paid for the ride. His face remained as impassive as a litter bin.

Welcome To France

The hotel was modern, emotionless and closed. I pressed a bell a couple of times and spent the next few minutes reading how to check in using a credit card. Finally, a man in a scruffy sweater and scruffy trousers with a scruffy face opened the door as you would a funeral parlour.

'give it time; get your bearings,'
I said to myself. I had three days
paid for in the hotel; after that I
had to find accommodation

My apology for disturbing him went unacknowledged. "I have a room reserved," I said and gave him the confirmation from the language school. He nodded and turned to the check-in desk while I held the door open with my foot. I blocked it with my briefcase and hauled the rest over it. He made it plain that I was a day early and would have to pay an extra day. With sleep deprivation taking its toll I lacked the necessary energy to hit him in the face. I consented. At this he swiped my credit card as if it were dirty and gave me a similar piece of plastic with a number on it. That was all.

My energy and patience draining away like jelly in a microwave, I heaved my cases up more stairs and along the corridor to the end room. One large bed, one bunk horizontally across the head, a TV set perched high in a corner over a sink no larger than a mixing bowl, all in dark puce – and that was my new home.

The shower was in a delightful shade of cream plastic; likewise the toilet, and both were shared by all on the landing. But it was cleaned after every use and for the moment seemed adequate. Towels were minimal. This was Formule 1. "You aren't staying here long, Mr M; don't make yourself comfortable." I was too tired to argue. And where was the Gallic charm?

Lesson 2: The French haven't mastered the art of warm welcome. Or perhaps they have and have found it unprofitable, a waste of time or beneath them.

For the rest of the day I was in a coma.

Around 6.30pm I surfaced. No more new recruits had checked in, although I knew others had been employed. A woman, whose lips were pursed by long-term constipation, explained in a desultory manner that shops and bars were a long walk from the hotel and were now possibly closed. She conferred with a man, then another and no-one seemed to have or wanted to give me a definite answer. They had given me some information, not conclusive, and it was now my decision. Public transport wasn't available.

When you could eat half a prairie cow with all the trimmings, overpriced, dried-up *madeleines* from a vending machine are a poor substitute. They failed to conjure up the same memories as for Marcel Proust but they had to do, together with coffee from a machine and water from the tap. I was walking nowhere in my state. So much for French food.

Lesson 3: Shop opening times are different.

"Give it time; get your bearings," I said to myself. I had three days paid for in the hotel; after that I had to find accommodation.

Showered, shaved and duly attired, I presented what was left of myself the following morning at 8.30. There were three other recruits, who seemed to be equally lost, bewildered and unsure. But they spoke English, were all in the same boat and joked about similar experiences. How can the British laugh at adversity?

We were picked up by the over-exuberant owner of the school and taken to be introduced to our new colleagues, who gave us the once-over like new arrivals in Stalag Luft 3. In the first hour we played questions and answers. One colleague explained the ins and outs of finding a place to live but we had to wait until the end of the course to find out if we were staying in town or being transferred to Paris, Le Havre or Rouen.

My car had been written off by a drunk before I departed for my new life so for the time being my movements were restricted. This I hoped would aid decision-making. After twelve years of rural living I didn't want life in a large city. I couldn't afford it. With no cash to buy a car I needed a flat nearby. That idea was soon dashed when I discovered that most of the work was at company premises. Information intake was becoming a little too much for my tired and muddled head but I knew there was no going back. I had to find a way.

Rights & Duties

We were given several print-outs on how to apply for a *carte de séjour* at the *mairie*, open a bank account, etc. We were also given another valuable document: a *contrat de durée indéterminée*, a work contract. This was a full-time commitment. I had received other documents before I left the UK but they had no relevance until now. The company had followed all legal procedures carefully – there are many cowboys in this business! – but this was my first contact with French paperwork.

There is lots of it and, as someone told me, "You must keep it by law." There are time limits on certain documents but others, like the *bulletin de salaire*, you keep for life. This is no simple affair; it's a full A4 page encyclopaedia explaining in detail plus accumulations what the French Government is taking from you.

My salary was derisory (half that of a newly qualified teacher in Britain) so it was reassuring to know that twenty per cent was being taken away at source. Income tax is paid separately. After these calculations, who needs laxatives?

At least I had my passport to The System – health, education, unemployment benefit – even if I was paying dearly for it. Unless you are out of it (*exclus*), it is difficult to realise how generous the advantages are when you need them. Or how long the Government can continue to pay them. If you find yourself in trouble, and once you have proved your case with the necessary documents, your Rights will be recognized.

Lesson 4: All French people know their Rights (Napoleon's *Code Civil*).

They aren't so hot on Civil Duties, however, as you also discover rather quickly. Rights doesn't translate into Responsibilities.

At least with a contract in your hand you can buy a house, rent a flat, take out a loan and consult your personal *conseiller* at the bank. He will be short on advice but will try to blackmail you into buying life assurance or stock market investments. These you can offset against tax. Avoiding tax is a legitimate pastime. Magazines are on sale in January every year to help you. Do your calculations carefully – share prices go down here too!

Now that I was on my way, I was going to be staying around Head Office. The Boss wanted to use my business experience. Only later did I discover he didn't want to pay for it.

A flick through the Yellow Pages (Minitel was beyond my ken) for estate agents and *notaires* and I was off into town. In 1991, flat-hunting was more in the realm of *notaires*, who must be called '*Maître*' – they just love their formality. Estate agents were just springing up as the French were being forced to accept mobility by company downsizing. Before this, a house purchase had been for life, not for profit.

the French will take every opportunity to remind you of the paucity of British cuisine, despite never having tasted the likes

Equipped with the necessary vocabulary (many a word spoken in jest . . .), I explained what I was looking for. The heads shook. "At that price there isn't a lot on the market. And nothing furnished."

This is where information given was proving unreliable. Not one office asked for my address. I had to call back. It was my first encounter with *Système D*. In polite terms, this means 'Sort things out for yourself'. In commercial terms, it means 'I am only here to take your money, not to help you find a place to live.'

Lesson 5: Giving doesn't come naturally to the French and is even considered a weakness: e.g. roundabout priorities, queuing at the baker's, passing on narrow roads.

Finding A Home

I had been happy to leave the burgeoning boorishness of England, the acceptance of the lowest common denominator as the norm. Here there was elevation to more cultural fields, more respect for the intellectual and aesthetic – the French have been brainwashed into believing that this is the route to more lofty realms.

In a Formule 1 this love of beauty is very much in evidence – from the metal, prison-style tables in the breakfast recess to the meaningless prints on the walls. Still, these rooms are meant for passing tourists (English, Dutch, etc.), who have little appreciation of the finer things in life (this is an ingrained belief and the French will take every opportunity to remind you of the paucity of British cuisine, despite never having tasted the likes), or for French businessmen and their girlfriends, who have little time for art appreciation.

In the first week I had visited all the agents in the area and had seen two grim studios: one where you put your mattress on top of the bathroom built in the centre of the room and one in a council block where you could hear neighbours discussing unemployment benefits five flats down the corridor.

Another thing you notice immediately: when people leave, they take everything, including light bulbs and connecting wires. Where and when are romantic dreams supplanted by grim reality?

Lesson 6: Don't expect much here and you won't be disappointed.

When agents show you around, you have the impression that they have their minds on more enjoyable things. Renting a flat at less than a thousand francs (around £100) a week is hardly worth leaving the office for, so they aren't prepared with the keys or bothered about the condition of the premises. I saw two places where even the rats and the spiders had moved out. Usually I viewed at their convenience. Perhaps service comes with a smile when more money is involved.

Two weeks were stretching into three and my credit card was bearing the weight. I was eating from cans with plastic spoons and a Swiss army knife in an ever depressing hotel room.

Then the sun began to shine: one of my students was vacating her flat. An equipped kitchen, a bathroom, a small wardrobe and a 'room' in an eighteenth century block, in the middle of a golf course. The choicest spot in the neighbourhood – or almost.

I feared the worst in rents but was relieved and surprised. It didn't come that easy, however. Nothing does here. First I had to undergo a gruelling interview with the proprietor and his sister. Twenty-year-old French was falling from my mouth like half chewed bread. What a pretty sight I must have presented. They seemed to like what they saw – an innocent, honest man, falling apart at the seams and with nowhere to go – and we concluded the deal on the spot, thus avoiding agency fees. Not that I understood all the details of the *bail* (lease) – who was I to dispute?

you think you had left Victorian values behind in the sixties. Not here. Women in bars, especially alone, are 'of ill repute'

When I finished signing and initialling all the pages, the sister then spoke in perfect English. She had been working in London for the last eight years. "Thank you for trying," she said. I was trying not to throw up in anger and frustration.

Lesson 7: In negotiations, the French hold everything back until the victim has committed. They then reveal their hand.

Negotiating means 'I win, you lose, patsy.' Win-win negotiations don't apply here. Sometimes this situation can be avoided by careful preparation of questions that crave their commitment (the words 'blood' and 'stone' come to mind).

But at least I had a pleasant roof over my head, albeit only when I had borrowed two months' rent as a *caution* (deposit) – blood and stone come to mind again. A stained carpet, a fridge and a cooker of indeterminate age, and a rickety shelf in the bathroom: perhaps that is why they didn't carry out an *état des lieux* (inventory of fixtures and fittings).

Fortunately one teacher had just left and another was leaving so I managed to borrow some articles of furniture. Telephone installation took an amazing two hours so I could call my family to relieve them of further worry. Lady Luck, who had deserted me over the last four years and had even succeeded in kicking me several times when I was down, was making a few apologies.

Bars

But my pockets were still empty. My salary was being paid by cheque at the end of the month. Then I could open a bank account. For the time being I had the use of the company car – occasionally. My flat was six miles from the school and the bus service was hardly convenient to my hours of work. Some of my English colleagues helped me with advice and I did receive unsolicited help from the French secretary, which I appreciated; no commitment, but help.

I was still looking for some Gallic charm and a friendly bar.

After a week in my flat to acclimatize I stepped out one evening into the village. Four bars and they all close at 8pm, but I can buy a beer or a calvados at 7 in the morning. Two bars close to the school were open after 10pm, with inflated prices and the atmosphere of a chapel of rest. Golf club prices were twice that of the village and members looked at me as though I had scurvy. Later I learned that one must be formally introduced. And the bar closed at 6.

A French bar isn't the place you meet people or go for a chat, at least not in this region. You order your coffee or beer or *ballon de Côtes* (glass of red wine), say hello to the barman and stare at the wall, TV or this new quick way of giving your money to the State: *Rapido* – or *Lotto* without waiting. Try making a conversation and you end up watching a human being biting his fingernails, shaking his leg or playing with his cup wishing that he was anywhere except talking to you.

Nor do you meet women. You think you had left Victorian values behind in the sixties. Not here. Women in bars, especially alone, are 'of ill repute'. *Correct*

French people will tell you, with some pride, that they never go to bars, not because they don't like coffee or beer, but because they are *correct*. Or tight-fisted. However, they will go in groups, when they will make a noise in order to be noticed.

Lesson 8: Not all French people go to bars.

Bars in Rouen seemed to be in a similar vein. With the drink/driving problem, meeting the populace had to be confined to other places.

Finding a good baker's, butcher's, etc. was much easier. It's food, so advice is readily forthcoming, if misleading. Colleagues, as poor as you, will direct you to the cheapest shops. Clients will recommend the most renowned, but you will meet very few people there because it's too expensive.

The standard opening gambit of the British – "We've just moved into the area" – cuts no ice with local tradesmen; they simply aren't interested. They have a business to run and your money to take. Exchange the formalities, state what you want to buy, pay and go. They ask no more of you; ask no more of them. 'Repeat purchase' is difficult to translate into French, as is 'brand loyalty'. Choice of supplier is purely subjective or practical. When you have made several visits, you will be recognized but don't expect the cloying, superficial gushing you left in the UK. And don't expect to be acknowledged in the street. You only exist in a business environment and won't spend money on the pavement.

The choice of native food is impressive but if you are looking for the diversity you found in your local Sainsbury you will have to import. Friends will bring in supplies of Marmite, custard, etc. Wine choice too is limited, as the French are highly developed in the art of self-protection. They will talk of "a good Bordeaux" but will only name the top wines, not their usual tipple – it might reflect on their choice and reveal something of their character, which doesn't come up to standard.

Lesson 9: French people's wine knowledge isn't as wide or profound as you would expect.

Ask most resident Brits what they miss most and the response is virtually universal – the pub. Even if they rarely used one in the UK. In the big cities, social life is easier but in my experience much more effort is needed here, especially in the provinces. For many years the French government actively discouraged social grouping and communal gatherings – they led to the Revolution, so old habits die hard. Social events lean more to the rigidly formal. Etiquette and set pieces are much valued and followed blindly, without question: this dish with this sauce, this wine, cheese before dessert, etc. You soon tire of this system.

The French like to tell you that the British are *coincé* (jammed or stuck, emotionally). We are also *insulaire* because we live on an island. Most of the French I have met – and I have met a few – are *renfermé* (shut in, locked up – and they have thrown away the key). Spontaneity is rare, calculating is not.

> **customer satisfaction isn't always part of the sales contract. Try taking something back ... You didn't buy it here ... Do you have the till receipt?**

You will frequently hear the word *intentionné* – acting in self-interest, with an ulterior motive. This forms the basis of much of French life. It is endemic, inbred. Unfortunately they think everyone is the same, so generosity – pecuniary or of spirit – is regarded as another weakness.

Caveat emptor: the artisan butcher, baker, *charcutier* is proud of his work and his products, often overly so. Quality on the whole is very high but the bigger the reputation the higher the price and frequently the less friendly the service. He knows what he is doing; you are merely the customer. In food and drink shops you have to submit to the theatre of customers asking advice about cooking, serving, etc.

Lesson 10: 'Knowledge is Power' is well developed in the French.

To establish superiority, they will drench you in information about their job or product. Ask another question and the usual answer is *"Je ne sais pas"*.

If they think a sale is in the offing, you frequently discover that your ideas of the truth don't coincide. You are the client, you make the decision. Customer satisfaction isn't always part of the sales contract. Try taking something back. "You didn't buy it here." "Do you have the till receipt?" "What exactly is the problem?" You even encountered this surly approach in the Paris Marks and Spencer before it closed down.

Cars

After following a steep learning curve I got around to buying a car.

It is rare that second-hand cars are cleaned up before sale so you do have the chance to see the original state. Garages will give it a cursory once-over when the sale has been closed. Usually ash trays, carpets and seats are covered in cigarette ash, bread crumbs or dog hairs and often all three. Rarely is bodywork polished. But things are changing. Over the last six years keeping your car clean has become fashionable. Franchises have sprung up everywhere but most people still consider car-cleaning a waste of time.

Major dealers are only interested in selling new or nearly new vehicles; older ones are traded privately. There isn't a lot of control and you can guess the ones I came across. Leaving your address for future possibilities usually falls on deaf ears. As with estate agents, you have to call back, but when you have little to spend . . .

Sales people regard themselves as superior beings, so you will be pumped full of all the positive aspects but negative aspects will be skipped over nonchalantly. Point out a scratch, dent, faulty tyres or a dead battery and the reply will be "*C'est pas grave*". When your interest seems to wane, you will be left until you have found another model.

I have seen two instances of a major change in mileage (denied vehemently, implying I was a liar) and one where the car being sold was manifestly not the model advertised (again the implication being that I was ignorant of the make). After the guarantee has finished, servicing becomes expensive if you go back to the dealer, so repairs move into DIY territory – need I say more? But I did manage to get a small bank loan after all my outgoings were analysed and to buy a car.

Today the *contrôle technique* (MOT test) has become more important so there are some safeguards. On the other hand, the *contrôle de papiers* (document check by the police) has become more frequent under this government, so if your papers aren't in order you can find yourself with a pile of problems.

It was a shock when I first looked for insurance. Rates were virtually double UK levels. Now there is little difference – accidents in France have decreased, theft and vandalism in Britain have increased. After searching around, I managed to find a reputable company to accept my no-claims bonus but, like banks, they take no risks.

don't expect to keep your car scratch-free – the French don't care much about theirs, so why should they care about yours?

A year into my contract I had my first accident, waiting for the lights to change. The fixed French response to almost anything is: "It's not me. I'm not responsible." I was lucky. The driver could hardly deny it and he turned out to be a respectable man who appreciated my British phlegm. The *constat* (accident report) was duly signed and the expected delay by the insurance company didn't materialise. They paid up quickly and without dispute. This, I assume, was because all the paperwork was in order and uncontested. There are some horrifying stories.

You will see many cars in need of body repair; this is because the accident was their fault and they don't want to lose their bonus, or the insurance company won't pay, or one of the vehicles wasn't insured.

Lesson 11: Don't expect to keep your car scratch-free – the French don't care much about theirs, so why should they care about yours?

Gallic Charm?

At last I had some independence: a place to live, a car to drive around, a bank account and documentation to prove it. With my pitiful salary, I had now developed routines and was reasonably acclimatised (read traumatised). At least I had new points of reference.

Seven months passed. Then one day I was accosted in the village by a couple of neighbours I had met briefly. "Oh, we are so happy to have you here. It's an honour to have an Englishman in our midst. You must come round for a drink sometime . . ." – all in French of course and with unctuous smiles.

"Swipe me," thought I (well, not exactly). I really wasn't sure how to reply because I wasn't exactly overjoyed to be in their midst, but my parents had taught me to be polite.

"Our son is studying English," they continued before I could catch my breath. "Is there any way you can help us to find him a job, get him on a course in the UK, etc."

To cut a long story short, before it hurts, I agreed to find some information. I made lots of telephone calls, wrote to places for brochures and less than two weeks later presented it to them at their house. Reluctantly, they invited me inside. As an afterthought, they offered me a drink – the smallest Martini I have ever been served.

After that, nothing. They passed me with a cursory wave from time to time and smiled wanly if I saw them on the golf course.

Word gets around. They weren't the only people to ask. Same oleaginous approach, same results. At last I had encountered Gallic charm – it is turned on when they want something or, as I was to find out more often, when they are trying to get out of a corner.

Lesson 12: The French are always there when they need you.

But I am an old cynic. Haven't you realised?

*France has many things to
recommend it; I'll leave you
to decide what*

There are some good things here. *La France profonde* is wonderful: peaceful little corners everywhere and not difficult to find. Yes, the food and wine are good but local menus can become rather predictable after a while and regional dishes can be overplayed. There is much more space, roads are less congested (but more dangerous) and generally in better condition.

The pace of life is much slower, although with globalisation the French have no alternative but to play catch-up. (They don't like it but their fear of being left out is much stronger.) People are much more content with smaller things. The British obsession with going somewhere, doing something is coming, but slowly. The shopping habit is much more discreet.

Dumbing-down in the media is in full swing but there is still a strong tendency to favour more cultured standards. (Remember: the French killed their royal family.) Most of it is a façade but it is better than the British alternative. Modern Britain is a bear pit compared with France.

To end on a more cynical note, beware of the following phrases:

Pas de problème – there always is.
En deux mots – impossible.
Franchement – this goes against the grain.
Soyez raisonnable – they want to win.
Je vous rapelle – a veiled threat.
C'est pas ma faute – it usually is.

Living here in retirement or having a holiday home isn't the same as earning your crust here. But for me, after thirteen years in France, returning to England is scarcely an option. I am caught in the pension trap. A well paid job or a mammoth win on the Lottery would be the only ways to get back on the housing ladder.

France has many things to recommend it; I'll leave you to decide what.

Enjoy yourself or, to use a popular French phrase, "*Profitez-en.*"

Luck And Hard Work

Mike and Suzie Broderick wanted to
move to Provence but ended up in Languedoc-
Roussillon — more by luck than design. What they did
design was their own house and their own business,
which took rather more than luck.

When we consider where we were about four years ago and how much we didn't know then, we realise that our journey to this corner of France was influenced by chance meetings, luck and an incredible amount of goodwill.

Our story starts in Southampton, where we had lived for many years, holding professional jobs in local government and the NHS Trust. Both in our fifties and regular visitors to France, we began thinking in 1996 about a new life, new challenges and taking things a bit easier, and started the process of looking for property during visits to Provence.

It soon became apparent that property in that area was out of our reach financially, so, as we had limited time in France, we employed a researcher who lived in Biot to look into suitable areas and prices. She rapidly came to the conclusion that we should be looking much further west and this led us into Languedoc-Roussillon, an area that seemed to have everything we were seeking.

Chance Encounters

Languedoc-Roussillon is a region of great contrast, with mountains at both ends – the Cévennes in the northeast and the Pyrenees in the southwest. The countryside varies from plateaux to deep river canyons and each turn in the road opens up a new vista. The Aude valley was particularly attractive to us when we were looking for our new home and we made several visits to the area, viewed many established houses, saw many estate agents, but just couldn't find something that was ideal for us.

we shook hands on the deal
with the vendor, who was to
become our friend as well as
our neighbour

On one visit we found an interesting winemaker's house in a village in the Razes area. It was built on the side of a hill; on the upper level it had the original office with the grape yield markings still on the wall and on the ground floor huge wine tanks built into the walls. We decided to put in an offer but were outbid by another person.

In retrospect, it was probably for the best that we were outbid, as we found out that there was a plan to locate the largest landfill site in the area – the rubbish tip for the whole Aude department – just five kilometres or so down the road. Feelings were running high about this and local protests included 'Village for Sale' signs at the entrance to many villages, protest messages painted on roads and the dynamiting of roadside culverts to prevent access to the proposed site!

It was on one of our visits to the area that we met, purely by chance, the nephew of the author Arthur Girdham. Girdham has written several books about the Cathars and it was partly his books, plus encouragement from friends in England, that led us to research certain aspects of the Cathars and their relationship with Rennes-le-Château, a small village not far from where we now live. On the same visit, we met many other people who proved to be helpful to us, both during and after our move to France.

On our return to the UK, we spent a great deal of time researching the local history and in particular the story of Rennes-le-Château, which is well documented by others. Our research led us to a discovery that is, as far as we know, unique. This work is still continuing and will hopefully be published in the near future.

By another chance, a friend in the area telephoned to say that he had heard of some land for sale and asked if we would we like him to view it. A couple of days later a fax arrived with all the details with a request that we should fly down to see it, as it was so lovely.

Falling In Love

We made a special visit to see the land that we had been told about, looked at it in the rain, in the sun, loved it immediately and decided there and then to buy it. In comparison with the price of land in England, what we paid for 1,500 square metres with stunning views of the foothills of the Pyrenees was incredibly little. We shook hands on the deal with the vendor, who was to become our friend as well as our neighbour, returned to England and set about designing the home that would be our B&B business and, hopefully, see us into retirement.

Our immediate family were very negative at that time, making comments like "you don't speak the language", "you don't understand the tax system", "you won't be able to go to the cinema or theatre like you do here", "what will you do for friends?", "you won't have a job", and so on. Indeed, we felt a great deal of pressure to change our minds. Now, their attitudes have completely changed, as they can see that we can speak French, we can cope with life, we have made good friends and we have a good life here.

Friends and work colleagues were much more supportive at that time, interested in our plans and enthusiastic about our proposed new life, and, we suspect, a little envious, wishing that they too could turn their dreams into reality. Some colleagues used phrases like "you're so lucky", to which our normal reply was that it wasn't about luck; we had worked hard for this opportunity.

We completed the plans for our bungalow and *gîte*, then contacted three builders in Aude, but were surprised by the variation in detail of the quotations. We were impressed by the detail and the overall price estimates of one builder, arranged to see him, and were invited into to his home to discuss details. Having accepted his quotation, we were issued with a contract, which we employed a professional company to translate, and then financed the construction by selling our home in Southampton and renting a property in Eastleigh.

Doing this for a year enabled us to make the stage payments for the construction and invest money whilst still earning our salaries. We bought a large van and rented a garage in a neighbouring village in Aude to store much of our furniture. Whilst making regular visits to the site to check progress, it became easy for us to move our goods and we became experts in packing our van so that no space was wasted. This may sound like an expensive option, but having the van enabled us to move large items after we had arrived in France, and we returned it to the UK after about three months, selling it back to the company we had bought it from.

Building A Dream

During the construction phase, we had to learn a great deal of technical French in order to have discussions with our builder and, by attending evening classes in Southampton, achieved much of this in the year leading up to our departure. We had only contracted for the shell of the building, internal insulation, plumbing, sanitary fittings and electrics, so we had to install the heating, kitchen and lighting and do all of the finishing work ourselves.

Looking back on it now, we felt that we seriously underestimated the amount of finishing work that needed to be done and, even on a new house, the work to create the garden, paths and parking area.

In November 2002 we made the final move with the remainder of our furniture, our three cats and our van. Because of the tardiness of the electrician and the plumber, we had to stipulate a moving date and insist that the house was habitable on that day. Immediately prior to leaving the UK, we had to have our cats examined by our vet and certified fit to travel. As they would never be returning to the UK, they didn't need a 'passport' but had to be moved within 72 hours of certification.

Our enquiries with the ferry companies were less than satisfactory, as the cats would have to spend the whole trip in the van on the cargo deck and we would be charged a ridiculous price per cat for the privilege. As the ferry company flatly refused to let us take the cats in their travel cages onto the passenger decks, we decided to use the Channel Tunnel for our journey, which although longer in mileage was shorter in time – and we could stay with our pets for the whole journey.

> *the cats took all this in their stride – with the exception of being taken outside on leads for a few days to be shown the garden*

We arrived at our new home on the day we had stipulated, but the plumber took a further week or two to complete his contract and the electrician took even longer. Having been connected to a temporary 15 amp supply from a post across the road, we had to juggle the things that we used at any one time, or the contactor would trip out and we would then have to go to the post over the road to reconnect the supply. The lesson that we learnt from this was that French tradesmen don't complete work when they say they will and seem to have a completely different view of deadlines from ours.

Overall, our builder did an excellent job and the plumber, when we could get him to turn up, did also. The electrician was less satisfactory and, as we were to find out much later, had completely ignored our written instruction to put most of the cabling in the roof. An English neighbour who had seen much of the construction work told us that it was like spaghetti under the floor tiles with copious amounts of cable trunking running in all directions. This, plus a great deal of repair work necessary to the walls where trunking had been inserted and outside light cables protruded from behind shutters, convinced us never to use this person again.

Settling In

Our first few days in our new home were very busy. The cats took all this in their stride – with the exception of being taken outside on leads for a few days to be shown the garden. Their protest consisted of going rigid and rolling over, then waiting to be picked up and taken in again, whereupon they resumed being normal cats.

With Christmas looming we had to install our wood-burning stove and erect the entire flat pack kitchen before the plumber could finish his installation, including our gas hob. Luckily for us, having chosen a good builder, the walls were absolutely square and upright and the floor was level, making fitting the kitchen much easier. As we have no mains gas in the village, the supply to the hob was from bottled propane situated outside and the plumber was able to install this for us. We have found that one bottle of propane costing €25 lasts us about six months.

Very early on in our new life we realised that, apart from the local supermarket, we had no idea where to obtain the building and decorating items that were to become essential. We turned to people we had met on visits leading up to our move for help and advice and very quickly gained a sort of 'starter pack' of local knowledge.

We found that prices for similar items varied greatly according to the town and supplier and that some things, such as paint, are very expensive in France whilst other things, such as tools, can be very cheap. It was a revelation, for instance, to find out that plumbing fittings come in inch sizes as well as metric measurements and that the paint we had brought with us didn't have the same density as the French varieties, which had much more coverage and were the correct ones for our needs.

We had a slight setback after ordering and paying for fifty square metres of tiles plus cement for the terrace. A promise of two weeks extended to eight weeks as first we were told that the lorry had been in an accident in Italy, and then that the tile factory was on annual holidays. We weren't too pleased about this, as we were trying to complete the work on the terrace in time to let our *gîte* at the beginning of the season. Eventually, after many phone calls and visits to discuss the situation, the tiles arrived and the company gave us the free use of their truck as compensation.

> *we felt like fish out of water. We didn't know anyone, we didn't understand very much and we had to survive*

We enrolled for French lessons very early in the New Year. Although we felt that we were at 'advanced beginner' level, we were soon to find out how much we didn't know. In these early days progress was slow, but we started to build up a vocabulary and felt a little more confident about speaking to our neighbours, if only to say hello.

Luckily, one of our next-door neighbours spoke some English and suggested that his wife come with us to the local supermarket to help us understand the labels. Most things on the shelves are easily identifiable, but Suzie has a life-threatening nut allergy, so it is very important to understand exactly what is on the labels. Our neighbour's wife was a great help; when you discover, for instance, that bacon is called *poitrine*, it is like a revelation to the uninitiated and toasted bacon sandwiches are re-discovered!

Our early venture into French bureaucracy was, so say the least, interesting. We soon discovered how difficult this would be with our limited command of the language and we spent a great deal of time in various offices, as we seemed to be constantly directed from one to the other. However, people really did try to help us and eventually we succeeded on most issues.

In this area, there has been a great influx of new people, many of whom come from the UK. This has brought new prosperity to the region and its commerce with the result that a cultural organisation has been set up in our local town to help newcomers with the transition to a foreign country. Called CCMFE (Centre Culturel & Multimédia Franco-Européen), it provides French lessons and bureaucratic support in addition to organising social events. This organisation has been of great help to us in dealing with various French organisations, plus helping us to understand the various official documents that we often found, and still find, confusing.

Fish Out Of Water

In the early days, we felt like fish out of water. We didn't know anyone, we didn't understand very much and we had to survive. I remember, one day in Quillan, our local town, our being so overwhelmed by all the signs, the adverts and the conversations of the local people that we felt we couldn't understand anything. It was a rather strange feeling of being totally alienated from the world that we had known and were familiar with in the UK, where we understood everything and could converse with others. Luckily, we had already made some friends, many of whom were recent arrivals like ourselves, and so we were able to move forward, but it was a very strange experience.

Making new friends has been surprisingly easy, sometimes through chance meetings in the supermarket or DIY shops, sometimes through CCMFE, sometimes thorough other people with whom we had already become friendly. Most of our friends are of a similar age to ourselves, a few much younger. All have come here with similar outlooks: to have a better life than they had in the UK, to enjoy the warmth and the sunshine and, to appreciate the culture and beauty of the area.

Although we work very hard on our home and garden, we try to take at least one day per week purely for exploring the area. As we run a B&B, we feel that it is important to have extensive local and regional knowledge. As we travel around, we find things that are unusual. For instance, we have found a salt-water fountain (source) in the middle of a field, discovered a local sculptor who exhibits his work in a field adjacent to his house, visited the most incredible rock formations, which will probably have eroded away in the next fifty years, and seen the most amazing church, which has its access through a fissure in the rock upon which it stands.

Making A Living

We knew that it wouldn't be easy to establish a B&B business here. There are many existing B&Bs, *gîtes*, holiday homes and hotels, so we decided to specialise as a mainly vegetarian B&B because, if you are a vegetarian in France, feeding yourself can be very difficult at times, as a great deal of meat and meat products are consumed here.

Our main problem has been getting known and we spent quite a lot of money advertising in UK publications, none of which produced the results we were hoping for. We designed and built a comprehensive website (www.audexperience.com), which is regularly updated, but our breakthrough came when we placed two advertisements in the Aude Tourist Board brochure. This has produced better results and we are impressed with the range of countries that receive this publication, having received enquiries from as far away as Denmark.

We don't think that running a B&B, however good it is, will provide all we will need financially; therefore, it is necessary to have an additional income such as a pension or savings, as we anticipate that it will take some time to become known and to get fully established.

Our village has about 120 inhabitants and nestles in a small plateau in the foothills of the Pyrenees. Like most villages in the area, it has a number of councillors who look after the business of the village and a committee that arranges social events. The Easter following our arrival was our introduction to one such local event with a meal organised for the villagers.

Arriving at about midday at the *mairie* for drinks whilst two lambs were being roasted on a spit, we suddenly discovered that we were supposed to bring a plate, glass, knife, fork and spoon each. No one had told us of this requirement, so a quick dash home was necessary. On our return most people had gone into the dining area to start the festivities, which involved much eating, drinking copious quantities of local wine and singing until quite late. There then seemed to be a brief pause, after which it all started again. Many people seemed unusually quiet the next day!

Our neighbours have been very good, patient with us and helpful in explaining things that we don't seem to understand too well. Although it is still early days, we have been accepted by our immediate neighbours, who now call us "nice English French people". Our neighbours on one side actually said that to us in English and the ones on the other side, who don't speak English at all, said that "together we make a good team". They, like us are new to the village and, even though they are French, feel that it will be some time before we are all fully accepted into the community.

> *there is neither drunkenness nor aggressive behaviour, just people out enjoying themselves*

The soil on our land is mainly clay with a great deal of rock mixed in. We struggle with gardening, as we need a pickaxe to remove the stone, then the clay either sticks to everything or is so solid you can't break it. One day a tractor pulled up outside and the driver asked us if we would like the contents of the trailer – a whole load of horse manure and straw. As this is very beneficial for clay soil, we accepted this example of local generosity without much hesitation and now have the start of a wonderful vegetable patch.

Instances such as this make us feel that we are becoming more accepted by the villagers, the majority of whom have been here for much, if not all of, their lives. It must be difficult for local people to adjust to the influx of foreigners, which, although contributing to the prosperity of the region, also results in property prices increasing dramatically. In villages like ours – where three years ago there was only one permanent British family and now there is us as well, plus three British holiday homes – it is easy to understand that the local people might feel they are being 'taken over'.

Taking Stock

Would we return to England? At the moment we feel that a permanent return is unlikely and there are several reasons for this. Having experienced the trauma of an aggressive burglary about eighteen months before we moved, we feel safe here. For example, our local town has an international folk festival in the summer and, even though there are often hundreds of people on the streets late at night, there is neither drunkenness nor aggressive behaviour, just people out enjoying themselves.

People are friendly and polite; shopping can be a pleasure, as the vendors are welcoming, helpful, anxious to please and tolerant of our inability to be fully fluent in French at the moment. We don't feel as stressed as we were when we were employed, even though we work much harder, as everything we do is for our benefit and that of our friends who have chosen a similar life here. The pace of life and the attitudes of minorities in the UK are of concern to us and, realistically, we couldn't afford to buy property again of the standard that we now enjoy.

become involved in your local community, its culture and events because you have chosen to be part of it; it has not chosen you

Overall, our move to France has been successful and, although there is still much to do, many places to explore, new people to meet and a new life to build, it is pretty good really.

So what advice could we offer to anyone contemplating a similar move? Perhaps the first priority is to research your chosen area as much as possible and to visit it as often as you can at different times of the year, having due consideration for the locality of shops and amenities. If you are contemplating buying an older property, you will need to think carefully about renovation costs and the length of time the work might take; even with a new property, don't underestimate the amount of work or the length of time required to obtain goods, as we did, or the amount of money needed.

Become involved in your local community, its culture and its events because you have chosen to be part of it; it has not chosen you. Most of all, take time to discover your region and what it has to offer you, make determined efforts to learn French and then enjoy your new life as we have already found we do.

Into The Unknown

Martina and Peter Nowottnick moved from their
native Germany to the Ile-de-France, where Peter was
to start work for a recently formed company. While he
soon felt at home in his new surroundings, Martina
became increasingly isolated and depressed.

Our adventure of living in France started in July 1997. At that time, I (Peter) was working at a university in Hamburg as a research assistant in microelectronics and applied computer science. Working within an international research project, I got contacts with many European colleagues, including the development team of our French partner company. In spring 1997, this team spun off a new company, just when I was about to finish work on my PhD, which was related to the results achieved by the project. When I started looking for jobs, I got an offer from this new company, working in the microelectronics industry, on telecommunication-related products (hardware/microchips and associated software).

So, I had a job offer to start working in France. Martina, my wife, and I decided to accept the offer and to take the challenge to move to France. The main factors influencing this decision were the prospect of learning an additional foreign language by living in that country, and of getting a new life experience (living as a foreigner in an unfamiliar country) with the opportunity to get to know that country. For me, as a young engineer, the career opportunities were tempting: starting work as one of the first employees in a start-up company, which provides a very friendly, open, dynamic, and also challenging work environment with the option of taking responsibility within the company quite soon.

As we didn't have children at that time, it was relatively easy to take that decision. We weren't risking too much (except for Martina's job, which she had to quit). And I would have had to relocate anyway, as my limited work contract at the university was ending that August. The new company asked me to start working as soon as possible.

Have Suitcase, Will Travel

Thus, in mid-September 1997, I started working for this company, moving with just a suitcase and a few boxes of books and documents to France. Martina had to continue working and therefore had to stay in Hamburg. I stayed in a simple hotel close to the company's offices (St Quentin-en-Yvelines, around twenty-five kilometres south-east of Paris) for the first three months.

From my temporary home, I (or we both together, when Martina came over at weekends) started looking for an apartment or house to rent. We had little money, and we didn't know how long we were going to stay in France, so we didn't even consider buying a property. We looked almost everywhere in the area surrounding St Quentin-en-Yvelines, finding very nice villages in the neighbourhood.

It quickly became apparent that the area close to St Quentin (including the town itself), as well as the area towards Versailles, was too expensive or the apartments were in such a bad condition that we would have had to invest too much to make them habitable. Therefore, we had a look more to the south of St Quentin, about ten to fifteen kilometres away, where we finally found a small, but nice apartment with a private garden in Les Ulis, a town with about 27,000 inhabitants.

The population here consists of many different cultures and people with skin of every colour. Most of the people living here are French citizens, a high percentage having African or Arabic origins.

The search for the apartment would have been very difficult for us without the help of two colleagues. Our assistant provided me with useful information about ways to find rented accommodation. She pointed us to a newspaper specialising in private real estate offers called *De particulière à particulière*, which was very helpful and gave much better offers than the estate agencies provided. And the second great help came from one of my colleagues, who speaks very good German, who helped me by calling some of the owners who were advertising apartments and came with me to the first visits I made. **I spoke almost no French when I arrived here** and I had no time (and no money) to take an intensive French language class.

> *getting integrated here in our new environment was a long and painful process. And the French language has a large impact on whether you are accepted*

In order to be able to rent an apartment in France, you need to have a French guarantor. This can be a severe problem for foreigners. We were lucky and the owner of our apartment accepted my father (who is also German) as guarantor.

Renting & Renovating

We got the apartment at the end of the 1997 and started renovating it. Although the apartment was offered as *"habitable sans travaux"*, there was quite a lot of work to do: removing all the old wallpaper (some of it seemed to date from more than twenty years ago before), renew all paintwork, including window frames and doors, change carpets in one room, remove the old PVC in the kitchen and WC, and so on.

We did all of this work ourselves, which took quite some time (as I was already working in my new job). But as a result, we got the apartment in exactly the state we wanted it, even if it had cost a lot of energy.

The apartment was worth the effort. It is located on the ground floor of a small apartment block (ten apartments on five levels) within a beautiful *résidence* in several segments, each consisting of about a dozen such buildings. The buildings were at that time about twenty years old, but looked as if they had needed a face-lift for at least nineteen years! And we have our own small private garden.

In mid-January, we actually moved into the apartment, which was not yet completely renovated. In March we completed the major work when (with the help of my parents) we put tiles on the walls in the bathroom and on the kitchen floor. The owner of the apartment paid for the materials, but not for our labour. The move itself went smoothly. We engaged a German removal company, which was paid for by my new employer. At that time, we had two rabbits and a guinea-pig. Taking them with us was no problem, even on the aeroplane that we took for the journey from Hamburg to Paris while our furniture was travelling by road.

> *everyone was very tolerant of my hesitant attempts at speaking French, which greatly helped me to gain confidence*

Getting integrated here in our new environment was a long and painful process. For me, it was much easier than for Martina. While I was working in a young team with open-minded colleagues, Martina had stopped working for the transition to France and found no possibility of working here in France, so she had no 'natural' entry point.

And the French language has a large impact on whether you are accepted here or not.

French Frustration

Our experiences in learning French were very different. As I have said, we both arrived in France almost without speaking French and having had no opportunity to take French classes beforehand.

At first, my colleagues were very considerate and tolerated me speaking English, although they had difficulty speaking English themselves, just as I had difficulty understanding them speaking French – and some of them speaking English too! Anyway, it was a Franco-American company, so a large part of the business had to be done in English – this greatly helped me to defend my position!

After about a year, I started slowly to understand more and more of the French that was used in the office and I was then 'forced' by my leader to start speaking French myself. Again, everyone was very tolerant of my hesitant attempts at speaking French, which greatly helped me to gain confidence with their language.

Nowadays, I am almost fluent in French conversation, although expressing complex (non-technical) facts and writing French is still difficult for me. But I get lots of compliments on my level of spoken French from other people.

Martina had much more difficulty learning French. Just after we moved, she learned by chance from a German lady she met on the aeroplane that the Sorbonne in Paris offered French classes for foreigners, called *cours de civilisation française*. Registration for this course turned out to be the first entrance barrier: all documentation, all information where to go (you needed to go to three different places in two buildings) and all additional explanations were given in French only! This means you have to be fluent in French to register for a French class. Martina just managed, thanks to being accompanied by the German lady, who spoke French very well.

The language course at the Sorbonne was very theory-oriented. The pupils were faced with too much grammar and too little practice. For somebody like Martina, who had no opportunity to speak French outside the class, the teaching method wasn't effective or satisfactory. The teacher wasn't able to take into account individual requirements and didn't cover any item outside the topics covered by the textbook. After four months of intensive work in the class every morning and several hours at home every afternoon, Martina passed the final examination with a 'good' grade, but wasn't capable of having a simple conversation in French. This experience created a lot of frustration and blocked her access to the French language for a long time.

At the end of this four-month language course, in which Martina had put great hope and on which she had spent a lot of effort, but which didn't help her to speak French at all, she fell into a deep hole of discouragement and passivity. She needed another six months to get over it and to get in contact with a local organisation called Friends of the German Language and Culture. The lady Martina spoke to referred her to another organisation, the Accueil des Villes Françaises and gave her the phone number of the person responsible for the German *Kaffeeklatsch* ('coffee gossip' group), as she thought her own organisation wouldn't be the right place for Martina to go.

Coffee Gossip

Martina finally called the *Kaffeeklatsch* organiser and found her to be not only a sympathetic listener but also a woman of action. She provided Martina with the details of how to join the AVF (the meeting times and an exact description where to go) and assured her that she would find friendly, helpful people, even though she didn't speak French. Furthemore, she promised Martina that she would contact her straight after her return from holiday. For the first time since we had arrived, Martina felt positive and looked forward to the future.

Martina went to the next meeting and found herself facing a large group of people, who were all chatting and laughing while drinking coffee and tea and eating cakes. The day she had picked to go was the celebration of the *galette du roi* (Twelfth Night) in January 1999 and many AVF members were there. Immediately, somebody came up to Martina and showed her to a table of English-speaking people. She was welcomed very sincerely and the same day was introduced to everyone she needed to know. This made her feel, from the first minute, that she really belonged to this group.

Within the AVF, Martina participated in the French conversation group and the German *Kaffeeklatsch* and started to regularly go walking with a group of members. All of them were friendly, open-minded, patient and very helpful. Some had lots of sympathy for her and her situation. The whole situation remained difficult, as Martina was still somehow isolated by the language, but she no longer felt that coldness around her. The AVF saved Martina and gave her many real friends.

In the second year of our stay here, we had the opportunity to take some French classes in different language schools through my company. These classes helped a bit to intensify our learning, but with just those classes we would never have succeeded. For me, contact with my colleagues was the most important factor in learning French; for Martina, French conversation in the AVF and the personal contacts from this helped most. Martina also participated in a French class in Palaiseau, which was organised by another association and specialised in basic French, using conversation groups. These courses are individually tailored to the participants' requirements and progress.

Impasses & Inconsistencies

Another step in integrating into French society was to get all our paperwork done. With this, we ran into a classic impasse of bureaucracy. As residents of a member country of the European Community, as it was then, we needed to apply for a *carte de séjour*, which is supposed to be just a formality – no difficulties are to be expected . . . To obtain this card, we had to get some personal papers from Germany (either translated or as an international form) and to present some French documents, among other things my social security number. To get this number, we had to contact the *Sécurité Sociale*. But it turned out that the *Sécu* wanted to see my *carte de séjour* before being able to assign me a social security number!

At that time, I was incapable of dealing with French administration. Thankfully, our company secretary and director's assistant helped me to get out of this impasse. She had to telephone many different offices of the *Sécu* many times and had to explain the situation over and over before being able to resolve the problem. I don't remember all the details of how she finally convinced the office to assign me a temporary social security number without seeing my *carte de séjour*, but it was tough.

> *it was difficult to find*
> *open-minded doctors who*
> *would accept and support*
> *alternative birth methods*

Coming from Germany, we weren't familiar with the French health system. The first time we consulted a doctor here, we were a bit surprised to see a notice informing us about treatment costs and doctors' fees. At the end of the consultation, we got a bill, which we had to pay immediately. We weren't at all used to paying doctors directly; in Germany, they are paid via the social security and health insurance systems.

We got our *carte vitale* quite soon after we arrived here. This card is supposed to be used in doctors' practices, hospitals and chemists' to prove your entitlement to treatment and to avoid your having you to pay for consultations and medicine. But in our first year, nobody was equipped with a card reader for the *carte vitale*, so you always had to have the printed copy of your certificate with you, so the medical services could read the information. Even today, five years later, almost no doctor accepts this card for payments. It is just used to carry your social security identification in electronic readable form.

Classical Delivery & Consumer Education

Our contact with the French health system became closer with the arrival of our two boys (Florian in 1999 and Lucas in 2002). Thankfully, the pregnancies were both straightforward and the births uncomplicated. It was just difficult to find open-minded doctors who would accept and support alternative birth methods.

The main problem turned out to be the fact that midwives and nurses in French hospitals are well trained to work with women who have epidural anaesthesia when giving birth but not for natural birth methods. Martina didn't want to have epidural anaesthesia and therefore needed more care during her long hours of labour, which unfortunately nobody in the maternity ward was able to provide. So we were left more or less alone within this difficult situation, until the labour reached its end. The personnel in the maternity ward were a bit inflexible and wanted to follow strictly their traditional methods. We therefore had to accept some compromises between our own wishes and the applied reality.

Something we learned from our experiences with the pregnancies and birth of the two boys is that you have to ask if you need help or if you want something. People are willing to help (if they can), but they usually don't offer their help. This is different from our past experience, where people often came and asked if we needed help. This is true for almost every area of our life – not limited to medical or service personnel, but also true of colleagues, neighbours and even friends.

Florian has been going to *école maternelle* (pre-school) for two years now. During this period, we have observed some specifics of the French school system. Furthermore, I have got some interesting feedback from my colleagues when comparing the French education system with the German one. The most obvious characteristics of the French system for me are the following: school days are too long, with homework in the evening and school on Saturdays, a lot of learning by heart sometimes without the necessary background of understanding what is learnt; often pupils aren't sufficiently encouraged to participate, so they learn as if they were a 'consumer'; and, last but not least, insufficient school time is allocated to music, art and sport.

Some of my colleagues have confirmed that on leaving school they had a very thorough general education, but they had missed some aspects of getting self-confidence and being able to take responsibility. Of course, this cannot be generalised, as I have talked to only a few people.

Free Time & Friends

The way we organise our free time here in France is completely different from what we had experienced in the past in Germany. The most significant difference is the way activities are organised. Before moving to France, we sang in two choirs in Hamburg. Like most choirs in Germany, they were linked to a church and we didn't have to pay anything to participate. In France, you have to pay an annual fee (which could reach a significant amount) if you want to sing in a choir. We recently started singing in a choir here, limiting ourselves to alternately participating in the rehearsals (except for the main rehearsals before a concert) to avoid needing a baby-sitter every week.

*after six years of living here, I
would describe the environment
we live in as friendly but distant*

The same applies to sporting activities. In Germany, you can take part in most sports within clubs. Typically, to be a member of a club, you pay an annual fee, for which you can participate in several sports (except very expensive disciplines); some clubs even offer certain disciplines free. Here in France, we were confronted with the fact that you have to pay individually for each sport you want to take part in, which can easily add up to large amounts. You need a health certificate (which you can get from any doctor) for all kinds of sports, even for basic activities like gymnastics; this applies equally to a four-year-old child who just wants to do some sporting activities and to adults planning to enter competitions. As we have two children, we weren't (and still aren't) able to participate in many activities.

Our integration into French society is going on very slowly. After six years of living here, I would describe the environment we live in as friendly but distant. We get on well with the neighbours and don't have any acceptance problems as foreigners. This may be related to the presence of many foreigners (because of the nearby university and a research centre). But we don't have close contacts with French people. In my opinion, several factors are responsible for this. The daily schedule of an average French family doesn't leave much room to meet other people (working late, children's homework, dinner, hobbies?) and the little time that is left is often spent within the family.

I have experienced a strong separation of professional life and private life; thus colleagues don't usually become good friends. And, as we have observed quite often, French people (at least here in the Ile-de-France) are quite reserved. Maybe this is related to the linguistic inadequacy we have to cope with, but it might just be their mentality. The result is that most of the friends we have made here are foreigners – not necessarily Germans.

But there are exceptions. Martina got into closer contact with French women (and some turned into friends in time) from the *Kaffeeklatsch* group, which is a culturally very diverse group composed of people of many nationalities. And, on the playground close to our home, she met a Frenchwoman with two children about the same age as ours. That day, Martina wasn't sure whether she should ask her to stop by one day or not, because in the past all attempts to get into contact with Frenchwomen had failed. But she summoned all her courage and asked her – with success!

We now have a very good relationship with this family; they could almost be considered as good friends. It may be relevant that they don't originate from the Paris area but from the south of France and the woman doesn't work either (like Martina). When we talk to them about our impression of getting into contact with people here, they confirm that they had the same problems when they arrived in the Paris area . . .

Impressions & Advice

All in all, we aren't able to say whether living in France has fulfilled our expectations, as we had no real expectations before moving to France. But one thing is clear: if we had known in advance what to expect here, we wouldn't have moved to France without better preparation. In particular, learning the language would have been much a higher priority.

you need to speak French to be able to start living here or at least you need somebody around you who can help you with the language

On a positive note, we like the way French people behave in general (they are usually friendly and open, but keep a certain distance) and how they act with small children (very open and affectionate, and children are easily accepted within a group of adults). Also in the associations we have joined (AVF and choir) we experience a lot of kindness and feel very welcome. Something we like about French people is that the start time of appointments is often not that strict, e.g. it is 'normal' for a rehearsal to start fifteen minutes later than scheduled.

As we are both busy during the day, we also like the markets on Sundays, and the fact that the shops are open much later. Motorways are better and less crowded (because of tolls).

On the negative side, we sometimes dislike some aspects of the French mentality, e.g. talking and complaining about things but taking no action, and parents often forcing children to behave or act in a certain way. In addition, the price of housing (at least in the Ile-de-France) is extremely high, but buildings are often in bad shape.

Some final advice from our experience: try to get as much information in advance as possible, for example about lifestyle, bureaucracy, French mentality, the school system, etc; have somebody in France help you get started, e.g. try to find a group like the AVF, which has the aim of helping people who are new to the area. You need a French citizen who is able to explain how living in France works. There are many unwritten rules you should know.

But again, the most important aspect is to know the language. You need to speak French to be able to start living here or at least you need somebody around you who can help you with the language.

No Regrets

Janet and Jonathan moved from Buxton
in Derbyshire to Normandy, having decided to
give life in France 'a go'. Although they were well
prepared, they discovered that nothing was
quite as they had expected.

W̶e both loved France. Jonathan knew the country from family holidays and school trips to Paris and Lyon and the surrounding area. His family also have a holiday home in the Quercy region. I had travelled all over France as a child with my parents; my father, a Francophile, had invested in a struggling vineyard in the Loire Valley so we spent a lot of time there with French family friends. On average I was in France two months a year from the age of ten to eighteen. After that, as a student, I hitched around France for three months (when hitching was safe!) and subsequently came every year for holidays or to stay with family friends. The only region I have never visited is Brittany!

It was an opportune time for us to move, as I was divorced and, even though I had just been promoted, I was bored with my life. Jonathan had just finished his studies and didn't know what he wanted to do with himself professionally. So, realising we had nothing to keep us in England, we decided to give it a go!

Moving Experiences

Our choice of area was determined by my finding a job which suited my qualifications and salary expectations. (I had a B'ED in French/English, an MA in Applied Linguistics and a TEFL qualification.) I found my first post by looking in the *Guardian Educational Supplement* and that is why we landed in Normandy.

We spent thirteen very happy years in the region and moved to the Béarn area in Pyrénées-Atlantiques in September 2003, due to the fact that the group Jonathan works for had bought a plant in the region and had offered him the post of President of the company.

The initial transition was surprisingly easy – probably because I had spent extended periods in France over a period of eighteen years and because we both had a positive attitude in moving here and were determined to make it a success.

The actual move from England to France posed no problems. As we were already living in France, we hired a van and drove over to the UK to load it up ourselves. However, the move from Normandy to the Béarn was a nightmare! We specifically chose a company that was registered with a professional national association (AFNOR), which is a 'guarantee' of quality and service, and opted for the five-star package – which means the company does everything: from packing all items by professional packers, to cleaning rugs before loading and cleaning the property ready for the new occupants. What a joke!

The removal lorry broke down and they couldn't send a replacement; they underestimated the number of people needed for packing and loading, which meant two employment agencies turned up at the gate asking me how many people I needed (is this what they meant by professional packers?); they underestimated the volume to be transported – all this resulting in a thirty-six-hour delay, our rugs left on the lawn to dry with black clouds overhead threatening to wet them again, the new owners moving in as we moved out and my driving ten hours overnight to be in time for the signing of the contract for the new house.

> **as we had been introduced 'privately' to the seller, we didn't have to pay estate agents' fees – just a backhander to the 'finder'**

The unpacking followed the same line: they underestimated the time it would take and had to leave for another job. So, instead of having our clothes hung in wardrobes and pictures on walls, we did most of it ourselves, and, amongst other things, found that Jonathan's shirts and pullovers had been used to wrap fragile items and dirty mugs hidden in boxes of books.

On arriving in France my boss had kindly booked me into a hotel near to work. When I realised that my limited funds were going to quickly run out on hotel bills and restaurant dining, I found a room in the local Foyer des Jeunes Travailleurs, which is basically a hostel for young people who can't afford to pay rent for an apartment or a house when they first start work, or are new to the region, and need time to find their feet. This wasn't the safest of places! I stayed there for nearly two months – saving my salary towards a deposit on an apartment and for furniture. Luckily, when Jonathan joined me they allowed us to share a room – not normally permitted.

Armed with character, bank and work references, together with three months' deposit, I found a two-bedroom apartment and we stayed there for two years. We realised that we were paying the same amount of money in rent as we could be paying in mortgage repayments and started to look for a house within our means.

Bombs & 'Black' Builders

We looked in local newspapers, estate agents' windows and *notaires'* notice boards. The buying process was surprisingly quick and straightforward, but we were a little apprehensive as a surveyor's report wasn't necessary.

For our current house in the Béarn I spent a lot of time surfing the internet and made appointments by phone. I wouldn't like to generalise but I found that

French-run companies were considerably cheaper in the pricing of their properties and their fees than British or German-run estate agents. However, after we had viewed around twenty properties, a wily estate agent said he knew of a house that would suit us. He was right! As we had been introduced 'privately' to the seller, we didn't have to pay estate agents' fees – just a backhander to the 'finder'!

> ***I walked into my living room to find the best example of still life modern art I had seen outside the Guggenheim***

The farmhouse in Normandy had been built in 1812 and little had changed since then – unless you call blocking up original fireplaces, installing a chipboard kitchen and a 'Cell Block H'-style bathroom extension improvements! As we only had rooms on the ground floor, we decided to extend into the roof area, creating two bedrooms and a bathroom. Originally this had been used to store hay and on clearing it out we found, amongst other things, candlesticks dating from around 1850, a trunk of clothes from the end of the 19th century and, carefully hidden in the beams, a leather pouch full of detonators from German Second World War bombs. The village had played a strong role in the Resistance.

We had quotes from what we thought were reputable local firms and eventually selected one, agreeing on a timeframe and costs. It turned out that the quote wasn't anywhere near the final bill! The builder had underestimated the amount of cellular concrete needed to lay the floor upstairs and the number of people needed to do the job, and he decided that the roof beams needed strengthening with iron joists – all at his cost, as these weren't hidden problems.

After a stream of different temporary workers hired by the company 'on the black' had come traipsing through the house, some working until 10pm on Saturday nights, the job was finished three months after the agreed final date. To cap it all, on one of the days they were laying concrete upstairs, I walked into my living room to find the best example of still life modern art I had seen outside the Guggenheim. Unbeknown to all, concrete had dripped through gaps in the beams onto the coffee table (complete with plant, candles, and fruit bowl), the antique Indian carpet below it and the footstool beside it, covering everything in a smooth, grey, fast-drying film and splashing the surrounding furniture and walls. I called the manager, who shrugged and walked away – expecting me to clean up the damage! He refused to contact his insurance company – so we deducted the cost of all the professional cleaning from the final bill. He wasn't a happy man!

Moral of this experience: Only pay a deposit for any work to be done, keep all paperwork - even if it's just scraps of paper with rough drawings or figures on, and don't pay for any of their mistakes or oversights.

And a word of warning: Be very wary of employing people 'on the black' (i.e. paying in cash, thereby avoiding VAT and social costs); a jealous neighbour of friends of ours 'shopped' their plumber - which resulted in a visit from the tax man and a hefty fine for both parties. If you don't have official receipts, you have no comeback with insurance companies should something go wrong. We have just found out that our entire central heating system was installed 'on the black' - so instead of having ten years' guarantee, we have none!

Check if there are local or national grants available for the work to be done; very often you can have part of the cost of the project deducted from your annual tax bill, especially if you are renovating an old house and the work involves insulation, heating and sanitary improvements - but only if you have legal receipts!

Check at your local town hall if the improvements need planning permission or need to be declared. There are numerous regulations, from the positioning of 'Velux' windows to the building of a swimming pool, some national and some with local derogations - so be fully informed. The conversion or addition of a room means an increase in your local tax bill. There was a rumour in our village in Normandy that the local council was sending up helicopters to photograph residential areas and isolated houses, to count the number of windows and compare the result with their records. I don't know whether the mayor started this rumour, but he told me later that he had a steady stream of people coming through his office to declare 'forgotten' work and there was a considerable increase in village funds by the end of the year!

We got married in June 1998 in our village in Normandy. The mayor said he was delighted as it was the first 'foreign' wedding he had celebrated in his town hall and hung the Union Jack and the French flag outside in our honour. We were also married in the local church; we had no difficulty in booking the church even though we aren't Catholic, but the Catholic priest couldn't marry us as I was a divorcee. So we had to find an Anglican priest willing to marry us. After two interviews and some very personal and searching questions directed at myself (including details of my sex life with my ex-husband - I had to bite my tongue!) he finally agreed - based on the fact that my first marriage hadn't taken place in a church but a registry office.

Fluent French?

I spoke what I thought was fluent French when we first moved here - having taught languages and visited the country for years. What an illusion that was!

What with local accents and dialects, slang and trendy expressions, the influence of street language, French rappers and Americanisms on the language, the different sense of humour, the addiction to acronyms and the national pastime of playing with words, I realised that the English National Curriculum hadn't prepared me for the realities of daily life. So, for me, it was a case of opening my ears and reading as much as possible to bring myself up to date.

For Jonathan the situation was different. He had studied French to A Level but in practice was very much a beginner, especially orally. It isn't much use knowing the difference between the present and imperfect subjunctive when you want to explain that your brake pads need changing! He was determined to speak the language as quickly as possible, so spent an inordinate amount of time watching television and listening to the radio, doing exercises in books designed for immigrants and school children, and working part-time in a bar.

We cannot emphasise enough the importance of learning the language – especially if you wish to integrate fully into French life, society and, of course, work. We are still shocked by the arrogance of 'Anglo-Saxons' who, arriving in this country (either on holiday or, even worse, to live), make no effort to speak French – not even a "*bonjour*" or "*merci*" when they go into a shop.

Why are you coming here? Are you going to join one of those sad communities such as some in Dordogne or Lot, where English immigrants have clanned together to eventually push out the entire French population of the village, including the local baker, grocer and bar owner, to create a 'little England', complete with a cricket team that French people are barred from joining? If that is the case, stay put!

Shortly after arriving in France, we were kindly invited to social gatherings by my new colleagues – who, as it was an English-language school, were mainly British. Having spent several evenings (at which the French language was banned – despite the presence of French people) listening to never-ending complaints about the French, their country, lifestyle – you name it, we heard it – we realised that this pseudo-colonial attitude wasn't for us. We wouldn't choose this type of people as friends in England, so why should we have to here? Being able to speak the language certainly helped us to integrate into the community quickly, to get to know our neighbours, to find employment, to understand the French mentality and diverse culture and history, to read newspapers, magazines and books, to listen to political and social debates, to understand their jokes – basically to live a normal life in France!

Job-Hunting

I was employed from England in the school, where I stayed for two years. As there was no opportunity for promotion, I moved to a company which was involved in the 'reinsertion' of unemployed people – mainly women and immigrants – into active life; my job description was to set up and manage a language learning centre for adults, with the emphasis on languages in the workplace. I was the only non-French person, and it was only when I joined this company that I really had the feeling that I was truly in France. Again, once the project was up and running, I saw no promotion opportunities and went back to my first 'love' of teaching children. I worked in a secondary boarding school which wanted to create a bilingual department, so I had the pleasure of discovering both the French public and private sector at the same time. More about this later!

Jonathan decided that he needed French qualifications (those bits of paper count for everything here; forget about experience!) so he signed up for an intensive international sales and marketing degree. He came out with the highest marks in his year and his French improved immensely. He scoured newspapers to find a job, but also sent out his CV to companies that he would like to work for. (If applying for a job, don't expect a letter in return – either to acknowledge receipt of your application or to tell you they aren't interested; it is beneath many companies to do this.)

before you embark on anything to do with officialdom, get a good night's sleep

He was quickly snapped up by a French company, but the surprise was his subsequent employment by one of the companies he had targeted on the off-chance. Much later, I had a similar experience, where a university I had contacted a couple of years before got in touch to offer me a post, which sadly I had to turn down. So despite the rumours, yes, CVs are kept on file, and yes, it is worth the price of a stamp to send your CV on the off-chance. For information on companies that may interest you, contact the local Chamber of Commerce, who have business directories, look in the Yellow Pages, and look on employment sites on the internet, such as www.anpe.fr (the national employment service) or www.monster.com.

I decided to set up my own company a few years ago and, knowing the French predilection for red tape and the relatively high costs of start-up in France, decided to sign up for a course at the Chamber of Commerce. For a nominal fee, I was given a very sound grounding in accountancy (nothing like the British system), the types of companies that can be created (very important – especially as far as social and fiscal charges are concerned), marketing and day-to-day running. They provided a wealth of information and support and are available to answer questions after you have started.

Before you embark on anything to do with officialdom, get a good night's sleep – this will help you keep a clear head and will keep your patience and tolerance levels up. Arm yourself with multiple photocopies of your birth certificate, passport, marriage certificate, previous marriage certificate and annulment (if divorced), driving licence and *carte grise, carte de séjour, RIB* (bank details), an official letter with your name and address on, such as an electricity or phone bill. Also have the originals with you and, if you can, get any English documents translated by an official translator, i.e. one who can put an official seal on them. Last but not least, paste a smile on your face – you'll get there in the end!

As many town halls in rural areas are open only for very limited (and often not convenient) times, many official documents are available for downloading and printing off the internet – together with relevant and useful information.

School Work

Having taught for several years in a French secondary school, I feel I have a good insight into the education system. I was employed in a fee-paying international boarding school which also accepts day students; it mainly followed the French national curriculum as well as offering SATS for bilingual English students and French-as-a-foreign-language courses for non-French students. Being Head of Languages gave me the opportunity to work in both sections. I worked with students from the ages of 11 to 20 preparing them for the *baccalauréat*, SATS and university entrance exams in the USA and the UK.

My overall impression was one of being left very much on one's own to cope – whether you are a student or a teacher. Teachers come into school, teach, and then go home. You teach only your subject. Your responsibility to the student is the giving of information as stated in the yearly *programme* (curriculum), making sure that you have completed the *programme* and checking that the student has retained it. That's all. Consequently, if, as a student, you are a slow learner, unmotivated, or have social/personal/family problems, you must deal with them elsewhere – school is not the place for them.

more credit is given to a pupil who knows the English irregular verbs by heart than to one who is able to go into a shop in England and successfully buy a bag of sweets

Success in the French system is based on the ability to absorb, retain and regurgitate facts. Little room (or credit) is given for the use of imagination, creativity, discovery, or the giving of opinions. Team spirit and class unity are not priorities. You are expected to aim to become a well-rounded individual.

You are judged by the marks you get during the school year – and your average mark (*la moyenne*) in each subject at the end of the school year determines whether you move up to the next year or whether you repeat (*redoubler*) the same year. Consequently in one of my English classes of fifteen-year-olds I had one nineteen-year-old boy. To succeed, students have to study hard – very hard.

When you first arrive in secondary school, you are put in a class and, if you don't repeat, you will stay in that same class until you leave. Even though each class has a *professeur principal* (similar to a form teacher but with fewer responsibilities), his or her role is more administrative than pastoral. They don't necessarily see their class every day and hardly any time is allocated on the timetable for them to make contact on an individual level with their charges.

I was *professeur principal* to pupils in *6ème* (eleven-year-olds) *3ème* (fifteen) and *1ère* (seventeen) and, having been head of year in England, was appalled by the lack of pastoral care and guidance expected from me. My job was mainly to lead *les conseils de classe* (teachers' meetings at the end of each term, where parents and two student representatives are welcome), at which we would discuss the progress and most importantly the average mark in each subject for each student; to lead *les conseils de discipline* (the same people but to discuss serious disciplinary matters); to organise class trips; and to make sure report books and any other paperwork were completed. If I wanted to build a relationship with my students, this was done in my own time and of course with the cooperation of the student and his/her parents. I found that I had often to deal with pastoral matters with my class during English lessons – which took precious time from my completing the year's curriculum.

From a language teacher's point of view, more credit is given to a pupil who knows the list of English irregular verbs by heart than to one who is able to go into a shop in England and successfully buy a bag of sweets. I was appalled by the lack of communicative language skills taught throughout all the years; I organised many school trips to England and the USA and many of my seventeen/eighteen-year-old students were unable to hold even the most basic of conversations with their hosts, yet they were able to mechanically recite whole chunks of Shakespeare and Milton – without understanding half of it – because it was part of the *programme*.

External national exams happen at the end of the *3ème* (age fourteen/fifteen). This is called the *Brevet* and students are tested in maths, French and history/geography. You must pass this exam but it is entirely worthless. The *baccalauréat* happens at the end of the *Terminale* (age seventeen/eighteen). This is the most important qualification, but as most students who reach this stage pass the exam, its value in the job marketplace has somewhat diminished. But, as I said earlier, the pieces of paper are vitally important.

There are several types of *baccalauréat*, depending on your interests, and you choose at the end of the *2nde* (age sixteen). The *bac 'S'* is the most prestigious – being mainly orientated to maths and science – so because of parental and media pressure most students opt for it, whether they are suited to it or not. Other common *bacs* are *'ES'* (economics-based) and *'L'* (literary-based). Unlike A Levels, the *baccalauréat* continues to give a broad education in several subjects instead of an in-depth study of a few subjects. So a *bac 'S'* student will still be expected to study a language whether he or she wants or has the ability to or not, and as his or her yearly marks are counted in a sort of continual assessment, it is important that at least the *moyenne* is reached. Consequently the pressure on students to study is very high.

Right from primary school, children and parents are encouraged to buy *cahiers de vacances*. These are small books full of exercises based on the last yearly *programme* in each subject, which are used either to catch up on what hasn't been understood or to revise and be ready for the following year's *programme*. In May and June, supermarket shelves are filled with these booklets, and there are news items on television and radio encouraging children to study during their long summer holidays – and they do! Even though the *cahiers* aren't mandatory, I know of one maths teacher who collected them in from her class at the start of the school year!

Hypochondriacs & Oenologists

We have had some health problems in France, as well as a serious car accident, and have found that the health care system is of a very high standard, with excellent facilities and very efficient, caring staff. Basically, you can make an appointment with any general practitioner (*médecin généraliste*) you choose; you don't have to register – and if you don't like his opinion you can go to another and another . . .! You will be given a prescription – often for more medicines than you actually need (doctors support drug companies and generic products are only now making inroads into the market).

The state covers seventy-five per cent of the cost of your doctor's bill and prescription and, if you have a *'mutuelle'* (a private health insurance scheme, often offered as a perk by your employer), the other twenty-five per cent is covered by this. The result is that the health care system is now deeply in debt, as, broadly speaking, the French are a nation of hypochondriacs! Talks in government circles are currently taking place to create a national register, which will stop the practice of going to consult several doctors for what is often a minor problem or, even worse, trying to find a sympathetic doctor who will give you a sick note!

The system is exactly the same for dentists and opticians. There are no long waiting lists for dentists or orthodontists, but we have found – both in

Normandy and in Pyrénées-Atlantiques – that the average waiting time for an eye test is six months, due to the lack of qualified opticians.

> ## *we only come across traffic jams during peak holiday periods, or when going to or leaving Paris*

For serious problems your general practitioner will refer you to a specialist. I had a serious skiing accident and subsequently was found to have no meniscus and snapped ligaments and tendons in my knee. I was given treatment immediately, with regular follow-up sessions, and finally six months of twice-weekly physiotherapy sessions – all paid for by the state and our complementary insurance. I was also told that I am eligible for micro-surgery; when I am ready to fit it in to my timetable, I can phone and give a week's notice for the operation.

We both enjoy travelling and have found the decreases in flight costs (except those of Air France) and the increase in the number of provincial airports using cost-cutting carriers such as Ryanair very advantageous when planning business trips, short breaks or long holidays. Jonathan occasionally travels by *TGV (high-speed train)* and finds it clean, quiet (mobile phones are banned in some carriages), safe and efficient. The motorways are fast, empty (compared to England!) and in excellent repair (thanks to toll booths – you get what you pay for!) with clean and well-run service areas. We only come across traffic jams during peak holiday periods, or when going into or leaving Paris.

Skiing is another of our hobbies. Obviously where we live now it is on our doorstep, but when we were in Normandy, thanks to the good motorway network, we were able to go skiing for long weekends quite easily and at very competitive prices.

We both enjoy good food and wines, of which there are many regional varieties. Although fast-food outlets and take-away services are available, these are mainly restricted to tourist and urban areas and have certainly not replaced traditional restaurants. We often go for weekends to different regions to discover their local wines and dishes, staying in one the many excellent-value *chambres d'hôtes* (B&Bs) available across the country. A word of warning to curry lovers: Aim for the major cities, as Indian restaurants are very thin on the ground. Vegetarians are also poorly catered for outside the main cities; it is a lifestyle choice that many French have great difficulty in understanding.

If you enjoy trying wines from different countries, stock up before you come here! It is practically impossible to find Australian, South African or any New

World wines in France; even worse, try convincing the average Frenchman that these wines are worth tasting – now there's a discussion that will bring out the vocabulary! Jonathan and I have both had great fun at the dinner table when serving foreign wines to French friends; we hide the label with a napkin on the pretext of catching drips from the bottle, let them pontificate on the quality, flavour, colour, etc. and then triumphantly reveal its origins. I'll let you imagine the rest!

Jonathan also enjoys playing golf, but it is a sport that is still in its infancy. There aren't as many courses as in the UK and they aren't always well-funded or well maintained and are often more expensive.

> *the pleasure of buying a warm baguette and eating it straight away has not diminished*

We have invested in satellite TV so that we can watch European sport, English films and comedy series in the original version. Despite the excellent efforts of the French at subtitling and dubbing, the subtleties of British humour aren't often conveyed.

English In France

In our village in the Béarn, according to the last census (1999), the population is 1,750 and rising. I don't know of any other English people in the village, but there are several Spanish – owing to proximity of the border. However, there are several holiday homes, belonging to Dutch and Germans. The village boasts a baker's, a bar, two mini-markets (in fierce competition with each other) despite the hypermarket being a ten-minute drive away, a chemist's, a vet's, a bank and a post office; the last has had its opening hours restricted recently and I don't think it will be too long before we see it closing totally.

It is very difficult to get to know people anywhere, let alone to make friends. However, having got beyond the stereotype image of an English person – i.e. a royalist football hooligan who doesn't know how to cook and lives permanently under rain clouds – we have made many French friends, from all walks of life, but mostly through contacts at work.

In Normandy we found it particularly difficult to get know our neighbours, as most people worked outside the village. Here in the Béarn, contact has been very easy, as most of our neighbours are farming families and consequently more accessible. However, we made a conscious effort to introduce ourselves when we first arrived and that certainly has made a big difference. We now get on very well with all of them and our relationships are based on mutual help and respect. I now know how to make a real *sauce béarnaise* and two of my neighbours make great scones! One good way of meeting local people is by contacting the town hall to see if there are any clubs and associations that may interest you, and most villages have social occasions and festivals that you can become involved in.

We have both met and made good friends with colleagues – mainly French – at our various workplaces, and have had the same type of up-and-down moments one experiences in any job, be it in England or in France.

When we first decided to move to France, we didn't have any particular expectations but came with completely open minds. We knew that it was up to us to make the effort, be it socially or professionally, if our lives here were to be a success. Fourteen years down the line, we have no regrets and, even though we could afford to, we would never return to the UK. We still feel that we have much to discover and enjoy in our adopted country and no, the pleasure of buying a warm baguette and eating it straight away has not diminished.

Of course there are negative sides to life here. Everything that is French is the best; anything that comes from outside France should be treated with suspicion (I once brought some top-quality venison sausages back from England and took them to a neighbour's barbeque; he initially cooked only one and cut it into ten pieces so that everybody could test it – needless to say the rest were cooked and devoured very quickly). Paris is still the centre of the world, especially to Parisians, and consequently anybody who lives or works outside Paris is considered a second-class citizen. Professionally speaking, it is still thought that the later you stay in your office the better a worker you are. The cost of hiring a taxi is scandalous – especially in rural areas (so much for tightening up the drinking and driving law). And sadly, racism and homophobia are still widespread and are expressed quite openly.

It only takes a glance in our freezer and cupboards to see what we miss most – bacon, sausages, baked beans, Marmite! We have recently returned from an extended tour of Ireland and we both agree there is one institution that cannot be copied or bettered anywhere in the world – the good old local pub!

Our advice to anyone considering moving to France would be: Learn the language and take off those rose-coloured glasses – it isn't all 'sun, *pastis*, straw hats and stone cottages in rolling vineyards'; it's real life!

An Englishman Abroad

Tim Stapleton went to France because he liked
French girls. After marrying one (twice) and settling
in Cher, he has trouble imagining leaving.
But life in France isn't all roses.

Imoved from Billingshurst in West Sussex, in 1992, after studying for three years in London. I moved to France because I loved the country and liked French girls. I had visited France often, as a kid on French exchanges, and as a student with friends – boating in Normandy, walking in the Pyrenees, and wandering around Paris and the rest of the country on a low budget seeing the sights, museums, etc.

I first worked on an organic goat farm in Isère (in the south-east), where a friend of mine had been. I had been living in London for my studies and was fed up with city life. The change was complete; herding goats, milking, sitting in fields with a bottle of *jus de pomme bio* – *quel bonheur!* So the transition was easy.

Love At First Sight

I came down to the Isère for the summer in 1992, when I was twenty-two, and decided I wanted to stay. I returned to the UK to sort out a few things from my London flat. There wasn't really any packing involved – being a student, I just had a bag of dirty washing; the rest of my junk I left in London. I came back in my Morris Minor to look for work on the nearby ski resorts, but had no luck, so ended up staying another six months or so on the farm.

One day, while I was sitting in the farm kitchen at the end of a long day, a beautiful Parisian girl stuck her head around the door and asked to speak to "Teem". I jumped up and presented myself, hoping she wouldn't notice my ripped and muck-stained working clothes. She said she had come down to visit her sister in a nearby village, and was looking for somewhere to stay.

She had visited an English-run B&B in the village, but it was too expensive for her budget, and the owners had suggested she asked me, as I was living in a house with a spare bedroom, albeit with very few facilities (i.e. no toilet or hot water). So she asked if she could stay with me, which met with my approval, and we settled on her filling the fridge with beer in lieu of payment.

Valérie then seduced me by preparing the most amazing feasts for me when I arrived home from working in the fields, and we would sit up gazing into each other's eyes, by candlelight, over a fabulous bottle of wine until late in the night. When she agreed to come and milk the goats with me at 6am I realised that we were made for each other. The fact that her English was as poor as my French at the time only made the relationship better, as we were obliged to use body language to communicate.

After three or four more months living in blissful poverty on the farm, we went to Las Palmas in the Canary Islands for six months to help my grandparents pack up and return to the UK – they had been there twenty-five years so it was quite tough. We managed to get to know each other very well during this time, in French, English and Spanish.

> " *my witnesses were my two brothers . . . when asked to put down their professions, I wrote Clown and Magician* "

When we came back to England, Valérie became pregnant, I proposed to her in a Sussex bluebell wood, she agreed and we started making preparations for the weddings – in the UK and Franc. We went to France to collect wine and Champagne for the various parties and to find a place to set up home afterwards. We drew a big circle on the map around Paris, within two hours' drive of the capital. While visiting Sancerre for the *vin blanc* we saw a *petite annonce* for a small house to rent quite cheaply, so we booked it to settle in after the weddings.

Two Weddings & Three Farmhouses

We 'first' got married in June 1994, in Maule, in Yvelines near Paris, a wedding presided over by the Mayor. I was new to French bureaucracy and slightly cross about having to have a medical before getting married, and about the forms I had to fill in giving endless details about myself and the witnesses I had chosen for our wedding. My *témoins* were my two brothers, who were both students at the time, and when asked to put down their professions I wrote Clown and Magician, not realising that this would be read out during the ceremony. Much hilarity ensued, although I am not sure if the Mayor really appreciated it.

He got his own back when, in answer to his question about whether I would take Valérie as my wife, I answered "*Ouai*", in the peasant accent I had learnt in the country – a bit like 'Yeah' in English. I was slightly embarrassed when he said, "In France, Monsieur, we say 'Oui' not 'Ouai'", in front of all my family and -in-laws – it put me firmly back in my place.

The reception was typically French, with a '*vin d'honneur*' – Champagne and nibbles to which everyone is invited – followed by a cruise down the Seine for a more select group and a six- or seven-course dinner lasting late into the evening and dancing the rest of the night.

We had a second wedding in the church at the end of my parents' garden in Sussex a week later, to enable English family and friends to attend. The French wedding was rainy (a good sign, apparently: *mariage pluvieux, mariage heureux*), and the English one was in blazing sunshine, to the surprise of the French guests!

We moved into our new house straight away. We had no animals when we moved, fortunately, which made it much easier – we coped with just a few trips in our Transit van, plus my parents visiting with their trailer. If we had to move now, we would need two articulated lorries!

We rented our first house in Cosne-sur-Loire in 1994 for 1,500 francs a month – a one-and-a-half-bedroom converted stable in need of renovation. We renovated it, but just as we finished Valérie gave birth to Théo and we found another house to rent – with three bedrooms, completely isolated in the country near Sancerre, for only 1,000 francs a month.

The landowners really just wanted the house to be lived in, as it had been a family inheritance; they had renovated it but been forced to leave for job reasons. We got on very well with them and the neighbours, who were also part of their family, so we got the lease and I moved all our stuff in while Valérie was in the clinic recuperating after the birth. She and our first-born moved straight into their new rooms.

We lived in the rented country house for about three years, and had our second child, Eva, in 1996. We started looking for a renovation project, mainly through local papers in order to avoid paying estate agents' costs. We weren't in a hurry; our house was lovely, and so we waited until we both agreed on the same house. I tended to see the houses in too optimistic a light, while my wife was rather sceptical about my ability to renovate a house alone. We must have looked at about fifty that we didn't agree on, and bought the first that we did.

I was then playing catch-up all the time to build bedrooms as quickly as my wife could have babies

The house was abandoned, and hadn't been lived in for about ten years. We found it through a classified ad, but this turned out to have been placed by an agency. We could have bought our house cheaper, in retrospect, because we accepted what the agent told us – i.e. that the roof was good. We could probably have got 100,000 francs off the price if we had checked it out more thoroughly; instead of signing the *compromis de vente* the first time we visited it!

Still, the selling price was still only 220,000 francs for two hundred and twenty square metres of living space, plus an enormous *grange* and lots of land, in an ideal spot for us. The roof seemed OK but turned out not to be – it had last been re-covered in 1924! The house had a big attic space that had been used for storing grain. We needed to renovate this space, but it was only when we had put the stairs in that we realised that one half of the roof was in a bad way. It looked fine – all the tiles were there – but almost every nail had rusted through, so the battens were just staying up by friction.

So, during the six hottest weeks of our first summer, with help from my very supportive family, I stripped the whole of one side of the roof, replaced all the battens, cleaned the tiles, and re-laid it all, never having done a roof before! It wasn't too complicated really, and I got a lot of advice from the locals, but it was very time-consuming, and hard work in forty degree temperatures.

I was then playing catch-up all the time to build bedrooms as quickly as my wife could have babies! We had one more girl, Aimée in 1998, five months after the move, and then our boy, Sam, was born in 1999. The house now has six bedrooms, a large living room, kitchen, two bathrooms, two toilets, a large, light-filled studio for my wife, who is an artist, to paint in, and a small messy office for me. It is about a hundred years old, with almost a hectare of land and a very large old barn, which still needs a new roof.

We are two kilometres from a village with schools, cafés and two or three shops, at the end of a road with no passing traffic. The only real problem is the lack of mature trees; we have planted many but now must wait twenty years for them to reach maturity. We do have a very productive peach tree though, and a few gnarled old walnut trees, which are beautiful.

The village has a population of 609, including us, which means we make up almost one percent of the population! I am the only person here registered as an EU voter. We don't yet have broadband internet access, and the lady at France Télécom laughed a lot when I phoned to see if we could get it. The department has announced plans to roll it out across the department by 2007, so we live in hope.

Accent Accidents

I was a beginner in French when I moved. I found it fairly easy to learn and did so through work and by talking to friends. I was lucky in that during my first stay in France – on the farm in the Isère – I was taken up by a large group of young, party-loving locals, so I spoke French all day and until very late in the evening seven days a week. This was fun, but mentally the most exhausting time, when I had to concentrate hard the entire time just to understand, but it brought me on very quickly.

I was also lucky to have a very good English friend there who was already fluent and able to explain the more difficult nuances to me. I then found Valérie, with whom I speak French, so the only time I speak English now is when I am teaching the language or with my children, and occasionally with friends and family. It now takes me a few days back in the UK before I start speaking 'normal' English again – I find myself saying things like "It's not true!" and "Oh la la la la" in a low guttural voice – and I always swear in French, bizarrely.

We have had many laughs over the years, and a few embarrassing moments, with the *cou/cul* difference, for example. In French your *cou* is your neck, and your *cul* your arse; unfortunately, to the English ear the '*u*' and '*ou*' sounds are virtually the same, so if you say "I've got a sore neck", it is generally taken to mean you have a sore arse.

Fortunately, a similar thing happens in reverse: I have got a French friend who couldn't understand the shocked reaction in an English B&B when he asked the lady of the house if she could change his 'shits'! The UK accent seems impossible to shake off completely, but the French seem to love it.

I initially worked as an English teacher, using English in class and French in endless meetings. Teaching work was very easy to find, but I was lucky; it isn't so easy for most people, especially as I found a job with Greta, the adult education part of the National Education Ministry, meaning relatively good pay and fairly stable contracts. I still do a lot of teaching work; it is a good way to meet people and leaves quite a lot of time for other projects.

My various other jobs have been on a self-employed basis. I have been a translator, combine-harvester and tractor driver, I have renovated buildings for others and acted as a house-finder/advisor on renovations. I still work as a journalist, writer, computer trainer and e-learning technician/writer on various internet projects. I get on very well with my French colleagues and clients.

It is easier to work for someone than to work for yourself in France, unless you can be sure of having a lot of clients/business. Business hierarchy works quite differently in France. It is generally stricter, and there is always the *tu/vous* difference, which can be used to put people down, show respect, or create an artificial distance between people, and is quite hard to get the hang of. At first I used *tu* with everybody, which is generally accepted if you are English, but now tend to use *vous* too much, which can have the effect of making people think that you aren't their friend rather than that you are showing respect.

Being a foreigner in French organisations allows you to get away with lots of things that the French couldn't, but also makes you a representative of your country, with the inevitable stereotypes that go along with that. If you work for yourself, it is quite complicated; it is best to get an accountant. If you are employed, everything is relatively easy. Basically, you have an awful lot of costs, and obligations. If you aren't sure that you will have enough capital, and clients, to tide you though the first three years, then it can be risky. There are many advantages in having a certified accountant, as you can then qualify for a simpler regime of *microentreprise*, with much less paperwork required.

Une Famille Nombreuse

The tax system in France is very favourable to families like ours (*une famille nombreuse*), as the amount you pay is dependent on your 'charges', i.e. the number of children or other dependent relations you have. So far, I have never had to pay income tax in France, and would have to earn an awful lot of money with four kids before becoming liable for income tax. There are, however, a lot of other taxes to pay!

All our children are at school in France, and so far our experiences have been nothing but positive. We were lucky to have good schools, very local, excellent teachers, reasonable class sizes, no serious discipline problems. However, we have friends with kids in *collège* and *lycée*, who are doing a fifty- to sixty-hour week. This is difficult for the kids – they have to cut down on extra-curricular activities – especially since there are very few sports or other clubs in the state school system.

> *having children brought up in France with foreign parents gives them all sorts of advantages*

Team sports are always organised outside the school system, meaning parents must become taxi drivers, juggling the timetables. I don't know why there is so much homework and such long days – the *Bac* is certainly quite hard, with many subjects studied to a high level, and the marking scheme of everybody getting points out of twenty and a rolling average score that is read out in front of the class in a sort of league table means that students quickly see if they are slipping behind.

All our children were born in France and we have become experts on births, problems with anaesthetics and breast-feeding. My wife had decided not to have an epidural for Théo's birth, which was in a private clinic as there was no hospital with a maternity ward in Cosne. We went to pre-natal classes and she was the only one of the twenty or so future mothers present not to want one. There was no possibility of having a home-birth, as no *sages-femmes* would commit to coming out, and no facilities for water births or anything other than the standard. When we arrived at the clinic, they assumed she would have the epidural, and refused to believe that she really didn't want one. The nurse actually went as far as to say, "You'll never survive without one." I resisted the urge to hit the woman and we went ahead, and everything was fine. We later found out that private clinics make a lot of profit on the epidural, but not much on the birth itself.

Our next three were born in the large public hospital in Bourges, with no problems, in very modern facilities, with a single room with en suite facilities and bright, friendly staff. Medical facilities are excellent. One strange thing, around here at least, is that very few women breast-feed their kids for long, many not at all, and you rarely see women breast-feeding their children in public. There seems to be very little pressure to breast-feed, and no education about possible benefits - certainly none of the guilt associated with not breast-feeding as is seen in the UK now. French women only get three months' maternity leave after the birth, and may see it as too difficult to continue breast-feeding and working. Although the French breast is widely seen on beaches, it is uncommon to see it in town or on the metro, and perhaps French mothers feel they would be stared at, or worse leered at, if seen doing so.

Doctors are sometimes a little 'holier than thou', but generally good, and I have got a great dentist. It is best to get a *mutuelle*, a private, top-up medical insurance. This covers the part of medicines and doctors' visits not reimbursed by the social security system. If you are salaried, this will often be paid for by the employer, or subsidised.

> *a lot of cultural exchange*
> *seems to go on with the help*
> *of alcoholic beverages*

From all I hear, having kids in France is a much better experience than in England – with the possible exception of those wishing for a home birth or special birthing facilities, which may be easier to come by in Paris or other large towns but are difficult to find in rural regions like ours. Otherwise, I think that having children brought up in France with foreign parents gives them all sorts of advantages – bilingual with no accent in either language and greater understanding of other cultures, etc.

Foreigners In France

In terms of leisure activities, I enjoy sport, gardening, and DIY, and locally there are many facilities for these. I also love reading and listening to British radio, all of which are easy to do here with the internet (e.g. Amazon for books and a Sky Digibox). You can now buy the latter, with a card, on Ebay or through any number of suppliers – at a price. The BBC is now free-to-air, which means that any digital satellite receiver can get the seven or eight BBC satellite stations and the numerous radio stations. The BBC children's channels are a great asset, as it means the children can listen to other accents and 'enjoy' English in a learning environment.

I am now more into good foods and wines than before, thanks to a large extent to the wonderful meals that my wife cooks for the family.

We have made many friends of all kinds in France. We get on well with our neighbours and some of them have become good friends. Our local friends are all French, as I haven't linked up with the expat community, such as it is, and have never bumped into British or American people in the area, although there must be some. We have a large English family and group of friends who visit often, so I don't miss the English contact too much.

It has been easy to meet people through work and children. I am on the school's elected board of parents, which means I also have a lot of contacts through the school, and like to be a member of the local community. I have learnt to make *vin d'épine*, a sort of aperitif, and taught them to make home-brewed beer and sloe gin. A lot of cultural exchange seems to go on with the help of alcoholic beverages!

Although there are very few foreigners in this part of France, I was accepted very easily into the local community – more readily, in fact, than my wife, who is a Parisian! The equivalent of the North/South divide that exists in England is the Paris/Provinces divide in France. Very few people who live outside Paris would ever consider moving to Paris – though many admit to enjoying it for a short holiday, and very few Parisians I have met would cope with living in the *cambrousse* – the large muddy hole outside Paris, far from everything and everyone.

The Parisians who have holiday homes around here do sometimes give a bad example to the locals – you can be sure they will drive in the middle of the road to avoid muddying their wheels on the verge, and there have been many examples of *citadins* (city-dwellers) complaining about cocks crowing and church bells ringing and muck smelling.

I think I was also accepted more readily than the French-born people of North African origin. There are consistently about fifteen per cent of French voters who vote for the *Front National*, and there seem to be more people who are ready to admit to disliking foreigners. I guess it is the same the world over, but the French voting system gives minority parties much greater exposure – as seen in the last presidential run-offs.

I know of a family where the twenty-eight-year-old daughter has never introduced her boyfriend of six years' standing to her father for fear of his reaction to his Mahgrebian origins. I do think it is generally easier to be accepted in rural communities as a white Englishman than as an Algerian, for example, but only among a minority of the local population, and this is changing with increased exposure to outside influences.

Representing England

I find that the quality of life is better than in the UK. There is more space and less noise, housing is much cheaper, tax policy is family-friendly, wine and tobacco are still cheaper, especially for pipe and rolling tobacco, but the weekly shopping bill has increased a lot since the introduction of the euro. Single malt is cheaper than in Scotland, and DIY supplies much easier and cheaper to find – especially heavy raw materials (sand, cement, concrete, plasterboard, wood, etc.).

I miss my family and some old friends, Cadbury caramel eggs, English sausages for breakfast, the easy availability of fresh milk

France has lived up to my expectations, although it is not all roses – I have been very lucky. I like the fact that you are greeted with a *"Bonjour Monsieur/Madame"* rather than the stony silence in English shops; the peace and calm; the wine. I dislike the *vous/tu* difference that makes life needlessly complicated, the lack of understanding of how roundabouts and indicators work among certain, often elderly, members of the community, the paperwork, identity cards, etc.

I never thought I would stay; now I have trouble imagining leaving. I would like the children to experience an English-speaking environment for a year or two, but we couldn't afford to live in the UK. We could possibly go the States one day, as I also have US nationality, but we will probably stay here. The children can always choose to go to university in the UK if they wish.

What do I miss about the UK? Sitting next to the fire in a country pub in the winter, or in the garden in the summer, with the pub atmosphere and camaraderie that is never quite the same in a café. I miss my family and some old friends (but they come and visit), Cadbury caramel eggs, English sausages for breakfast, the easy availability of fresh milk and English newspapers . . .

I would advise others to come to France, but not around here, please – house prices are going up fast enough as it is! It is close to home, but we enjoy a much better quality of life, largely thanks to the cheaper housing in this area. I think being an isolated Brit/foreigner in a largely French area has many more advantages than being in a British/foreign 'enclosure'.

I find that I am regarded as being representative of the whole of England and Britain and have learnt much about my English identity through thorough questioning by French friends and family. I am supposed to be phlegmatic, a lover of le fairplay and a gentleman, and I think I probably am more so since I have been here. My English accent has also become more English, I think, through teaching the language.

I am regarded by some people as being responsible for British political decisions (problems with British involvement in Iraq, lack of UK integration into Europe, etc.), in which case I tend to deny any responsibility, pointing out that I have become disenfranchised in the UK, and not yet enfranchised properly in France. Also the England-France sport matches are much more important than they used to be, and being English has never felt so good as when we beat the French and went on to win the Rugby World Cup!

Staying Despite It All

Bev Laflamme 'just happened' to move to France. Despite being married to a Frenchman, she was regarded as an illegal immigrant and told she had thirty days to leave the country.

Unlike many expats I have met here in France, I never aimed to come live and work in France. I originally wanted to come to Europe, and in fact I wound up in Germany, which makes sense seeing as I have a university degree in Germanic Languages. Moving to France just sort of happened. But here I am, and I expect here I am going to stay.

I am American by birth. I was born in St. Louis, but did most of my growing up in New England. My father's family hails from New Hampshire, which accounts for the French name, though most likely our family spent some considerable time in Quebec before heading south. (Or maybe they got thrown out of Canada – you never know!)

In any event, it was pure happenstance that my family moved to the town of Needham outside Boston just when the schools there started up a French-language learning program for third graders (age eight or so). Then I added German in high school.

From Silicon Valley Via Stuttgart . . .

Fast forward many years later . . . and I am working as an accountant for a Silicon Valley computer company, when I am offered the chance to go live in the UK for what was supposed to be eighteen to twenty-four months on an 'extended business trip'. A British colleague with whom I had worked on a project had suggested me for the post, knowing that I had expressed interest in working in Europe. I would like to believe it was because of my unique qualifications (MBA, accounting and two foreign languages) that I got the nod for the secondment, but in fact it probably had more to do with the fact that I was divorced with no children, so would be a far more economical choice for the job than the other candidate.

he convinced me that my two cats would be better looked after at his house . . . so they moved in a good three months before I did

My assignment in the UK wound up being cut short, thanks to an economic downturn, and I was forced to return to California. But during the eleven months I spent as European Service Controller I had had the chance to travel throughout northern Europe and meet the company's various business managers, including a Frenchman by the name of Pascal.

Back in Silicon Valley, I was not at all happy about my forced return, and started looking around for a new job. It finally dawned on me that at my age (by then I had just crossed the forty year threshold) it was probably now or never for finding a job in Europe – and so I wound up working in Germany.

Once back in Europe, I of course contacted my former colleagues, several of whom had been very helpful to me in the job-hunting and moving process. This was all made far easier through the increasing availability of personal e-mail in Europe in the early 1990s. And initially, it was through e-mail that I kept in contact with Pascal from Germany, though this quickly progressed to telephone calls and then regular visits – mostly involving me hopping the train to Paris on a Friday evening and returning late Sunday night.

After three years of this, I suddenly found myself unemployed. The *Arbeitsamt* didn't hold out much chance for me to find a new job, what with the high unemployment rates in 1994 and restrictions on work permits for foreigners. And then Pascal leapt to my rescue by asking me to move in with him "for the long term," as he put it. He had recently finalized his divorce and was not at all anxious to get married again. He was, however, offering me a "sabbatical" – free room and board with no obligation to start looking for work for a year or so. How could I refuse?

I still had several months to run on my lease in Germany (not to mention that my unemployment benefits would end as soon as I left the country), so I had the luxury of moving my possessions to France a carload at a time as I drove back and forth to stay with Pascal on the weekends. Shortly before Christmas, 1994 he convinced me that my two cats would be better looked after at his house than in Germany (since they wouldn't have to be left alone at the weekends) and so they moved in a good three months before I did. After the nine-hour flight to Germany from California, the six hour drive to Pascal's house was relatively easy for my little beasties, though they complained most of the way.

In the meantime, I made a number of trips to Stuttgart, the site of the French Consulate in Germany, to apply for a long-stay visa. My first interaction with the infamous French *fonctionnaires* (civil servants) was basically a disaster. Though I ran into an extremely helpful guard at the Consulate (a fellow American, married to someone working in the Consulate), I didn't pay adequate attention to his warnings that the information I was getting from the officials "didn't sound right".

The consular 'officials' (mere clerks, I now realize) insisted that they couldn't even give the forms out to anyone not in possession of a valid job offer in France. Somehow I wheedled the forms out of one of them (eight copies, all of which must be filled out "as originals"), but when I returned with my carefully completed forms, photos and fees, they again questioned my motivation for wanting to live in France. In desperation, I said that Pascal and I were going to be married. Surely the French wouldn't refuse that request, would they?

The official's face brightened and he said, "Well, in that case, you don't really need a visa!" He went on to tell me that I could simply move to France as an American tourist, get married within the six months of my tourist visa and then simply "regularize" myself afterwards as the wife of a French national. It sounded simple enough, except for the fact that I knew the tourist visa was only good for three months, not for six . . . and, of course, Pascal didn't want to get married.

I called Pascal to tell him this latest development. He didn't seem too disturbed by the idea, though he did call the Stuttgart Consulate, just to make sure I had understood everything correctly. (The officials at the Consulate had refused to speak either English or German with me. All the conversations, save with the door guard, had been in French, and my French was very rusty at that point.) Pascal called me back the next day to announce that he had been told exactly the same thing and that, if getting married was the only way I could come live in France, then get married we would – but within three months of my arrival, just in case!

. . . To Paris For The Long Term

I engaged a removal company to pack up my furniture and remaining belongings for delivery to Pascal's garage. The German removal van was expected to arrive the day after I did. In mid-March, 1995 I finally de-listed myself officially from the little town in Germany in which I had been living and made my entrance into France "for the long term."

This was in the early days of the Schengen Treaty, and each weekend, I was able to simply drive straight across the border at Mulhouse. The customs booths were still in place, as were the signs warning cars to be ready to stop, but there wasn't a soul to be seen anywhere at the frontier of the new 'borderless' Europe.

The next day, the removal van did indeed arrive, with just the driver to unload my things and put them into the garage. He was more than a bit miffed to find that the garage in Pascal's house was, in fact, in the basement and instead of a flat, paved driveway, he had to get my sofa, chairs, bed and other bulky furniture down a sloping, curved grassy path with paving blocks laid in for traction. The weather had been rainy for several weeks before, and the wheeled dolly didn't navigate the muddy drive particularly well. I called Pascal at work in a complete panic and begged him to come home to try to help with the process of getting my stuff from the truck into the garage.

We were married on May 6, 1995 in the *mairie* of the town of Forges-les-Bains (where we live), and we applied immediately for my "regularization" (since most of the documents required were the same ones needed to get married anyhow).

I had lots of adjustment to do with this move and the marriage and all, over and above the usual transitions to living in a new country. First of all, Pascal has two children from his first marriage. I had met them both several months earlier during one of my weekends in France. The son was in the midst of his university studies, lived with his girlfriend and seemed to be a pleasant and highly intelligent young man.

The daughter was just finishing *lycée* and coming up on the *bac* exams when we announced our plans to marry. There were obviously a number of unresolved family issues involving the divorce and the way this particular family and French families in general operate. In any event, the daughter and I didn't hit it off at all, and her visits turned into competitions between us to 'mark our territory'. (I have since heard that this is fairly common between daughters and their fathers' new wives, in just about all cultures.)

Sans Papiers

One day at the beginning of July, a mere two months after our wedding, Pascal arrived home to tell me he had given notice at his job. Though he had mentioned his interest in starting his own business, I had no clue at the time that he meant to do this right away, but apparently he had heard about a grant available from the government for new businesses and the deadline for the grant was rapidly approaching.

> *my application for a carte de séjour had been rejected and I had thirty days in which to leave the country*

So, we scrambled over the next few months to set up our business, which we run from the house. We bought some French accounting software, subscribed to a bunch of publications that promised to explain the secrets of business to would-be entrepreneurs in France and set up Fire Mountain Services, SARL. Pascal, a computer engineer, initially set this up to do information system consulting for small and medium-size businesses, though we also sell and maintain computer and networking equipment.

Pascal had considerably more confidence in my ability to manage the administrative side of this enterprise than I did. I did, after all, have an MBA and years of experience in accounting and finance (all in American companies). To an engineer, "all that paperwork stuff" is pretty much the same whether you are in Silicon Valley or in southern Germany or in the Paris area. In theory, he has a point (or so I can say now, after nearly nine years of dealing with billing, accounting and tax forms), but at the time, I was overwhelmed at the amount of material I had to learn within a relatively short period. (And, of course, the only available information for all this was in French.)

> **they shook their heads and refused to speculate whether I needed to fear the gendarmes coming to my door to drag me off in chains**

Our company opened for business on November 2, 1995. Unfortunately, our incorporation was five days too late to qualify for the government subsidy.

And then, four months after submitting my request for "regularization" to the *mairie*, I received a registered letter from the *préfecture*. They informed me that my application for a *carte de séjour* had been rejected (no reason given) and that I had thirty days in which to leave the country. The letter ended: "Please make sure to give a copy of this letter to the customs officials on your way out so we will know you have left."

Thus began my life as a *sans papiers*, an illegal immigrant, a wetback.

For nearly two years we tried various things to overturn this (obviously unjust!) decision. We appealed to the *mairie* for help. No, the new Mayor wouldn't see us or attempt to intervene with the *préfecture* on my behalf. (The Mayor who officiated at our marriage had retired and a new Mayor had been elected.) The clerks at the *mairie* just shook their heads and refused to speculate whether I needed to fear the *gendarmes* coming to my door to drag me off in chains if I simply refused to leave as requested.

Pascal appealed to a friend who had family connections within the *préfecture*, and a cousin was dispatched to take the *préfet* himself to lunch and plead my case over a good meal and a glass or two of wine. The *préfet* wasn't swayed. (I am still lobbying to have that particular *préfet* reassigned to Corsica!) Pascal visited a regional official and even took an appointment to see the local representative for the *Assemblée Nationale*. Both elected officials wrote letters to the *préfet*, who absolutely refused to reconsider my expulsion.

Unfortunately, this was the same era when the question of illegal immigration was very much a big deal within the French administration. Unemployment in France was at record levels and the Prime Minister, Alain Juppé, had started a program of repatriating illegal immigrants using charter flights that were quickly dubbed "Air Juppé" in the press. It was also the time of the hunger strikes staged in various churches around Paris by long-time illegal immigrants threatened with deportation. It was all over the news and the papers, and it didn't make me feel at all comfortable in France.

All this time, various friends, family members and vague acquaintances to whom I complained about my problem (i.e. just about anyone who would listen) wondered how I could be refused residence in France when I was married to a Frenchman and counseled me not to take it personally. At one point, Pascal drew up a job offer from our company, promising to employ me himself, thus getting around that particular objection. It didn't work.

After our first anniversary, we made a second attempt, filing a brand new dossier at the *mairie*. That didn't work either (I still wonder if they ever actually submitted the second dossier to the *préfecture*). At last, we broke down and spoke with an attorney someone had recommended.

She was a chain-smoking Arab woman who seemed equally clueless about what the *préfecture*'s objection to me might be. But she suggested that perhaps they were questioning the validity of our marriage, and that we should get all our friends (Pascal's friends, actually) to submit affidavits on my behalf – talking up the fact that we had known each other for years before deciding to marry, attesting to our stable relationship, to my outstanding qualifications and obvious employability, etc.

And just about the time we had assembled a dossier of all these recommendations (accompanied by a photocopy of both sides of the attester's *carte d'identité*), I got another registered letter from the *préfecture*, informing me that my case would be considered at a special tribunal on the stay of foreigners.

 the judges turned to me and asked me how I had arrived in France. I said 'en voiture'

When we handed this letter to the attorney, her jaw dropped and all she said was, "But this is where they send the Africans!"

She did agree to meet us in the lobby of the court building thirty minutes before the appointed time to discuss strategy, but she admitted that she had no experience with this particular tribunal. I wasn't feeling terribly confident that morning, but by the time the session was due to start, I was out and out seething. The attorney hadn't bothered to show up thirty minutes early, nor even by the time the tribunal was due to start.

As it turns out, she had been almost right. The tribunal was set to hear about a dozen cases that morning. Most of them did involve people from various countries in Africa: Mali, Senegal, Gabon, Burkino Faso, etc. There was one Turk, married to a French woman (and with their baby in tow) and then there was me and Pascal. One by one we were called up to the stand. The representative of the *préfecture* read off the report of the "problems" they had with each case, and then the judges posed questions to try to clarify the situation. The ruling by the judges would be only advisory, but the *préfecture* was said to abide by the judges' decision.

I was called early in the session, maybe third or fourth. Pascal and I went up to the stand together. The *préfecture* read off the charges: I had entered into French territory with the intention of staying for the long term without making my arrival known to the border officials. The judges turned to me and asked me how I had arrived in France. I said "*en voiture*" (by car). The spectators in the courtroom laughed and I took that for a good omen.

> *I started yelling every English-language obscenity I knew, as Pascal gently guided me out of the préfecture building*

Then I went on to explain (mustering up my best French, which wasn't easy at the time) how I had made multiple trips to the consulate, only to be told I could just come here, get married and then "regularize" myself, which turned out not to have been true. Of course I pointed out that no one had ever mentioned anything about getting my passport stamped on entry into France and that, even if they had, there hadn't been anyone at the border station who could have stamped my passport if I had stopped (which I hadn't).

As we were dismissed and my dossier was added to the pile for the judges to consider, into the courtroom rushed my attorney, resplendent in her black robes, with what appeared to me to be little white rabbits' feet attached to the ties at her neck. At this point, all I could do was walk up to her and say, in plain English, "You're late!" I sat down and refused to look at her, so she left.

After all the cases had been heard, the judges retired to render their decisions. We wetbacks cooled our heels in the courtroom, chatting among ourselves or with some of the spectators (in some cases fellow immigrants with tribunal appointments the following month, looking to see how the session operated). Of course we exchanged histories and sympathized with one another over our outrageous treatment at the hands of the local *préfecture*. After about an hour, the judges returned to read off the names of those cases for which they had found in the affirmative. My name was the very last one they read off.

Coming To Terms

About a week later I received another letter from the *préfecture* (not registered this time) directing me to appear at the *préfecture* in Evry promptly at 8.30am on a specific date. This was regarding the medical examination for my *carte de séjour*. It seemed a bit odd to both Pascal and me that medical exams would be done at the *préfecture*, but we got up bright and early to fight the rush hour traffic to ensure that I would be there by 8.30.

We were directed to the foreigners' desk, where the clerk demanded a check for a thousand francs for the exam and then asked if next Thursday would work for me, and did I prefer a morning or an afternoon appointment. We had just spent nearly an hour and a half in traffic so as not to be late for an appointment to make an appointment! I lost it. I started yelling every English-language obscenity I knew, as Pascal gently guided me out of the *préfecture* building and back to the car.

A couple of weeks later the *mairie* called to say that my *carte de séjour* had arrived and I could pick it up. Because we had now been married for the requisite period (i.e. more than a year), I received a ten-year *carte de résidente* with full working privileges, backdated to the date of my original arrival in France. And shortly thereafter, I received a thick envelope in the mail from the attorney. She was returning my file. Fortunately, she had the good sense not to bother sending me a bill for her 'services'.

Needless to say, after nearly two years of fighting this out, I didn't feel terribly welcome in France. In fact, it was probably pretty fair to say I actively hated France by this time. The one bright spot was that I could finally put myself onto our company payroll and start to draw a (small) salary from our business. This meant I could also finally have a social security card in my own name.

But on those 'bad France days' I could work myself into quite a stew about the bad drivers, overcooked vegetables, stupid bureaucracy, the impenetrability of the French accounting and business regulations or the frequent strikes by 'public service' employees. Basically I made a real pain of myself, moaning to Pascal about how things were or weren't done in "this dumb country" or how I had given up everything (my career, my way of life, my habits and customs, my rights) to be with him while he hadn't had to alter a thing.

He offered to move to the US with me, on condition that I would then be the one to support us by finding one of those high-paying jobs I was missing so much.

Since the one thing I really did like about life here in France was getting away from the pressure of big business and the need to constantly keep advancing up the corporate ladder, I eventually decided I had better find a way to come to terms with my current situation.

Along the way, I tried taking some classes in Paris. I joined various expat and foreigner groups (also in Paris) and, at one point, I even managed to find a two-month temporary job at the OECD. But all these things involved the need to commute into Paris on a regular basis. One other thing about my life in France I was coming to really like is living out in the countryside the way we do. To make a meeting in Paris, I generally have to allow between one and a half and two hours of travel time. This gives me a cushion for heavy traffic on the road to the RER station and for delays in making connections between the RER and the metro, or finding an alternate route if there are strikes or other disruptions of service. If all goes well, I arrive a good half an hour early (definitely not French!) and wind up having to kill time walking around the block.

In the end I just decided that I didn't want to take on activities that forced me to commit to the long commutes into and out of the city. So I was stuck back out in deepest, darkest Essonne, more or less on my own.

The AVF

After I had been living in France for nearly seven years, I just happened to discover the AVF chapter serving the towns of Bures, Gif and Orsay. I had done some work for Survival Books titles on France and the editor wanted me to add something about a group called Accueil des Villes Françaises. I had never heard of it, so I tracked down their website and found that the AVF has something like four hundred groups throughout France, all charged with welcoming newcomers to their respective areas. The closest groups to my home were each about twenty kilometres away, in towns I wasn't particularly familiar with, so I found what I needed for updating the book and promptly forgot about the AVF.

A couple of months later, my car needed some minor repair and so I went to the Toyota dealership in St. Rémy-les-Chevreuses. While I was waiting for them to finish the work on my car, in walked a short, cheerful woman the Toyota people referred to as l'Anglaise. She gamely tried explaining to the woman at the desk what the problem was with her car, but she was obviously struggling with the language. I offered to help with translation and soon the three of us had worked out a common understanding of her problem and what the garage would be able to do for her.

The garage employees had been remarkably helpful and quite sympathetic towards the woman, despite her inability to speak French, something I had not often seen this far outside the tourist track in Paris. l'Anglaise (whose name is

Sandra) explained to me that it was precisely for this reason that she now brought the family Opel to this Toyota dealership for repairs and maintenance.

> *I had finally found a group of like-minded souls and interesting activities not too far away from where we lived*

It turned out that Sandra wasn't English as all, but Australian. She lived in St. Rémy with her husband and son, and it just so happened that she pulled out of her purse a program booklet for the Bures-Gif-Orsay AVF group, to which she belonged.

Thanks to a large number of foreigners who live in that area, the AVF group offers a number of English-language activities as well as language circles and practice groups in other languages, including German. They also host day trips, hikes, cooking classes and crafts studios – just the sort of activities I had been looking for in vain in and around Forges. Sandra was the first of many people to tell me that finding the AVF group had literally turned her attitude around about being "stuck" in France. She encouraged me to call the English-language contact for the group, a British woman who lived in Gif, and then she called me later to make sure I had done so.

Ann, the British woman I had called, invited me to come to the next session of Coffee Break, spent time explaining to me how to find the hall in which the group meets and told me about the local AVF chapter. The rest, as they say, is history. I had finally found a group of like-minded souls and interesting activities not too far away from where we lived. Armed with some local maps, I soon found myself venturing out to AVF activities – Coffee Break, *Kaffeeklatsch*, French Conversation – and meeting not only other foreigners, but also French people.

And then again, there were the donkeys who had gradually worked their way into our lives, and now our home.

A Tale Of Two Donkeys

Hubert, one of the retired farmers in the area, had bought a couple of young donkeys to pull a cart he owned. Evidently Hubert had been a planting and plowing sort of farmer and didn't have too much experience with livestock and never seemed to have sufficient time to devote to their training. Since the donkeys were kept in the field just behind our house, we became great friends not only with the animals but also with Hubert.

Several times when Hubert had forgotten to lock the gate to the donkeys' enclosure, Pascal and I wound up retrieving them from wherever they had wandered off to, usually one of the other fields nearby. Eventually we started taking them for walks and inviting them over to "trim the grass" in our yard, and when they would get out on their own, they developed the habit of coming by our house first.

After a couple of years, Hubert decided that he wasn't up to training the donkeys for their intended purpose and he announced he had decided to sell them in order to buy a pony, already trained to draw a small cart. At that point we couldn't bear the thought of losing the donkeys we already thought of as ours and so we bought them. This, of course, involved both Pascal and me attending 'donkey school' in the south of France to learn how to properly take care of Annette and Martin, and the building of a proper shelter for our new charges. Having a couple of donkeys pastured next door to the house definitely makes you something of a celebrity in the neighborhood, too.

The House . . .

Because I was moving into Pascal's house, I had been spared the need to look for a place to live or to have to deal with estate agents or landlords. On the down side (and something that would bother me through the worst of my 'bad France days') I never really had any say in where we were living.

As I had feared, the fact of my moving into what had been the family home tended to aggravate the problems I had had with Pascal's family, especially his daughter, who was particularly upset when I chose to re-do what had been her bedroom in order to have a guest room for a friend of mine from America who was flying in for our wedding.

> *the maçons left their cement mixer and supplies . . . vowing to return 'on Friday'. As the old joke goes, they hadn't specified which Friday*

Subsequent changes and redecorating have all been subjected to the scrutiny of Pascal's son, daughter and sisters when they visit (though I did finally convince Pascal's older sister to consider painting her walls instead of wallpapering them – a small but telling victory!).

Forges-les-Bains is a small town of around 3,500 inhabitants, roughly forty kilometers south and slightly west of Paris. This part of Essonne is truly farm country, though some of the larger pastures and fields are gradually being sold off for housing estates.

Our house is out on the far edge of town on a narrow little road that starts in the neighboring town of Angervilliers. The end of the road that is Forges is well hidden by patches of woods and a couple of open fields that are still restricted to agricultural use only. Our house stands in roughly the center of a little triangle of land measuring around eight hundred square meters.

A few years ago, when the agricultural property next door came up for sale, I bought it so that Pascal could have the sort of large garden he had long dreamed of. It also serves as my contribution to the family home in the light of the way French property laws work. Since acquiring the donkeys, however, most of that space has been given over to pasturage.

Hubert was anxious to move his pony into the space that the donkeys had previously called home and, until we could make arrangements to build a shelter for them, they stayed in a nearby pasture, loaned to Hubert by another farmer in the area.

Meanwhile, we were told by the *mairie* that nothing at all could be built on the agricultural land I had bought – not even a barn – and our only option for building anything on the lot on which the house sits would be to construct a shelter of no more than twenty square meters. For this, we would need to file a declaration rather than obtain a permit and we would need to meet a number of specific requirements regarding the exact placement of the shelter on the lot.

. . . & The Donkey House

Pascal hired a *géomètre* (a sort of a surveyor) to determine the exact boundaries and size of both plots and an architect to draw up the plans for the shelter as well as to prepare the forms needed to file the declaration. There seemed to be little difference in the amount of paperwork required whether we were going for a declaration or a building permit and, in fact, we had to wait for our declaration to be approved before we could start building "the donkey house."

Once the approval came through, Pascal located the various handymen needed to complete the job. In what I have come to know as "typical French fashion" we negotiated with the neighbor across the street, who had contacts with a company that rents out digging equipment. Pascal and the neighbor spent one weekend leveling the site for the donkey house and digging a trench from the house to the site to carry the water and electricity connections. They also dug a number of holes to be used for setting fence posts. The neighbor's brother-in-law did plumbing and roofing work, so he was engaged to help on those parts of the project and he pitched in on digging the trench. The *maçons* had to pour concrete for what would be the floor of the house and this project took two or three days to complete, along with setting the fence posts at one end of the pasture.

There was some problem that the *géomètre* had encountered, so the setting of the posts at the other end of the pasture had to be delayed. The *maçons* left their cement mixer and supplies in the far corner of our yard and their shoes and jackets in our garden shed, vowing to return "on Friday". As the old joke goes, they hadn't specified which Friday.

Over the next three weeks, I would sometimes catch a glimpse of their large white van parking on the road in the early morning twilight and one of the workers would scurry into our yard to retrieve a couple of sacks of cement mix or a couple of fence posts, apparently needed on whatever job they were working on in the meantime.

Pascal located a carpenter to handle the construction of the body of the house after some effort (several of the carpenters recommended to him turned out to have recently retired), but he was fully booked for the next six weeks. We had received our permission to build at the beginning of November, hoping to have the donkeys in their shelter before the winter weather closed in, but the earliest the carpenter could start work was the first week in January. So we continued hauling hay and feed and water out to the donkeys in their borrowed pasture through Christmas and into the New Year.

At last, the carpenter called to announce he would start work in a few days. The structure itself took shape quickly and soon was completed, except for the roof. The neighbor's brother-in-law promised to get right on it and, one day, while we were off in Paris visiting the *Salon de Cheval* (an annual exposition dedicated to horses and equitation), the roofers turned up to complete the job.

The donkey house looked quite nice, though what was left of our yard had been turned into a giant mud pit and there was still work for Pascal to do to finish the electrical and plumbing work and refill the trench cut in the side yard. Pascal set up the electric fencing in the pasture area and we introduced the donkeys to their new home. At first they wouldn't go into it even when we put their food inside. Obviously they thought we would slam the doors shut on them, holding them hostage. By the next morning, though, they had overcome their fears and taken over their new home. We are still in the process of restoring the lawn and plantings in what is left of the yard.

How Many Are Your Husbands?

On my arrival in France, my spoken French was rudimentary at best. Not only did German words insist on springing onto my lips when my French vocabulary failed me, but I soon discovered that the French language and vocabulary they had drilled into us back in elementary school was probably at least twenty years out of date at the time. All around me I heard words and expressions I had never run into at school and words like *bicyclette* and *souliers* had been replaced by *vélo* and *chaussures* – or *pompes* or *godasses* . . . – without anyone ever telling me. This was all compounded by meeting Pascal's children, both young adults who spoke far more rapidly than I could hope to follow and whose use of the current slang expressions left me completely lost.

> *he started off by asking me, 'How many are your husbands?' . . . he was trying to ask was what time my husband would be home*

By far the worst was (and to some extent continues to be) the telephone. I had been through this while living in Germany. On the phone, the lack of a human face and hand gestures means that you have to divine all content from what the person on the other end is saying. There were considerable misunderstandings with Pascal's kids as well as with our customers, as I would have to ask them to repeat, sometimes several times, what they were trying to say.

I did take a month-long intensive French class in Paris. When Pascal set up his business, I found myself playing telephone receptionist while he was out attending to customers. It is rather embarrassing for a qualified accountant to have as much trouble understanding numbers over the phone as I did, but I blame the French with their strange numerical system that includes such oddities as 'sixty-fourteen' for seventy-four and 'four-twenties-ten-eight' for ninety-eight.

I often managed to infuriate or completely baffle the customers and the sales people who called with my less-than-perfect French. There were also those days when either my brain or my mouth simply refused to work in anything other than English. Several salesmen had commented rudely on how badly I spoke French (while I made a mental note never to deal with their companies).

Once in a great while, someone would offer to speak English with me – an offer I would eagerly accept. One salesman glibly started off by asking me, "How many are your husbands?" I am not sure how I sussed it out, but what he was trying to ask was what time my husband would be home. We normally wound up switching back to French.

Then there was our "customer from hell", a particularly demanding and unpleasant man from a small African country who quite clearly didn't appreciate having to speak with Pascal's 'secretary' when calling long-distance. (It apparently wasn't easy getting a line to France from wherever he was calling from.) On one call he made a couple of rather nasty remarks about how bad my French was, and suggested sarcastically that perhaps we should continue the discussion in English or German. I sensed an opportunity here and tried to say in French that maybe it would be best to continue our conversation in German, as it would be a second language for both of us and therefore put neither of us at an unfair advantage. He abruptly announced he would call back later and hung up.

Authoritarian Regimes

We had set up Pascal's sister as a 'silent partner' in our business because the French make a big distinction between a *gérant minoritaire* (i.e. a general manager who holds only an minority interest in a company and thus is considered an employee) and a *gérant majoritaire* (where the general manager is also the owner of the company and thus considered to be an evil, money-grubbing capitalist out to exploit the down-trodden workers). Under French law, my ownership in the company was counted toward Pascal's effective ownership interest, though that of his sister wasn't.

> **France is just crazy about categorizing people and businesses into regimes**

Given my immigration difficulties, I couldn't look for work at that time anyhow, so I became an undeclared (and unpaid) *conjoint associé* (the term used for a wife who owns part of a business and works for the company). I learned the French accounting system, French taxes and payroll 'on the fly'. Actually, I may be the only person in the country ever to have actually read the instruction sheets sent with most of the tax forms – not that I understood much of what I read. (Pascal usually admitted he couldn't understand the sections I asked him to explain to me, so after a while I stopped asking him.)

People were astonished to hear that I could figure out French accounting on my own, as there is a belief that French accounting is very complicated and much harder than 'Anglo-Saxon accounting', as it is called. Thanks to any number of books I picked up (almost all of them in French) I managed to put together a decent (if not entirely perfect) set of French regulation financial statements at the end of each year to file with the *Greffe du Tribunal*, as required by law. (According to the business publications we get, many small businesses here don't bother to file their statements at all.)

Then, Pascal's sister decided that she wanted out of the business. Though she was a partner in name only, she still had to declare her ownership interest on various tax forms, and she began to worry that this 'investment' might call other parts of her tax forms into question.

By this time, I was officially on the payroll, drawing my own social benefits, and there had been some changes to the law that made it much less onerous for Pascal to be a slave-driving capitalist entrepreneur (i.e. *gérant majoritaire*). Obviously, this isn't the sort of change of regime that happens often in France because it was extremely difficult to find information about what to do and how to make this happen. There was plenty of information about which regime to choose when setting up a business, but changing from one to the other seemed to pose a whole different series of problems, to get round which I wound up improvising.

All in all, it took fifteen months of calling around, getting rejected by various social benefit agencies and changing our business category with INSEE, the French statistics agency, before we were suddenly considered 'acceptable' to the agencies that had previously rejected us.

France is just crazy about categorizing people and businesses into regimes, and part of our problem turned out to be the fact that the management of a 'consultancy' is considered to be a *profession libérale* (a sort of private practice) while computer and office equipment repair (the category we eventually chose) falls under the *artisanale* regime, while the fact that we sell equipment too makes us *commerçants*, which is another regime altogether. Each regime has its own advantages and disadvantages, not only for the *gérant*, but also for the *conjoint associé* who works in the business alongside her spouse (namely, me).

It wasn't particularly surprising to me when Pascal suggested before we got married that perhaps we should have a contract. Both of us were divorced and he had his two children to consider, so a pre-nuptial contract (as these things are called in the US) seemed quite logical to me in our case.

What I didn't realize at the time is that in France, you must choose among the six available *régimes de mariage*, with little or no freedom to tailor things to your particular needs. We went for the *séparation de biens*, which is the regime usually recommended for second marriages, especially where one or both partners has children from the previous marriage. Basically, this maintains all property as either his or hers, based on whose funds were used for the original purchase.

This turned out to be a lucky choice for us, as this is also the least restrictive of the regimes for spouses who choose to go into business together. Under any of the regimes that grant communal property rights, the spouse who works in the family business is limited to a nominal salary (less than €3,000 per year), even if they work full time in a responsible position for the business.

The other thing I hadn't realized at the time was that, under French inheritance law, spouses don't inherit from each other. So we drew up a *donation entre époux* (mutual gift between spouses), which permits me to inherit twenty-five per cent of his estate, the rest of which goes to his children. In typical French fashion, the inheritance laws have recently been changed to reflect pretty much the same terms as our donation, though there are a few additional provisions for allowing a surviving spouse to remain in the family home.

School Influences

One would think that a person without children would have little or no reason to get involved with the schools in France. That, as it turns out, is just plain wrong. Schools are a major presence in French society and they affect every individual living in France, like it or not. Furthermore, schools figure prominently in politics, both at national and local levels.

It didn't take me long to learn that one avoids going shopping, particularly in the *hypermarchés*, on Wednesdays, when most schools are closed. Although most mothers of school-aged children in France work, many are part-time employees with their hours carefully planned to coincide with the school schedules, including having Wednesdays (or at least Wednesday afternoons) free. Shopping centers are generally a zoo on Wednesdays – mothers doing errands with the children in tow, and teenagers hanging out at the mall with their friends.

Then there are still classes on Saturday mornings, though Saturday was chopped out of the French work week some decades ago. Now and then, some brave soul raises the issue of doing away with Saturday morning classes, but this is generally met with staunch resistance from both the teachers (who seem to fear this would jeopardize their Wednesday afternoons) and the parents. If Saturday classes were cancelled, the reasoning goes, when would the children learn all that material that is covered on Saturday mornings?

The French were at one time quite proud of the fact that you could enter a French classroom anywhere in France on a given day of the school year and know precisely what lesson was being taught. I am told that schools aren't nearly as rigid as this any more, but I am not so sure.

A surprising number of working women are also guaranteed time off during the frequent school holidays. The school year starts at the beginning of September and, by the end of October, the students (or more likely, the teachers) need a break, so there is a week-and-a-half long holiday for *La Toussaint* (All Saints' Day). There are two weeks off at Christmas, followed by the two-week 'ski holidays' in late February or early March, and another two week 'Easter' holiday in April (even if Easter falls in March!). School finishes at the end of June (or even the beginning, for some grades), leaving two or three months of summer holidays.

Most clubs and associations in France close down during the school holidays and, in any event, no one dares to schedule meetings or activities while 'everyone' can be assumed to be away. The custom lately seems to be to park the children with the grandparents during most school holidays if Mom and Dad can't take time off, so even retired people with grown children still schedule their lives around the school calendar.

The local *boulangerie* and *boucherie* often close for part or all of the school holiday periods, forcing customers to rely on the shops in neighboring towns. In fact, it took me several years to convince Pascal that it might be advantageous to avoid vacationing (especially in the camper) during the school holidays, when the *autoroutes* are clogged with departing or returning traffic and vacation facilities are full booked.

Living where we do, on the far edge of town, we have just a short walk to the primary school in Angervilliers. Nevertheless, the children who live on the Forges part of the street must attend the school in Forges, some five or six kilometers distant. The town of Forges provides a bus, but the bus stop point is actually further away than the Angervilliers school. The children of the neighbors on either side of us have only just started school, and we have heard from their parents about the situation.

It is supposed to be possible to get permission from the Mayor to have your children attend school in a neighboring town. What it involves is the two towns reaching an agreement. In this case, Angervilliers to accept the students, and Forges to pay a tuition fee to Angervilliers to compensate them for taking on the extra children. However, since the towns are granted money to run the schools based on the number of students they serve, no Mayor wants to surrender precious state funds to another town.

 the French healthcare system can best be described as severely pigeonholed, as much of French administrative life and culture seems to be

Moreover, it seems that the number of school-aged children in Forges has been shrinking the last several years, and the town is threatened with the need to give up several school-related jobs. The Mayor has vowed to keep all Forges children in Forges schools. So, our neighbors' kids will go to school in Forges, hiking each day to the bus stop, or having Mom or Dad drive them and pick them up, while the kids living at the top of the street will hike to the school just a couple of hundred meters down the road.

General Health

The French healthcare system can best be described as severely pigeonholed, as much of French administrative life and culture seems to be. Each person in the health care system seems to have his own very restricted and constrained job, and it is fairly clear (at least to me) that none of them ever communicates with anyone else in the system.

the French have a very strict definition of friendship. You can only consider someone a true friend if you have known him virtually all of your life

Almost as soon as we decided I would be moving in with Pascal, he had me put on his social security card, meaning I would be covered for health insurance as his dependent. It didn't seem to matter whether or not we were planning on getting married and, as I later found out, there are plenty of unmarried couples sharing national health benefits like this. Of course I got nervous after my immigration problems started that any attempt to seek medical attention would just alert the authorities to send the *gendarmes* to come pick me up, but I needn't have worried.

French GPs don't seem to do very much except for a very general examination of whatever body part you have come to complain about, after which they write up prescriptions for medications and any specialized testing they deem necessary. In some cases, they will send you to a specialist – say a dermatologist or a cardiologist or a rheumatologist – who has the necessary expertise to treat whatever the generalist thinks might be ailing you.

The generalist doesn't keep much in the way of records, either, though this has changed since the *Sécu* required all doctors to use a desktop computer to produce forms and prescriptions. (It seems that the problem of doctors having illegible handwriting is an international concern.) Every doctor I have seen takes great pains to hand-write any notes to the specialists he sends me to. I, of course, open the sealed envelopes as soon as I get home (and before I make the appointment with the specialist recommended) to read what has been said about me. Pascal says I am not really supposed to do this, but no one has yelled at me about it yet.

There is also the matter of what to do when you get the results of the various lab tests back. Generally the written report sums up whether or not your results are within the normal ranges, and I am told that the labs routinely mail a copy of the results to the doctor who ordered up the tests. You must take X-ray films or other sorts of 'pictures' (sonograms, various types of scans, etc.) to show the doctor on your next visit, and some of the patients in the waiting room seem to have accumulated some rather impressive-looking dossiers, which they take to each and every medical appointment.

If you are employed, you must have an annual employment examination, which is supposed to cover conditions specific to the type of work you do. Obviously a generalist isn't qualified to do something like this (at least not in the French system), so you must go to a special 'work doctor', who apparently does nothing but employment examinations and who has no contact whatsoever with your generalist. My work doctor occasionally asks me if I am up to date on things like my gyne exams, mammograms, and vaccinations. I have learned by hard experience that it is much easier to just lie and tell her everything is up to date whether it is or not. I don't think she believes me, but she does note it down in her file on me and usually stops bugging me about whatever it is.

Degrees Of Friendship

The French have a very strict definition of friendship. You can only consider someone a true friend (i.e. *ami(e)*, the word we all learned in school) if you have known him virtually all of your life. *Un ami* or *une amie* is someone you have grown up with, preferably someone who attended the same *maternelle* (primary school) as you did. For those who have been forced by cruel circumstance to live at some distance from where they grew up, a friend may be someone you know from work or some other shared experience, but to be true *ami(e)s* it is normally necessary to have known each other for a minimum of ten or twenty years and, even better, to have endured some great hardship together (unpleasant boss, sadistic teacher, etc.).

I first stumbled onto this aspect of French culture when I was attending intensive language classes in Paris one summer. Our instructor, a cheerful young woman in her mid-twenties, had asked us to compose a letter to a friend describing what we had done over the weekend. After ten or fifteen minutes of work, we were then to read our compositions to the class for correction and comment.

First up was an Italian student, a curly haired character who clearly relished the role of class clown. He started out his letter (as we all had) with *"Chère amie"*, then went on to describe a perfectly ordinary weekend in terms that had us all creased with laughter by the time he read out his closing *"avec tout mon amour"* or something equally passionate.

Our instructor seemed a little bit embarrassed as she explained that the opening and closing of the letter were far too "intimate" for the purposes of the exercise, and that she could only assume that he meant to write a love letter to his girlfriend. The Italian laughed and said that, no, he just always felt it was appropriate to speak passionately to a beautiful woman and, after all, weren't French men well known for their romantic ways?

At that point, our instructor began a lecture on the French notion of friendship and the various terms and levels associated with people you know. I don't remember all the details, because the lecture developed into an impassioned argument over how the French could consider themselves such experts on love if they insisted on all these silly rules regarding which friends merited what titles and exactly how you should begin a letter to each category of acquaintance. (It was a warm afternoon and we were obviously getting bored with our regular language learning work.)

At one point in the discussion, I can recall our instructor accusing the Americans in particular of being almost profligate with their use of the term 'friend' as they use it to refer even to people they have only just met. But her point was clear. You might describe someone in French as your *copain/copine* but the term *ami(e)* was reserved for those with whom you had a particularly long-standing and close relationship.

Since then, I have noticed that most French people I know do tend to avoid the words *ami* and *amie* unless there is some particular reason to draw attention to the nature of the relationship. I suspect that much of this is the natural sense of modesty and possibly even a bit of *égalité* in the French culture. After all, if you are talking to someone you consider only an acquaintance, it may be considered somewhat rude to point out that you are speaking of another person you consider to be a true friend in the French sense of the word.

For women in France, however, the main source of friends seems to be the act of dropping off and picking up their children at school and that is one activity I am excluded from. And that is where the AVF has come in for me. As it turns out, one of the founders of my local AVF group is said to have started the group after moving to the area without children and finding herself with no means of meeting people.

The big advantage of the AVF, besides it being much closer by than any of the groups in Paris, is that the members include not only other foreigners, but lots of French people, mostly women. Thanks, too, to an active core of foreigners, there is a healthy exchange of activities reflecting both French and foreign cultures, languages and interests. Those French women who attend the language circles and who host the French conversation groups for foreigners are those most likely to be interested in foreign cultures, or at the very least, somewhat used to dealing with foreigners.

And of course, it is always a great relief to find other foreigners with whom you can compare impressions, both good and bad, of French living and culture without fear of giving offence. The French women I have come to know through the AVF seem much more receptive to our stupid questions about why things are done this way or that way in France. Some of them have lived abroad themselves and been through some of the loneliness, others are married to foreigners, while others are simply interested in learning about foreign cultures and lifestyles.

> *I am seriously looking into taking French nationality, though I once vowed never to tangle again with the administration here*

We all use *tu* with each other when speaking French and there is a general exchange of addresses and phone numbers as part of most activities to encourage members to contact each other outside of the AVF. It may be the sort of superficial friendships that the French so often accuse us Americans of having, but after seven years of being on my own, it is a welcome refuge.

Expectations & Realities

I have been living in France for a little more than nine years now and I think it is safe to say that I am adjusting reasonably well, all things considered. So well, in fact, that I am seriously looking into taking French nationality, though I once vowed never to tangle again with the administration here.

Living in France has certainly turned out to be very different from what I expected on my arrival. But looking back, I suppose that many of my expectations were pretty unreasonable. Take, for instance, the idea that by marrying a Frenchman I would have some sort of instant 'in' with the society and the culture as well as my own personal resource for insights into the hows and whys and whats of France and the French.

I was moving into Pascal's home, in Pascal's territory, where everything seems perfectly normal and ordinary to him. Although he has traveled extensively, mostly in connection with his work, he has only lived outside of France once – six months spent in the US attending training, accompanied by his French wife and children (both kids pre-school aged at the time). Not only was his time overseas relatively short, but being surrounded by his French family he was hardly being fully immersed in the culture the way I have been here. Consequently, he just didn't see the sort of adjustments I felt I had to make. In any case, I soon realized that I couldn't expect Pascal to ease my adjustment, because getting used to things was something I had to do on my own.

One thing I discovered over time is that I have to be careful about voicing some of my fears and aggravations about France and the French too freely even when I am at home. Pascal is, after all, French. And if I arrive home after a 'bad France day' ranting and raving about how poorly the French drive, or express my doubts about the competence of my French doctor or dissatisfaction with the national elected officials, I shouldn't be surprised to find my remarks put Pascal on the defensive.

It is difficult when a foreigner criticizes your country, even if that foreigner is someone near and dear to you. I have noticed that I tend to bristle when he raises issues about some of the stupid ways things are done in the US, even if they are the very same things I complain about to fellow Americans, and the same applies in reverse. I have to imagine he has been vaguely insulted by some of my 'innocent' comments or questions, such as "Why do French drivers ride right on your bumper like that?" (especially the time I told him if he didn't back off the car ahead of us, he was going to have to marry the driver . . .). Things here are dead normal to him and he has never really had any reason to question why they are done that way, or how they look to people brought up elsewhere.

Our life here is very different from anything I expected, and I continue to be surprised (and occasionally delighted) by new discoveries. First of all, I had no idea until after I got here that Pascal had ambitions of starting his own business. I had always felt that I could never run my own business. I am simply not disciplined enough and I like my employee benefits. But working as a team for the last nine years, I don't think I could ever go back to working for someone else – at least not in a high pressure, corporate business environment like I used to.

> *while I still have 'bad France days' and expect I will continue to do so, I think I have at last started to settle in here*

As a little girl, I dreamed of having my own horse, but eventually I came to realize that horses require lots of expensive care. But now we are donkey owners, and I am finding I prefer my easy-going donkeys to horses.

In some ways I realize that I will never be completely French. Though I am starting to understand and accept some of the more annoying aspects of French life (the strikes, the bureaucracy, some of the rather rigid attitudes), I will never be able to take them for granted the way Pascal does. But when I go back to the US now for visits, I find that many aspects of life there that I used to accept unquestioningly now strike me as stupid or wasteful and I wonder how I ever put up with life over there.

I live in France now. And I am very likely to remain here for the rest of my life. While I still have 'bad France days' and expect I will continue to do so, I think I have at last started to settle in here. I will continue to be a foreigner, even when I take French nationality. But I am a foreigner back in the US now too and moving back there isn't even an option for me any more. France is home now.

Picking The Right Place

Londoners Martin and Julia Hills bought a
holiday apartment in southern France and found
village life a shock. It took them two more moves to
find what they were looking for.

Julia and I moved permanently to France about eight years ago. We are both Londoners, by birth and inclination, and so are essentially urban, if not indeed metropolitan, people. The significance of that was to emerge later. Today, we are both in our sixties. We are interested in politics and the arts and have spent much of our married lives buying and doing up old houses to our tastes – mainly because the houses we liked and could afford always needed renovating. Julia had given up her job to raise a family and so it was she who principally developed DIY skills.

We have moved house more than most people – partly because, once we feel we have got a house 'right', it lacks challenge; and partly because of a disinclination to put down roots.

> *when, in the mid-eighties, we*
> *realised that we might be able to*
> *afford a holiday home abroad, the*
> *only question was where in France*

Julia's background was scientific: she had been engaged in veterinary research. I, on the other hand, was and have been for most of my working life, in one form or another, a professional writer. Indeed I still am, writing for a number of English-language publications in France. For many years I ran a Fleet Street marketing communications consultancy, which meant working in and across the allied fields of public relations, advertising, conferences, exhibitions, publications and all that kind of thing.

Why France?

In our case, for a variety of reasons, there was never much doubt. For years we had taken all our holidays abroad. We preferred the freedom of driving and, given the existence of the Channel and North Sea, came via France. In the course of our touring, we covered most parts of France, making a point of not rushing through to the destination.

Another factor was that my business, which was highly personalised, didn't have an unlimited future, as long-standing contacts moved on or retired, to be replaced by younger people who preferred advisors of their own generation. While technology enabled me to dispense with secretarial staff and even an office, it was clear that we should prepare to live on a much reduced income, and we were well aware of the differences in property and living costs between France and England.

Thirdly, we had had to accommodate and nurse both our parents in their later years and we were determined not to saddle our children with that burden.

Distance would help. On the other hand, our family remains in England and we wanted not to be so remote that visits in either direction would be too difficult or costly.

When, in the mid-eighties, we realised that we might be able to afford a holiday home abroad, the only question was where in France it should be. We considered somewhere in the north – we had become very attached to St Omer in Pas-de-Calais, where we had often stopped. There, we should be able to go over for weekends. Then we considered somewhere further south, like Dijon in Burgundy, which we also loved. That would probably rule out weekends, but could be reached without an overnight stop. We didn't then consider the south, because the distance seemed to preclude any but long holidays.

However, as retirement became increasingly imminent, we began to use our holidays to examine particular areas more closely and the changes in my working conditions opened the field more widely. We were also now taking into consideration the relative ease or difficulty of selling quickly should we decide to retire elsewhere.

It was on one of these trips that we first came to Var and instantly fell in love with the extraordinary scenery, carmine earth, mountains, vast forests, charming and picturesque villages, and – as we then thought – marvellous weather. I should also mention the light – you don't have to be a painter to see why the extraordinary clarity drew so many of them to Provence – and the smells: walks through the woods are inseparable from the pervasive odours of thyme, rosemary and all the other famous *herbes de Provence*. We were hooked.

On subsequent trips, we started to develop criteria. As city dwellers, we liked the contrast of country holidays and began assessing villages. The right one had to have a river. It must have a choice of basic local shopping, not just one butcher, baker or candlestick-maker. It had to have a sufficiency of bars and restaurants, from cheap and cheerful to places suitable for celebrations. We also considered seriously the financial side. If we weren't going to be there that often, could we let the place when it was unoccupied? Seaside places were easier to let, but they were more expensive and we would hate to be there in the height of the season. On the other hand, what would happen to our property in our prolonged absences?

Then, on a leisurely return from Italy, we happened on a leaflet describing the conversion of an olive oil mill into a small block of flats. The architect sent us a video and we bought off plan. The site was on a steeply sloping riverbank in Cotignac, a village we had already rated highly, a little north of the A8 motorway between Aix-en-Provence and Nice. At the rear entrance to the building, our apartment was at street level, but at the front, looking over landscaped gardens to the river, we were on the topmost two of four storeys.

The apartment had a large living/dining room, with cloakroom, kitchen and pantry off it on the lower floor, and two bedrooms and a bathroom on the entrance floor above. The stairs were against the two-storey rear wall, which was that of the ancient olive oil mill, and we had a south-facing balcony at the front. This had the advantage that, when the sun was low in winter, it penetrated the full depth while, when it was high in summer, the apartment stayed cool and shady. There was also a large power-operated skylight for through breezes.

A further advantage was that the deal included optional letting management, a facility comparatively rare at the time in inland parts of Provence.

Mistakes & Problems 1

Broadly speaking, the purchase went smoothly and, having visited the architect to choose details of finishes, we were able to arrange all the stage payments and completion without having to leave London. We had been careful to read up about French methods of conveyancing and felt quite confident that we needed no further advice. That was our first mistake. Well into the process we were told that planning permission for the original design had been rejected unless changes were made. One of these was that our large cantilevered terrace, leading off the main room, had been cut back to a small balcony.

We thought that this change would probably be sufficiently radical for us to pull out and get our money back – but we weren't sure and were reluctant to scrap everything and start over again. We regretted this later, as ours ended up the only apartment without a terrace and the disadvantages became apparent.

The next problem came when we took possession just before New Year 1988 to find that the floor and wall tile choices we had so carefully made had been disregarded and replaced with more expensive ones. This rankled and dented our confidence in the architect. The large terracotta floor tiles had been laid unevenly – we were told that this was the "traditional Provencal manner" and, with interior walls already on top of them, nothing could be done.

Worse, the essential treatment of the floor, entrusted to the architect's nephew, very much a non-specialist, were like a very old DIY joke. The boy had literally painted himself into a corner and the sole-pattern of his trainers was permanently imprinted the length of his exit route. Eventually the affected tiles were replaced at considerable inconvenience but, happily, at no cost to us.

Coming To France

Around 1992, the decline in my business – and the fact that it could be handled as easily from France as from London – decided us that the time had come to move. We put our house in Islington on the market and, reckoning that it was too small to live in full-time, also put the Cotignac apartment up for sale. The timing was far from ideal: the UK housing boom had collapsed and the adverse exchange rate had made the French property market, in those days always sluggish, grind to a virtual halt. It was unclear which property would sell first – in fact, both took over three years.

> **there are great savings to be made by letting your removers select the delivery date that suits them best**

As it turned out, the UK market began its slow recovery before that in France picked up and the Islington house sold first. We put the bulk of our UK goods in store and moved down to Cotignac in stages from late 1995.

Arriving, we set about disposing of much of our second home furniture, chosen with holiday lets in mind, to make room for their UK equivalents. Some we got rid of locally; other items that the children wanted were shipped back on the return leg of a part-load. It is useful in such circumstances to be aware of the French *dépôt-vente* system for disposing of second-hand goods. This is similar to the UK's junk shops, but differs in that the goods are sold on commission, the percentage rising with the time they remain unsold, to the point when ultimately the previous owner gets nothing. Another possibility that we discovered later is Emmaus, an international charity which will take most things in saleable condition.

It is worth adding here that, should you have the luxury to be flexible about arrival times, there are great savings to be made by letting your removers select the delivery date that suits them best, particularly if you are not moving enough to make up a full load.

We set about devoting the winter to transforming a place suitable for a few weeks' holiday into one for full-time occupation. This meant building in a great deal more cupboard space, which we did ourselves. It also meant discovering the differences between English and French DIY. Among the most obvious of these is that the product ranges in DIY stores and builders' merchants' are not identical. For example, in the UK we had extensive gradations of thickness of MDF readily available; in France, only two or three.

Also, certain products appear to have no French equivalents: we have still to find one for Unibond PVA adhesive, which, on a builder's tip, we find invaluable in cementing (you paint it in dilute form on the surface to be cemented and then mix it into the cement to ensure a good bond). Nor have we found knotting fluid for preparing new wood for painting or varnishing.

I have mentioned that Julia is the practical member of the team and she has found great reluctance on the part of staff at builders' merchants' to take seriously requests for technical advice from women. Staff at DIY stores seem less chauvinistic but can be less technically knowledgeable or simply less familiar with professional products.

Cotignac

We liked Cotignac very much and enjoyed the fact that our apartment was only a couple of minutes' walk from the centre. It is a pretty village of some 2,000 inhabitants set amid beautiful countryside – vineyards, forests, olive groves – and protected from the north by a high tofu cliff surmounted by the remains of two towers, said to have been erected as an early warning system against Saracen raiders. The cliffs hold troglodyte caves, part of a long history recorded by a local historian in a series of vast handwritten and hand-decorated tomes, and by a local heritage society for whom we helped design a series of exhibitions once we had done most of the work on the apartment.

This society, like the village itself, is very cosmopolitan, with expatriates from Australia, Belgium, Germany, the Netherlands, New Zealand and the USA, as well as the UK and incomers from all over France. For those seeking to improve their French, this can be a disadvantage, as so many people speak English.

Mistakes & Problems 2

A major difference between property rules in France and the UK affects multi-occupancy developments, such as blocks of flats. Where, in the UK, it is common for the developers or owners to handle the administration of common parts and outgoings and virtually to charge what they please in the way of service charges, in France the whole development becomes the joint property of its sub-owners.

we were startled, on being introduced to strangers, to find that they already knew all about us

They elect one of their number as *syndic* and that person either administers the property or sub-contracts the work to an accountant or estate agent.

As largely absentee apartment-owners, we had mostly been able to keep aloof from the running of the development, simply paying our dues on time. Early on we had attended the AGM of the co-proprietorship, which was conducted in French and was chaotic and rancorous, with people shouting all at once. After that, it was easy enough simply not to be there at such times.

However, as full-time residents, we became uncomfortably aware of the tensions that had built up. The role of *syndic,* or administrator, had passed to one of the few French residents, who had successfully reduced the outgoings. However, the bulk of owners were foreign – English, Belgian and American – who mostly let their apartments when they weren't using them. The *syndic* complained that the visitors' use of the swimming pool required vast amounts of chemicals whose cost fell on the full-time residents as well as on those who made money from lettings. Those letting resisted paying a larger share of the service charges and the *syndic* and his wife tended to find fault with their tenants.

This conflict found angry expression at the AGM and created an uncomfortable atmosphere at other times. Since we were no longer letting, we were on neither side, but couldn't avoid hearing the complaints of both. It was a great relief when we finally sold the apartment the following spring.

A different sort of problem, relating peculiarly to ourselves, was that we were totally unaccustomed to village living. We were startled, on being introduced to strangers, to find that they already knew all about us – we had reckoned without the village grapevine. We found the business of everyone living in each other's pockets uncomfortable and somewhat intrusive.

We also realised, when there all the time, how much the village itself had changed and continued to do so. Cotignac was expanding rapidly with endless building of new and undistinguished bungalows springing up everywhere. Throughout the ever-lengthening 'season', tourists abounded and on market days it was impossible to park anywhere near, though this didn't initially affect us. The boom was reflected in the changing face of the shops: every time one closed, it was replaced either by an estate agent's or a boutique selling tourist kitsch (though these often survived only a single season). The contrast between the hyperactivity of the season, with countless entertainments, and the cessation when the tourists went home became more marked.

Next Move

Having agreed the sale of the apartment, we had three months to find somewhere else to live. In all our many previous UK moves there had always been plenty of time, because of a combination of conveyancing delays and the fact that, at most times, one was somewhere in the middle of a chain of sales and purchases, any one of which could run into problems. Here, there was little scope for flexibility, as our buyers wanted a holiday home and were not selling. There ensued a frenzied search for the next place, for which we hadn't prepared.

We knew we wanted somewhere with a garden – Julia is a gardener (practical, again) and hated not being allowed to tinker with those surrounding the apartment block. We cast the net fairly widely but were not having much luck. Once again, we had reckoned without the village grapevine. Still less had we underestimated the friends we had made, albeit in the expat community and over such a short time, who seemed determined not to lose us – another total surprise.

As the sands ran out, we began seriously – but very reluctantly in view of the hassle and expense involved – to consider putting everything back in store and to rent until we found the right place.

Then a friend came up with a promising deal. A lady who had been trying to sell for some time and was becoming desperate enough to drop her price substantially had a house with a large garden a little outside the village. Could we see it? Of course. Did it meet our needs? Well, sort of. We saw it and, although it hardly conformed to our tastes – a modern bungalow – we decided that it was acceptable.

The house had been unoccupied for about a year and we viewed it first on our own with the loan of keys and later with the owner. When we agreed the sale, we drove Madame back to the apartment to arrange an appointment with a *notaire*. Cotignac has only two *notaires*, who work in partnership. It is the buyer's right to select the *notaire* and we chose the one who had handled our sale. Madame was vehemently against this as she had, apparently, had a run-in with him on some previous occasion. It wasn't important to us and we were prepared to use the other partner.

At this point a farcical element entered the proceedings. When we got back to the apartment and I was about to call the *notaire*, I found a message from him on the answerphone, asking me to call back. Madame suddenly waived all opposition to our using him, declaring that it was "a message from God".

An appointment was arranged and Madame and the *notaire* seemed to have arrived at a sort of armed truce. However, later stages were marked by periods of hysterics and floods of tears on the part of the vendor. Though wearing and time-consuming (not to say inexplicable), these further meetings completed our purchase without either problems or further divine intervention.

The house we had bought was an example of the off-the-peg designs widely offered in France then and now: formulaic, characterless but scrupulously disguising its breeze-block construction under approved stucco colouring. Like so many around, it reminded us irresistibly of Pete Seeger's song about 'little houses made of ticky-tacky'.

Although the house didn't greatly appeal to us, the garden did. It was long and slightly wedge-shaped and had quite a lot of olive trees dotted around, as well as shrubs and a few fruit trees. The house had a large terrace to the south shaded by two established *platanes-muriers* (trees which bush out hugely to give shade in summer but can be cut back to the rims to let light through in winter). It also had a wind-out blind to extend the shade on the terrace. The previous owner had added a huge garage, though with entry for only one vehicle, and this struck us as offering potential for conversion.

> *we had to reapply for planning permission <u>not</u> to do what had been allowed*

Before we committed ourselves, we talked to the planning officer at the *mairie*, who explained that, under the then rules, we could expand a great deal if we chose. He also urged us to put in a planning application as soon as possible as the zoning rules were under review. "Put in the for the maximum you want," he advised us, "because, once you have permission, you have ten years to complete whatever you want to do, regardless of subsequent changes to planning regulations."

Mistakes & Problems 3

We had never previously looked at houses that were unfurnished; nor had we ever bought a modern house. These factors were to present problems. Empty houses look a great deal bigger than furnished ones, so that this one proved to be smaller in reality than we had supposed. Such misconceptions aren't helped, for British buyers, by the fact that houses are described in France in terms of square metres of 'habitable space', which is to say excluding such things as garages, corridors and bathrooms, and so give no idea whatsoever of the dimensions of individual rooms.

The design of this kind of modern French house, like those on housing estates in Britain, tends to run to one very large living room, all other rooms being relatively small, so misjudgements about dimensions can be serious, as we discovered. Our bedroom, for instance, once it had our double bed installed, left only enough room to walk around it sideways!

Our unfamiliarity with modern houses left us unprepared for another snag. All our previous houses had been at least a century old, constructed at times when space-saving was not a consideration. Hence it was almost always possible to win extra space when needed. In contrast, new properties are designed not to leave a square centimetre unexploited – a great disadvantage for would-be converters. We got over the problem to some extent by converting the garage to a self-contained apartment with two rooms, cloakroom, shower room and utility area.

As advised, we had put in for planning permission for a more extensive conversion, including a partial first floor (we really don't like bungalows) and a roof terrace. The latter had to be redesigned, owing to the vagaries of local taste – in effect, the whims of the mayor (though this may become less evident as more powers go from individual municipalities to the new agglomerations). "Cotignac," we were told, "doesn't like large balconies or roof terraces." Cotignac also didn't like windows that were wider than they were high and doubtless many other things that we hadn't included.

In the event, we didn't get around to doing more in the way of major works than converting the garage. Curiously, this created a new problem when we came to sell. We had imagined that we could simply pass on our accepted project to the next owner to continue or abandon as he chose. Not so: we had to reapply for planning permission *not* to do what had been allowed. This cost us time and money in the critical closing stage of the sale.

Moving Again

Although we had never been very fond of the house, we had contrived to make it work for us tolerably well and the garage conversion was very convenient for putting up visiting family and friends. The garden was agreeable, though we soon realised that its size, 2,750 square metres or rather over half an acre, was not large enough to be left to nature but too large in the amount of work it required to keep it in order.

we hadn't appreciated how not being right in the village would reduce our involvement its life

We also found the location, some three kilometres outside the village, trying. We could and sometimes did walk in, but this meant traversing a very steep hill – bad enough going, terrible coming back loaded with shopping. We felt as though we were living in a suburb, with all the disadvantages of both town and country and few of the benefits of either. Inevitably, it became a drag to have to get the car out every time we needed a loaf or a bottle of milk and, when we did, it made more sense to go to the nearest town, where the choices were wider. We hadn't appreciated how not being right in the village would reduce our involvement in its life.

However, these matters were what might be described as low intensity dissatisfactions. What prompted the next move was that Julia's left hip, which had been deteriorating for some time, came to the point of needing a replacement and she could no longer handle a large garden.

After the last experience, we decided to put the furniture into store and rent a house in the village until we found what we were looking for: a larger house with a smaller garden, in the centre of wherever it was. As it turned out, the house sold quite quickly to an American family who wanted a house that they could let and also use for holidays. They chose an English-speaking *notaire*, as they spoke no French, which simplified the proceedings, although by then we were familiar with them.

We moved out at the beginning of October 2000, five years after moving to France and a little over four after the last move. We were able to find a large rented house in Cotignac, which meant we could put fewer things into store, and prepared for a long period of house-hunting.

In the event, we were there for only two months, having found our present house in Brignoles – which, again, had been unoccupied for a long time – and moved in just before Christmas 2000. It is a large house close to the town centre, on four storeys.

It was built in 1830 and was originally detached, although it is now effectively in the middle of a terrace. It has a huge garage, originally a coach house (which retains the original manger) with two further large rooms to the rear, beneath a large terrace at first floor level. There is a modest-sized walled garden behind, largely given over to trees, mostly fruit.

The move went smoothly, apart from the fact that Julia fell and broke her wrist just before it and was still in hospital when it took place. Friends from Cotignac rallied round to help with the house cleaning, which was of Augean stables proportions.

The house is on the busy N7 but a bypass is due to open soon and this should reduce the traffic, currently averaging 900 HGVs a day plus cars and the seasonal flow of caravans and camper vans.

Brignoles

The town is twenty kilometres south of Cotignac and has access to the A8. With a population of nearly 16,000, it is one of the larger towns in Var (where even

Toulon, the biggest, has only 170,000 inhabitants) and the smaller of two *sous-préfectures*. Like many French towns, its super- and hypermarkets are on the outskirts, so many people in the surrounding area hardly know the place or remember it only for traffic jams. Friends from Cotignac have been surprised at how attractive it is when properly introduced.

It has an extensive 'old town' area, which had been allowed to run down over a long period but is currently undergoing major restoration, property owners being encouraged by generous grants to take part. Among many interesting and historic buildings are the former palace of the Counts of Provence, now the town museum, and a former olive oil mill, now imaginatively converted into a municipal art gallery. It is a place of tree-shaded squares, narrow lanes, unexpectedly vertiginous flights of steps and ancient ramparts and well deserves its listing as a *ville fleurie*. Beautiful countryside is close at hand.

There is a large new *médiathèque*, a small studio theatre, a large open-air theatre and a two-screen cinema. The town is known for the quality of its public entertainment, which regularly includes a mediaeval fete, festivals of jazz and piano music, and free concerts and outdoor big-screen film shows in the summer. Brignoles also hosts the department's main agricultural show, on a scale comparable to a UK county show.

Mistakes & Problems 4

We don't think we have made many mistakes this time. The most obvious one is to have underestimated what it would take to put a place that had been badly neglected to rights. We were well aware of the poor state of decoration and general upkeep but it took time to appreciate just how much bodged and ill-advised DIY would have to be redone properly. The garden too proved to have been planned with more enthusiasm than common sense, with too many trees planted too close together for their eventual size – a problem we had also to deal with at the Cotignac house.

The first problem on moving in was to dispose of the huge amount of junk that the previous owners had left behind. The house had all the appearance of one whose occupants had had to flee it in an emergency, with clothes and toys abandoned and even a broken-down washing machine in the garage still fully loaded with garments. Fortunately, we have a large car – and, better still, friends with large vans – and the dump isn't far away.

It is my understanding that most house sales contracts, in both France and the UK, include a clause requiring the previous owners to clear out their rubbish. If this is so, it has been disregarded by every vendor we have encountered. It is hard to see how it might be enforced , without delays that might only make matters worse; if it isn't enforced, the clause might just as well not be there.

We have already had the roof overhauled and the two main floors rewired and re-plumbed and are tackling the long slow task of redecoration.

So far, the biggest problem we have encountered is to find last year that the wall on the stairwell had become very damp and the plaster was coming off in places. This turned out to be the result of a leak in an apartment next door. That was in February and the landlord's difficulty in evicting his tenant meant that the leak wasn't repaired until October. We now have to wait for it to dry out before the wall can be re-plastered and decorated, happily on our neighbour's insurance.

French & The French

Our French, upgraded from distant school days by courses of tapes, videos and frequent visits, was probably better than average when we arrived but we feel that it deteriorated during our time in Cotignac, because English was so widely spoken. We tried to counter this with informal conversation classes but there is still large room for improvement and we hope that the fact that there are fewer foreigners in Brignoles will help. We have managed to cope with films in French, if there isn't too much argot, but haven't yet attempted French theatre – though we were tempted by productions of Shakespeare in French.

A particular problem in this area is dialect. Many Provencal words have been absorbed into the local language and the more extreme cases of local *patois* can be virtually unintelligible.

We had French neighbours both at the apartment and the house in Cotignac and we got on well with all of them. However, we have found it difficult to make close friends among them, partly perhaps because the French seem to have ambivalent attitudes towards foreigners. They like the benefits they bring – Cotignac, for example, could never sustain its variety of shops, bars and restaurants without them – but they do tend to drive property and other prices up, even though there is little evidence to support claims that they take as holiday homes houses that young French people would buy if they could.

he arrived each day with the biggest cold box we had ever seen and had a daily three-course lunch with wine

Foreigners generally prefer old property or to build new, while the French broadly prefer modern houses.

There is the further aspect that *les Provençaux* are notorious in France for their clannishness. As a result, all the friends we have made here are from the international community. This matters less to us than to people accustomed to closer-knit village life; city dwellers are used to a degree of isolation.

> **he vanished, never to return,**
> **without even leaving his last**
> **bill as a memento**

As I have indicated, we are familiar with the business of 'doing up' houses and probably our most advanced French vocabulary is in this field, though local argot terms – such as *paillasse*, normally meaning a straw mattress but here a kitchen work surface – weren't initially obvious to us. Because we understand the processes of carpenters, plumbers, electricians and plasterers, we have had few problems with any of these specialists.

The only major building work we have undertaken so far involved the conversion of the Cotignac garage. We consulted friends as to which local firms were most reliable and were given a list in descending order. The supposed best had retired and we picked the next, who proved efficient as well as extremely amiable and helpful.

I should, perhaps, explain that, in this area, getting anything at all done can be problematic. During the slump, the French building industry reacted rather as the British one had earlier: firms which had traditionally employed all their own craftsmen laid them off. The craftsmen became self-employed and sub-contracted or worked directly for customers where they could. Long-standing apprenticeship schemes fizzled out. When demand came back, there was a desperate shortage of talent – and still is – and the attempts to recreate apprenticeships will take time to make up the deficit.

The problem applies particularly in areas like this, where there is a building boom, and is accentuated where, as here, there are many second home-owners who come down in the summer and want problems resolved while they are there. The temptation to exploit these 'rush job' requirements is irresistible and can make it hard to find help at the height of the season.

That said, we have been pretty lucky. Our original builder entrusted almost all the work to one operator of impressive and versatile skills. We were equally impressed by that fact that he arrived each day with the biggest cold box we had ever seen and had a daily three-course lunch with wine. At first, he declined to join us for lunch on the terrace but eventually unbent sufficiently to offer us some of his wine.

In Brignoles, our first plumber/electrician (the combination is common in France) was a delightful character – amusing and interested in what we were trying to achieve. He had no inhibitions about joining us for coffee and chatting about all manner of things. He was also a good and efficient worker – but totally unreliable. He would leave at the end of the day, saying, "See you in the morning," and disappear for a week or more. Eventually, he vanished, never to return, without even leaving his last bill as a memento.

His successor, in contrast, worked like a Trojan, wouldn't stop for a coffee and ate his sandwich lunch while still busy wiring or plumbing. Like all the others, he was charming and efficient and, with the obvious exception, someone we would happily use again.

Medical Matters

If you move to France as an EU citizen, at least from the UK, you are entitled to reciprocal cover for a period of two years. What we hadn't appreciated was that this was two calendar years, or part thereof. So, leaving in October, we were covered for only 14 months. Over that time, Julia was covered by my national insurance. I expected then to have to pay into the French social security system. However, conveniently, Julia became 60 at this time and so was able to cover me as her spouse.

I have mentioned that Julia broke her wrist at an awkward moment and that she subsequently had a hip operation. Both these events required in-hospital treatment and the latter a period of recuperation – in a splendid clinic near Hyères, where we were impressed by the facilities.

The clinic had indoor and outdoor swimming pools, both for therapy and for recreation, accommodation for families, educational facilities for children, and two gyms. Dining arrangements were divided between a number of rooms small enough to avoid a sense of mass catering, where there was a limited choice of menus and to which friends and relatives could be invited for lunch. There was also a small snack bar for less elaborate entertaining. Having subscribed to a *mutuelle* (a top-up insurance scheme), we had to pay nothing for any of this, nor for the physiotherapy following the wrist-break.

Later I had a minor operation which necessitated a couple of nights in hospital, again at no extra cost. As is customary in French clinics and hospitals, there are no wards – just two-bedded rooms, which may be had without sharing (for a price), also covered by the *mutuelle*. In all these cases, what might be described in other contexts as 'after-sales service' has been beyond reproach. Although our only other medical experiences were in the UK, we see no reason to doubt the WHO verdict that the French health service is the best in the world.

The 'faults' that exist in the system – that proprietary medicines are unnecessarily prescribed when generics would serve, that GPs tend to ask if there is nothing else one would like (in response, no doubt, to the French enthusiasm for pills and potions), and that everyone has free access to any number of specialists, all of which increase the cost of the health service and consequently contributions to it – are currently being addressed.

Conclusions

We very much like living in France and wouldn't readily go back permanently to the UK, even if it weren't unaffordable. We enjoy the quality of life, reasonably-priced food and drink, the climate (even if the weather is not always as fine as is supposed), the highly varied countryside. Perhaps above all we like the egalitarianism, where waiters, shop staff and others are treated with politeness and a respect for their professionalism they wouldn't enjoy in the UK. We have found no pet hates and even the bureaucracy, of which many complain, is fairly efficient and probably little if at all worse than anywhere else.

I can hardly describe our progress as triumphal but so far, apart from the setbacks I have described, it hasn't been a disaster. I am conscious that this might suggest complacency or self-satisfaction but, in fact, the problems we have had and the mistakes we have made simply generate a wish to get better at living in France and to engage more fully – and we have ideas about how to do so when we are less busy with house and garden.

If we have any advice to offer, it would be to approach living abroad by being open to new experiences and avoiding comparisons with 'home'. Picking the right place to live is essential. We would recommend seeing as much of the chosen country as possible before settling on a region or a specific location. As you home in on an area, be sure to visit it at different times of the year: not only does the weather vary but a spot that is full of life at the height of the season may seem quite dead at other times. We found it helped to draw up a specification of what you want and need as a yardstick against which to compare places – a scoring system could make this easier.

It is well worthwhile making serious efforts to speak the language as well as you can. Fluency is ideal but not essential provided you can make yourself understood and understand other people. Whether they can speak your native language or not, local people will appreciate your making the effort to speak theirs, even if you don't do it well.

> **" it is pointless to indulge in an
> unrepeatable past . . . our present
> and future is here and now "**

Do we miss anything? Yes, of course. We miss the cultural life of London. We miss the theatre, but we are aware that, had we been able to stay there, we would no longer be able to afford to enjoy it. At a more trivial level, we miss odd food items that aren't available here, though increasingly they are becoming so. We – more so I – miss the pubs, particularly the Fleet Street pubs, which were so much a part of my erstwhile milieu, even though they and Fleet Street aren't what they were. All this amounts to a nostalgia, but it is pointless to indulge in an unrepeatable past, and we try to avoid doing so. Our present and future is here and now and, though we have 'folk memories' of the UK, that is all that they are or should be.

Europe, All By Herself

Having always dreamt of living in France, Wanda Glowinska-Rizzi followed her brother to Paris from New York but soon fell in love with rural Creuse. Earning a living there proved more of a challenge.

My full name is Wanda Patricia Glowinska-Rizzi, which reflects a lot of who I am. Although born in Britain and of British nationality, I am what I laughingly call 'Europe, all by myself'. My father is Polish, hence Wanda Glowinska; My mother is Irish, so she gave me Patricia; and when I got married to a Frenchman of Italian extraction I decided to make this even more difficult and tagged his name, Rizzi, to the end of mine. It does make life interesting when people ask me to give my name over the telephone. And, when I am in a waiting room and the receptionist calls out, "Madame Glow . . . wo . . . ," I know it is my turn.

I was born in south London and lived in suburbia until I was 29 – except for my university years, when I lived in the City. In 1989, after a certain woman (I'm trying to keep politics out of this) got elected for the fourth time as Prime Minister, I left for a job in New York. Meanwhile my younger brother had got a job in Paris. After two and a half years in the States, where I had been working in a home for troubled adolescents and then as housekeeper to a rich American family, I went to join him and got a job teaching English as a foreign language.

From The Big Apple To The City Of Light

Paris is in a lot of ways similar to New York: the same bustle, the same dirtiness and the same treatment by cab drivers. However, Paris has such a sense of history and culture that I never realised how New York was lacking that until I left. The French are probably as patriotic as the Americans (and certainly much more so than the British) but they can fully embrace Europe without losing their cultural identity. And, surprisingly enough, I get the impression that there are more foreigners living in Paris than there are in New York. In New York people exclaimed over my accent and always wanted to tell me which part of Europe their family came from. In Paris I was simply one of many.

> *France felt like 'home'. We had often dreamt of living in France and now it was becoming reality*

Another thing that is interesting to note here is the difference between the US and France regarding foreign countries. I was in the US during the first Gulf War and in France during the second. In the States there was fierce patriotism and support for the troops without the majority of the populace knowing where Iraq was. This patriotism was for the troops only and not for the 'cause', as this was never really discussed. Also, although the war involved America, it was taking place in a foreign country and domestic news, no matter how trivial, took precedence. I remember reading *The New York Times* the day the largest number of US troops lost their lives; that news was on page three, while a burst water main took the front page. In France most people are able to say where Iraq is and can argue the pros and cons of going to war there. During the second Gulf War, even our local newspaper reported events on their front page.

Fortunately, I managed to adapt to both New York and Paris fairly easily even if sometimes adapting to the people was less easy. I quickly learnt to be careful of where I could travel alone in New York and not be too passionately British. In Paris, I was only one of millions of foreigners. And it still amazes me that often I would catch the last *métro* home alone at nearly one o'clock in the morning in all security – something that I would never have dreamt of doing in either London or New York!

A few years after my arrival in Paris, my father handed over his engineering business to my eldest brother and with my mother bought a house in Creuse. As a family, we had often taken our holidays in France. Perhaps it is because neither of our parents is English that our outlook has always been 'European'. To us, France felt like 'home'. We had often dreamt of living in France (I think the wine and cheese contributed to our desire) and now it was becoming reality.

Down & Almost Out In Paris

Unfortunately, while in Paris I was introduced to the French health service, as I had become quite ill. I had to undergo a number of operations and I well remember the time the doctor informed of the first. I asked him how long the waiting list was. He simply looked at me and then said, "Oh yes, you're British." Sure enough, the longest time I have ever had to wait is three months, and that was for an exploratory knee operation. On the whole, I have only good things to say about the French health service. I am concerned though that, top-heavy with administration, it is going the way of the National Health Service in Britain. But let me get back to Paris.

When I arrived there, I got a job as a nanny to a small boy. But the job was depressing and difficult, as the father worked at home so I was never able to relax. He also wanted to learn English, so I wasn't allowed to speak French (or try to, as my school French was nowhere near adequate for living in France). I was terribly frustrated at my lack of progress. I remember watching American 1980s police shows and trying to lip-read in an effort to understand what was going on.

Needless to say, I didn't last long in that job, especially as part of my salary was a small room with a dirty bed and the toilet was at the end of the communal corridor. The change from New York was immense, as there I had had an enormous bedroom in the basement with my own fairly luxurious bathroom. And there were times when I questioned my sanity. I had left my three-bedroom detached house in London suburbia for ten square metres of grubbiness.

I then got lucky. In a free English-language magazine and on the same day, I saw two adverts: one for English teachers and the other for free accommodation in exchange for looking after two girls. Like a dream, it worked out for me. I got invaluable teaching experience and use of the washing machine that my evening employers allowed me to use during the day. Life was getting better. I joined a French-English conversation club and made many friends – both Anglophone and Francophone. My French was improving, even if not as quickly as I would have liked. I bought a car and, with friends, started to explore France.

Unfortunately, as in most big cities, you need money to live well in Paris. I loved living there but my last year was difficult. I was living in the 6th *arrondissement* (district), which is terribly 'chic', but the only place I could afford which was close enough to work was a *chambre de bonne* – a thirteen square metre room, on the seventh floor (with no lift) that used to house the servants who worked for the people in the larger flats below. Mine was fully equipped, which meant that I could talk on the telephone, have a shower, cook dinner, be on the toilet and watch television all at the same time! However, the seven flights of stairs (although great for exercising both my thighs and my memory) was playing havoc with my poor health, which meant that I was unable to work full-time, which in turn was playing havoc with my bank balance.

I moved into another ground floor flat when I changed jobs. But my luck was beginning to run out. The company where I taught English went bust, which meant that I had only a few hours' work a week in a research laboratory. So, after yet another series of operations in 1995, my long-suffering friends packed my stuff into a van and I went off to my parents' to convalesce.

Convalescing In Creuse

They had bought a large stone-built house in central France. The area is predominantly rural and relatively poor but it more than makes up for it with its rich landscapes. It is heavily forested and criss-crossed by rivers and lakes; small stone villages nestle amongst the rolling hills and the wildlife is abundant. I fell in love with the place and decided to stay.

However, this rural paradise has a sting in the tail: no work. Creuse is part of the Limousin region (famous for Limoges porcelain and Aubusson tapestries) of southwest central France. Population density is low with 130,000 human inhabitants and 400,000 cows. To a large extent, the modern world has passed it by, which means that industry is virtually non-existent and almost no one speaks English. I was registered with the unemployment office but, as I had been working part-time in Paris, my monthly benefits didn't amount to much. I eventually set myself up as a self-employed English teacher and translator and got a small grant from the government to buy equipment.

Being self-employed in France is not easy. The social charges are high and, even before you earn money, you have to pay. My grant was small and hardly covered the cost of the books and computer that I had to buy, let alone essential luxuries such as electricity. After eighteen months I was forced to stop, as I simply couldn't do enough work quickly enough.

> " *the only problem was that my town hall had never organised a wedding where one of the parties was British* "

Although in general the people of the area are welcoming, work is a different matter, as unemployment is so high. I remember I went for an interview for an English-teaching job in an adult education centre. They gave the job to a French person, as when speaking I had made several errors in French. I hadn't applied to be a French teacher and thought that it was my level of English that was more important! I did learn a very important lesson though, which is probably true of all rural areas: what you know is important, who you know is primordial.

Marriage & Home-Making

Just before leaving Paris I had met my future husband, but, as I was leaving for the sticks, nothing came of the meeting. Once I had got myself set up in a flat, I organised a house-warming and invited friends down from Paris. One of them brought Jean-Pierre with him but, much to his chagrin, in all the hassle of moving from Paris I had completely forgotten him! The weekend was nevertheless a great success and, when he went back to Paris, we kept in touch. In February 1997 I went up to Paris for a weekend and Jean-Pierre met me at the station. As they say, the rest is history.

In June of the same year, we decided to get married and buy a house (neither of us was exactly a spring chicken, so perhaps we knew more of what we needed in a partner than people in their twenties). We found the house first. Surprisingly, it wasn't at all what I had envisaged buying when first moving into the area.

Creuse is full of beautiful ancient villages made up of granite-built cottages. But, as Jean-Pierre quite rightly pointed out, buying an old house that needed renovating or lots of 'tender loving care' wasn't practical under the circumstances. For the moment he was in Paris working full time and studying for a Masters degree in computer studies. The last thing he wanted to do was travel 350km each way to spend his weekends on DIY.

The house was built in 1980 and was habitable straight away. Even though it didn't have a lot of character, its position more than made up for that. It was in a small hamlet on the side of a valley overlooking the main village. The garden was large and sloped down to a river and included two centuries-old granite houses. Our offer was accepted, so we had to go about getting a mortgage.

> **66** ***in France paperwork is sacrosanct and nothing can be done without the correct documentation*** **99**

A number of people had told us that getting a mortgage was easier as a married couple than if we remained single. As we had already decided to get married anyway, it made sense to get married straight away. And that was when the fun started!

We chose to get married in the small town where I was living, as the town hall was in a medieval castle and was simply much prettier than the 1970s building in the town where Jean-Pierre lived. In France a priest or any other religious practitioner cannot legally marry you; it has to be done by the Mayor or Deputy Mayor. So we decided to make the civil service a small family affair and arrange a big church wedding for later.

The only problem was that my town hall had never organised a wedding where one of the parties was British. They gave me a list of documents that I had to provide: a birth certificate dated less than three months previously, a *certificat de célibat* (a certificate proving spinsterhood), proof that I didn't have a criminal record and so on. I argued: I was born thirty-seven years ago and my birth certificate was dated the day my birth was registered; how could I prove I was a spinster; and how could I produce a 'non-criminal' record?

The British Consulate in Bordeaux came to my rescue. They sent me a copy of the French law covering the validity of my birth certificate, told me that a signed declaration from me stating that I had never been married would replace the infamous *certificat de célibat* and explained how I could get my 'non-criminal' record.

But my trials weren't yet over. I was told to get a blood test. "What for?" I asked. To make sure that there would be no problems with blood incompatibility for our children. "But I can't have children," I replied. They shrugged. In France paperwork is sacrosanct and nothing can be done without the correct documentation. So I took my blood test demand to my doctor. He looked at me and said, "But you can't have children." I shrugged. He signed my certificate without taking a blood sample and at that point I handed over my fiancé's request and asked him if he would sign his as well.

As late as the Thursday before the Saturday we were due to be married, we were still unsure as to the whether the wedding could take place because Jean-Pierre was still waiting for a document from his town hall. Miracles do happen, though. We got married on 29th November 1997. We had arranged everything in under four weeks! We obtained our mortgage and on 17th December we signed for our new house. As my husband is French, the buying process had been relatively painless. My husband had, of course, been able to negotiate easily with the various people and understood any correspondence we received. If had had to do it alone, I think I would have had many problems.

The house was in a hamlet of only twenty-two inhabitants – a big change from London, New York or Paris. We were very lucky to find neighbours of roughly the same age as us (Creuse has the highest average population age of any area of Europe) and with pretty much the same sense of humour. We have since become firm friends. Our acceptance by the other neighbours took a little longer.

I remember one Sunday evening my father, husband and I were sitting in the garden enjoying a beer when the 'patriarch' of the village arrived with some eggs. We invited him to have a drink with us, and he willingly accepted. As he was leaving, he turned to us and said, "I said to my daughter, 'I know the new neighbours aren't French but they're alright'." "But I AM French," wailed my husband.

Holding Hands In Rural France

As in many rural areas, a car is essential for both work and leisure. We are lucky where we are in that the nearest supermarket is only six kilometres away and the nearest mainline station twenty kilometres away, and we are well served by major roads. Popping out for a 'bite to eat' could mean a sixty kilometre round trip – and you can forget about take-aways. Leisure activities here are based more upon visiting family and friends than in big towns. In the summer, if you like outdoor pursuits, you have everything literally on your doorstep: fishing, swimming, walking, off and on-road cycling, horse-riding . . . Also, the villages come alive with fairs, fêtes and shows. Winters are spent visiting friends or going out to restaurants and cinemas.

I must add that, although I quite often went to the cinema in Britain, here I go rarely. There are two main reasons for that. The first is that I object to paying to watch English-language films dubbed into French, especially as I know that very often the translation leaves an awful lot to be desired. The second is that in general I don't like French films (or French television come to that). I find that the acting is stilted and when they try to copy American films or TV series (which in general aren't fantastic to start with) it is a recipe for disaster. I think that this is a cultural difference that can be seen mostly in comedies. French humour is more like American humour than British. It is an obvious humour and quite slapstick. British humour is much drier and subtler. We take a situation and adapt it so that we can identify with it and see it happening to ourselves. Our humour must be unique, because I will watch my father and husband doubled up over something while my mother and I look on bemusedly, and the reverse is true for them.

Meanwhile, working for other people wasn't continuing as I wished and I made the decision to set myself up in business again. This time it was different. I had had the chance to build up my network of contacts so I was getting referrals from friends and friends of clients, etc. I had also spied a business opening in the area due to the rising number of British people buying houses. When my parents had bought their house, they had fallen foul of some Brits working for the estate agent. Not knowing anyone in the area and speaking minimal French, they were pleased to find someone who said they would help them with finding plumbers, builders and the like. My parents never thought that they would get this service for free, but when they discovered that the commission was more than the actual work carried out they realised that they had been 'had'.

I decided to give English lessons and do translations again but I also added a 'hand-holding' service. This means that I help at the *notaire*'s or with France Télécom or I can find builders and get estimates. I work a lot with estate agents, who realise that clients are comfortable knowing that I am there to help them and not simply trying to sell them a house.

Unfortunately, the more I work the more I hear about people being ripped off by both the French and by fellow Brits: British 'estate agents' who are registered neither here nor in Britain and have no professional insurance; builders who never made it in Britain so try it on here, knowing that people who don't speak French won't know the regulations either; and French estate agents who neglect to tell buyers about a right of way in front of the living-room windows. If in doubt about an estate agent, ask to see his *carte professionnelle* (work permit). This means that he is registered as an estate agent and more importantly is up to date with his professional insurance.

Among some French people, we Brits don't have a very good reputation here. This has been exacerbated by the fact that house prices are increasing far faster than local salaries. On the one hand, we are bringing money into the area; on the other, we are pushing prices up beyond what the locals can buy. It is a two-edged sword. The only consolation is that the British tend to buy old, run-down houses and do them up and the French prefer starting from scratch and building something new.

I enjoy my work immensely, as each day is different. Each year I seem to add another activity to my business: I teach, translate, interpret, present activities in English on the local radio, do internet research for local businesses, act as English Press Agent for the Creuse Tourist Board; I even wrote a chapter of *The Best Places to Buy a Home in France* for Survival Books! I meet different people all the time and find myself in situations from the sublime (being taken out to dinner in a chic restaurant) to the ridiculous (immersing my naked upper body in cold, dirty water in an attempt to stop a broken main flooding a house). I sometimes feel I should write a book on my experiences!

Essentially, I am lucky in that I have found something I love doing in an area where unemployment is high. I have been doing this for five years now while in Britain I never lasted more than two years in any one job.

Proof Of Existence

Setting up the business was relatively painless (which is something of a miracle, given French bureaucracy) and the Tax Office was extremely helpful. This isn't to say that it is easy all the time. When I was getting my first job in Paris, I was told by my prospective employer that I needed a *carte de séjour* (residence permit). So I went off to the *préfecture* (the local authority) to obtain one. The person at the desk asked me if I had a job. I replied that I would have the job once I had my *carte*. But the person replied that I could only have a *carte* if I had a job. When I asked how could that happen if I needed the *carte* to be employed, he simply looked at me and gave me a very Gallic shrug.

when the Russians knocked on our door to deport us to Siberia, birth certificates were the last thing on our minds

Fortunately, my employer, having met the situation before, agreed to give me a limited contract that would enable me to get a temporary *carte*. Once I had that, he would give me a permanent contract and I would then have to change my temporary *carte* for a permanent one. Talk about a 'chicken and the egg situation'!

I would like to add here another little story about the rigidity of the French *administration*. When my parents came to live in France, they took all their official papers from Britain and went off to the local Social Security office. The *fonctionnaires* (civil servants) checked the forms from the UK Department of Social Security, inspected their passports and then asked for their birth certificates. My mother duly produced hers and my father offered his naturalisation papers.

"We need your birth certificate," they said.
"I don't have one," replied my father. "I was born in Poland before the war and a lot of records were destroyed."
They looked at him in horror. "Well, if you don't have your certificate, do you have your mother's?"
"When the Russians knocked on our door at two in the morning to deport us to Siberia, birth certificates were the last thing on our minds."
"Have you written to the Polish Consulate?"
"I could write to the Pope but it won't make any difference. What is lost is lost. But I do have my British passport, my British naturalisation papers, my demobilisation papers, my forms from the DSS and my British driving licence. Won't they do?"
"No. Without a birth certificate technically you don't exist. We'll have to get advice."

they have a meeting. Then they have another meeting. Two years after my first meeting with them I am still waiting for a response

The situation was finally resolved six years later. My grandfather had been in the Polish Army, which had entitled his family to travel at a reduced rate on the railways. When they were deported, my grandmother took her handbag with her and in the bag was the pass that the army had given my father, containing a photo of him when he was seven. Of course, seven decades later there was hardly a strong resemblance but the French Social Security accepted this as evidence that my father was who he said he was!

Rejuvenation In Creuse

Despite these sometimes irritating problems, I love living here. There is no way that I would return to Britain. It is true that the pace of life is slower here and that you have to adapt. The corollary is that there is no pollution, no traffic jams and, if you have a job, little stress. 'If you have a job' is the key here though. Coming to Creuse is like taking a step back through time. The villages are quaint with their stone-built houses, small smoky bars, medieval churches and lack of satellite dishes. You can drive through twenty of them and see no one. Even in the towns ('towns' is a relative word here: Guéret, the capital, is the largest and has only 15,000 inhabitants; La Souterraine, the next biggest, has around 5,000) the shops are closed on Mondays and for two hours at lunchtime – which of course makes for very some frustrated tourists during summer.

Unemployment is high. The area is highly agricultural, farms usually being small family-run concerns. Even with the heavy subsidies that farmers get here, they cannot really compete with the big industrial farms that are being created. There is an idea of helping them to diversify – B&B, organic farming, farm visits, etc. – but these things take time and the majority of the people here are resistant to any change. There is a big problem with depopulation, as the young leave to find work in the cities. They come back when they retire but this means that the average age of the population is around sixty. If something isn't done soon to stop this exodus, Creuse will become one vast retirement home.

The question is: what can be done? I have spoken to the Chamber of Commerce with ideas for activities or means of attracting foreign investment. They listen, they agree and then they have a meeting. Then they have another meeting. Two years after my first meeting with them I am still waiting for a response. I have to tread delicately, though. I am a foreigner and new to the department; it would be presumptuous of me to tell people what I think should be done. I do for that very reason, however, have another outlook and can give them the benefit of my experiences of other countries.

I think that this area would lend itself greatly to teleworking. With modern technology we no longer need to be in an office every day. We can keep in contact with almost anyone in real time. No rush hours and sitting in traffic for hours or getting crushed in an overcrowded train. And, if necessary, Paris is only three hours away by train and London is a short flight away from Limoges (65km from Creuse). But for the French, Paris is the centre of the world and the idea of decentralising isn't one that is readily embraced by them.

Another idea is to develop 'green tourism', which is a form of tourism that respects the nature of Creuse and the Creusois. I don't mean that there should be coach loads of people staying in holiday camps with discos and nightclubs. This area is ideal for unwinding, getting back to nature, enjoying the many outdoor sports on offer or simply doing nothing. These are both ideas that would help the area without destroying its character.

If I had a choice, would I live anywhere else and would I have done anything different? Although France and Creuse are home, I may not stay here for the rest of my life. My husband and I have no children and with his computer expertise and my English-teaching experience we could probably get jobs almost anywhere in the world. I would certainly like to see more of the world while I am able to appreciate it. So, who knows? And as for doing anything different – well, I really wish I had passed my French O Level!

The Seoul Of Paris

Hyunsook Ahn Charras followed her future
husband from South Korea to France with her eleven-
year-old son. Adapting to French ways was a life-
changing experience for both of them.

I was born in South Korea, where I met a Frenchman, who was to become my husband. We started living together in Korea in 1998, but we got married in France. My husband worked for a French company in Seoul from 1997 to 2002, then moved to another French company in France. That is why we had to move to France in September 2002.

I have an eleven-year-old son from a previous marriage, to a Korean. Since I got divorced, I have taken care of him and I took him with me to France. Although we had lived in Singapore for two months and travelled in Japan, Taiwan, Malaysia, the Island of Saipan and Great Britain, we had never lived in France before.

DIY In Paris

It was easy for me to move to France. I didn't have pets when I was in Korea and I didn't bring any furniture to France. Some clothes, Korean books and photos were all that I could take with me in the aeroplane without extra charge. My husband already had some furniture and we bought some more after arriving in France.

To begin with, we lived in a four-storey house with one of my husband's sons and his girlfriend in Villebon-sur-Yvette, a town of 11,000 people to the south of Paris, from September 2002 to November 2003. My husband had already lived for more than ten years in this area before coming to Korea. Then the young couple moved to Paris, so we sold the house, which my husband owned, and the three of us (me, my husband and my son) bought an apartment in the same town.

I think that the real estate system in France is well organised, although it is very competitive. We used the same estate agent to sell and buy. When there were prospective buyers, they visited the house, but I didn't need to explain much to them because the agents had told them everything about the property. Concerning the legal process of property registration, my husband managed all this.

> *I didn't speak any French*
> *when I arrived and still*
> *regard myself as a beginner*
> *in the language*

Our apartment, which is on the first floor, was built thirty-five years ago. There is no lift, but the garden is pretty big and well kept. The apartment itself measures 109 square metres. We have five main rooms, a kitchen, a bathroom, a shower room, a WC, two parking spaces and a cellar.

Before we moved in, we did some renovation to the apartment. We painted some walls and put up wallpaper ourselves to save money. We were able do the work without hurrying because we had plenty of time and could come and go easily, as the new apartment was located in the same town as our house.

However, we also had to replace the work surfaces in the kitchen because all our appliances, such as washing machine, cooker and dishwasher, didn't fit the existing framework. I discovered that manpower in France is more expensive than in Korea. So I found some Koreans who could do the work in my kitchen instead of having French workers. It cost less and was easy for me to tell the workers what should be done because I spoke Korean with them.

During the move, a cupboard which was very old was broken. The removal company had insured it for a certain amount but, because there aren't many people who can repair old furniture, the cost of repairing it was more than that of buying a new one. For four months, we were unable to use it while we tried to find someone to repair it. In the end, we bought a new cupboard at our own expense, as the removal company wouldn't cover us for a replacement.

To reduce costs we had to go to Leroy Merlin [a large DIY store] several times and find things that we needed. In France, many people seem to like to assemble their own furniture and renovate their houses by themselves. This is quite different from Korea. When we buy furniture, the furniture company delivers and assembles it; the cost of delivery and assembly is included in the price of the furniture. So I am still not comfortable with going to shops like Leroy Merlin to buy things and assemble them by myself.

Gender Differences

Since I have been living here I have found many differences between Korea and France. But I was able to adapt easily to my new environment because my husband helped me when I was faced with problems. At home, my son and I speak Korean. That makes me less lonely; I miss my country less. And my younger sister does business with Italy, Spain and France. She comes to France every three months and stops by at my house to see my family. I don't feel that I am too far from my home town.

Nevertheless, learning French was and still is a challenge for me. I didn't speak any French when I arrived and still regard myself as a beginner in the language. It has been difficult to learn, although I have had lessons and studied at home.

In French all nouns are female or male. It's funny! Verbs, adverbs and adjectives in French change according to the subject. You always have to pay attention to the grammar and must be alert to whether the subject is male or female. The order of French sentences is different from that in Korean. Korean phrases start with the subject and finish with verb; objects, adverbs, relative pronouns and everything else come between subject and verb. There are also some difficult French sounds which don't exist in Korean.

My first French lesson took a place in Paris city hall. It was very cheap and the content of the lesson was very good. The teachers were serious. But there are always too many people who want to take the lessons for the number of places. I failed to continue the lessons because my application form was delivered late. (The school accepts applications only by letter and they are given priority according to the order of arrival of the letters; it is first come, first accepted.) I was sorry that I couldn't continue lessons in this school even though I had had good marks during my second term.

But you can find small French classes organised by the town where you live. I found one in the neighbouring town. It doesn't cost much and I am satisfied with the lessons.

Above all, I put effort into learning French by reading newspapers and books, watching TV, talking to French friends and self-studying, as well as attending lessons. Of course, my husband corrects my French. But during the week he doesn't have much time to help me with it because he works. Only at the weekend are we able to talk much in French. I think that my husband is my best teacher and I am very happy to learn French with him. We can also communicate in English.

When we came to France, I could speak English better than French. But in France, I couldn't find many French people who could speak English. For example, when you need to complete paperwork in a French administration office, you will hardly find anyone who tries to explain things in English. French officials speak to foreigners as they do to French people. When I am faced with this kind of situation, I repeat what I don't understand and ask the person to write it down.

Patience Is A Necessity

You need patience to wait for documents to be produced. The administration procedure is very slow and inefficient. The following is an example of my experiences with French administration.

When I applied for a residence card, I heard from one of my Korean friends that I should go very early to be among the first twenty people. It was eight o'clock in the morning when I went to the *préfecture*. There were already ten people in front of me. The *préfecture* opens at nine o'clock but foreigners come one or two hours earlier and wait for an hour or more in the cold.

There were two women taking care of services for foreigners. But neither of them tried to speak English. As you can imagine, most foreigners who apply for a residence card have just arrived in France and have a language problem. Some are probably already taking French lessons; some may not be. But most of them can speak better English than French.

> *I am really impressed by the history and old buildings of Paris. But the French should change their old-fashioned thinking*

I saw Indians, Japanese, Arabians, Chinese and other foreigners among the twenty people in the queue. It took ten to fifteen minutes to complete each person's documents because there were always problems understanding what needed to be done to complete the procedure. I believe it would have been a lot quicker if the two women had been able to speak English.

Most documents are refused and need to be redone. Many foreigners must come back two or three more times to complete all the documents. As for me, my documents were accepted without much problem because I am married to a Frenchman.

I was supposed to go back to the *préfecture* three months later. Two and a half months after my application, I was instructed to come at nine o'clock the following morning. When I arrived there, at nine, I had to take a ticket as on my first visit and there were seventeen or eighteen people in front of me. In other words, the instruction they sent me requiring my presence at nine o'clock didn't constitute an appointment. So I had to wait for two hours to hear that my son's documents could not be processed until I had a residence card.

My son is Korean like me. I had applied for his residence card at the same time as mine. When they received my documents and my son's, they didn't tell me that I could only apply for a residence card for my son after having obtained my own.

I was even more surprised to hear that my documents weren't dealt with by them, but by the town hall where I live. They told me this and asked me to go my town hall. They had received my documents and my son's three months previously and now told me they couldn't deal with them any more, gave me back the documents, and didn't even apologise for their mistake. How stupid can you get?

I think that the French are inured to slow administration. When my husband has to deal with French administration, he often complains about the slowness of the system and the number of documents to be completed but just accepts it. You can imagine how foreigners feel! French people, especially those who are in foreign services, should be more efficient and take good care of documents. I have often heard that many foreign people suffer at the first stage of obtaining a residence card by wasting time and money and being emotionally hurt.

> *it is good that French schools receive foreign children regardless of their French speaking ability and that they have good integration programmes*

The French seem very pretentious. They need to learn how to help foreigners. To speak English to foreigners is a gracious attitude when the foreigners cannot speak French yet. Paris is one of the most visited cities in the world. I am really impressed by the history and old buildings of Paris. But the French should change their old-fashioned thinking.

A Good System

In Korea, I worked as a hospital nurse for four years. At that time I spoke only Korean at work. Then I worked for four years in a Korean trading company that imports medical equipment from Canada, England, France and Italy. I sometimes travelled to those countries on business and spoke English with suppliers.

I don't yet work in France. I am trying to find a job in medical field. I know that there is great demand for nurses in France, but first I would like to find a job in a medical or pharmaceutical company as a marketing manager or representative. Failing that, I can try in Korean companies in Paris. It will be good to work for a Korean company in France since I am a native Korean and I speak French and English.

When we arrived in France in September 2002, my son joined a school in a neighbouring town. He participated in two classes. One was for foreign children (of all ages) who couldn't speak French at all, like my son. This class was only for intensive French lessons. The other was a normal class, where my son learned history, geography, mathematics, music, sport and other subjects with other French children. He spent half the day learning only French, the other half all other subjects! I think it was a really good system.

My son stayed at that school for one year and then moved to a school in Villebon. Now he is in *CM2* and his classmates are the same age as him. Children must adapt rapidly to a new environment.

My son is going to *collège* this September. I am happy that he gets on well with his school and friends. He speaks French pretty well now, even though he still makes errors in written French. His pronunciation is almost like French native speakers.

Before coming to France he couldn't speak a word of French. However, he didn't have any difficulty entering French primary school without speaking French. It is good that French schools receive foreign children regardless of their French speaking ability and that they have good programmes to integrate foreign children.

On the other hand, if foreign children come to Korea I don't think their parents would want to send them to normal Korean schools because learning Korean isn't popular. Primary and secondary schools in Korea aren't able to give special education to foreign children, and most foreign children in go to international schools.

The number of students in a class in French primary schools averages twenty to twenty-five, which is the half the number in Korean classes. My son has two teachers: one teaches French, art and history, the other teaches science, mathematics, music and sport. In primary schools in Korea, a single teacher takes care of a class of thirty-seven to forty-five students.

Undressing & Making Friends

I had a funny, though very reasonable, experience when I took my son to a GP to get a certificate of physical health to submit to a school. The doctor asked my son to take off everything except for his pants. I had heard that people are asked to take off their clothes when they go to a doctor in France, and I think it is a good thing. The doctor can examine them properly. He also takes time to examine his patients. You cannot expect this in Korea, where you aren't asked to take off your clothes unless you have skin problems. (This was a strange experience for my husband when he went to a urologist in Korea and he wasn't asked to take off his clothes to be examined.)

I cannot get used to making appointments to go to a doctor. In Korea, you don't need to make an appointment at small clinics or with GPs. So it is often crowded in small clinics, and the doctors cannot take much time to examine their patients. I think that Korea should apply the reservation system to all hospitals, including small clinics.

I took some time to make friends in France because when I first started living here I stayed at home most of the time reading books and studying French. There are more houses in town where I live than in Seoul, where there are many high-rise apartments. There, I could meet neighbours every morning and evening – at least two or three times a day. It isn't easy to meet neighbours in the street when you live in a house unless you invite them to your house.

I have made some French friends – and foreign ones as well – by taking French lessons and joining in some local activities. I have also made some friends thanks to my husband. These were my husband's friends and are now mine as well. When we want to meet them or invite them for dinner, it is my husband who contacts them. I am a bit passive with these friends!

I have been very active in making my own friends. First, I met some Koreans and other foreigners in my French class in Paris. Second, I found a group of graduates at my university in Paris, which organises three or four meetings every year. Third, in the town where I live, I joined an association which welcomes foreigners and organises many activities: the Association des Villes Françaises.

I participate regularly as a foreign member in activities of the local AVF, which is an association that covers three towns and helps foreigners adapt to local life. The group is more than thirty years old and all its members are very kind and open to foreigners; they like to share different languages, cultures, cooking, etc. Most of them speak English quite well. The association offers many activities through which foreigners can make friends. This particular association seems well developed because the towns welcome many foreigners, unlike other areas. I particularly appreciate the French conversation group,which is held in the home of French member. I have a chance to see other foreigners from all over the world and to learn about their countries. I have met two other Koreans in the conversation group. I am happy to know this association and I appreciate the kindness of its members.

I don't think it would have been different if I had had a Korean husband. Maybe we would have had more Koreans as friends through my husband's work if he had worked for a Korean company. The most important thing in making friends is being active and trying to understand other people.

The Good & The Bad

The quality of my life is much better here than in Korea. In France, most people take at least a month's holiday every year. Koreans can take maximum of ten days a year. Also, Koreans work longer hours than the French. Not working at weekends in France has been the norm for many years.

Before I moved in France I worked from Monday to Friday and also every other Saturday. Sometimes I played golf on Sundays. Apart from that, I didn't have any leisure activities. Now I have more time to take care of my son, to do household chores and to participate in local activities. Mainly, I spend my leisure time learning French: for example, taking French lessons and participating in a French conversation group. I also like to make things for decorating the house, like curtains, napkins, tablecloths and so on.

At weekends we go to exhibitions of painting and sculpture and dance performances in Paris. I appreciate the fact that I have so much opportunity to enjoy cultural events in Paris, which is well known for its artistic life.

Before moving, I didn't have many expectations about France. As a foreign country, it generated fantasies about the different appearance of the people, romantic places, wines and *chansons*. It is true that Paris is very lively, with many foreign tourists, and has preserved its old and historic buildings. Paris more than lives up to my expectations.

But there are also some disappointing things. The Paris underground is old and very dirty. There is no air-conditioning, whereas the underground in Seoul is very clean and new and has good air-conditioning. When the *métro* is full of people in summer it is terrible. And there are often accidents and strikes, so trains are delayed. All the transport companies – buses, taxis, trains and underground – call a strike at the same time. That is a big problem for the people who live in the suburbs of Paris and go to work in Paris. And even though they cause us much inconvenience with their strikes, they don't try to improve their service.

> *most French people don't make the effort to speak English. They seem very proud of their language – or themselves*

Nevertheless, Paris is very attractive and lively. I like to sit outside a cafe and look at people passing by. In Korea we don't have this opportunity because most cafeterias or coffee houses decorate their interiors elaborately and it is hard to find cafes which put seats outside on the street because there is so much pollution. Also, I love exhibitions of all kinds in Paris. France is full of art – both in itself and through its many artists.

For the time being we will stay in France – maybe indefinitely. First, my husband has a job with a long contract and wants to retire from this job. Second, even though my son had language problems initially, he likes school and has made already some friends; I don't want to give him another change. Living costs in Seoul are much lower than here, but the Korean education system is inefficient. That could be the third reason.

It helps if you can drive. Most supermarkets are located in a commercial centre which is used by two or three towns, and these commercial centres aren't easily accessible on foot.

I would also advise people to learn a bit of French before coming. Because French is quite different from English, it is important to know some key words and everyday expressions in order to adapt to your new environment easily. If you can at least say or ask in French what you need, you will get less of a shock! Most French people don't make the effort to speak English. They seem very proud of their language – or themselves?!

Realising The Great Ambition

William Jaques had wanted to live in the
South of France since the age of 16. He finally
moved there – with his new wife Brenda – 40 years
later, but they soon found that life in a château
wasn't their idea of paradise.

At the tender age of sixteen I hitchhiked from Lewisham in South London to Dover with a map of Europe, a tent and £11, boarded a ferry for Calais and, aided by a thumb, arrived in Paris two days later. It was raining but warmer. A brief encounter with an Essex school teacher and his girlfriend on a street corner encouraged me to join them – in the back of a car on the top of a car transporter that took us the length of France to Montpellier – and so I ended up in the beatnik, pre-hippy world of Agde, where I lived on the beach in total happiness with twenty or so other young people from Europe and elsewhere.

The downside: every week the police came and checked us over and, true to form, several of our number got a free train ride to the nearest border. My turn came and my train trip ended at Tarragona.

This was about as far from paradise as could be imagined. At that time, the Spanish military police were still under Franco's influence and they adopted an aggressive attitude towards anything or anybody they didn't understand. There was a lot of bad feeling towards them; locals opposed to the government used to blow up level crossings, post boxes and sometimes policemen. So they normally had a round-up of potential terrorists at midnight and took them to the police station for 'questioning'. The normal procedure was to beat the victims on the arms, legs and feet. If nothing untoward was discovered, they went 'free' (after confiscation of all known worldly goods). I needed medical treatment and spent three days in hospital, after which I had my second free trip to the nearest border. I didn't return to Spain for twenty years.

One of the hospital nurses was a young, recently qualified French girl, who spoke perfect English and was also 'working' her way round Europe. She told me that the best place on earth was my previous resting place in the South of France. I believed her and so started my great 'I want to live the South of France' ambition.

A Property In Three Parts

After a few years in the Merchant Navy, I returned to the South – around Montpellier – for some weeks every year and got to know the land, some of the people and, most important, the local history. It was never the right time to actually make the move until in 1988 I met Brenda, my new boss, and eventually married her at the advanced age (for us both) of fifty-five.

Together we bought a business in Hythe in Kent with a view of France from the bedroom window, prospered and, on one of our regular trips to the South of France, finally made up our minds to buy something for the future. A quick look at estate agents' windows and we started looking seriously; at that time, in 1991, property was a bargain by British standards.

To start off with we didn't know what we were looking for but suddenly, whilst looking at a very large house near the Rhone, we realised that if we intended to come and live here in the foreseeable future we would need an income, as we were both many years away from an old age pension. Property renovation and resale was an answer and the easy (?) option. Various optimistic agents drove us in small battered cars to see many, very different, types of property, from a £3,000 town house to a £100,000 château; nowadays they drive a Mercedes or similar.

> *the buildings had been unoccupied since well before the war – except by rats, mice, lizards, scorpions, spiders and a large white owl*

One day, while viewing properties in Gard, we saw and settled on a collection of buildings that were between 350 and 400 years old and were open to many options: somewhere to live and something to let or sell. What we bought was in three separate parts. The first part consisted of an old barn over a garage. The upper level of the barn had been used to store hay for the horses that worked the vineyards, and the ground level had been let to the local carpenter as a workshop. Below this was a *cave* where the animals used to be kept: there was a pigsty, a sheep room, a cow byre and a horse stable – complete with 'floors' consisting of layers of dung. The rabbits and the chickens lived together in a small, afterthought extension.

The second part of the property was an old silkworm hatchery complete with the wires to which old mulberry leaves were still attached and the required chimneys in each corner to keep the worms warm. Below this were two bedrooms where the grape pickers used to live for a month a year (complete with beds and chamber pots) and a kitchen with a cold-water tap. The shower and toilet were on the terrace, exposed to the elements – and the next-door neighbours.

The third part was an old stable that had been converted into very basic living accommodation; the last inhabitants had been German prisoners of war, rounded up before being retuned to Germany. The collapsible bunk beds were still there, as were many scratchings on the wall and a few very secret items hidden in the stone walls, which we were to find during the renovation.

Apart from the grape pickers and POWs, the buildings had been unoccupied since well before the war – except by rats, mice, lizards, scorpions, spiders and a large white owl, which was living in the roof. The property had three wells built into it; we discovered two of them when floors started to collapse as we excavated the topsoil. The communal village toilet was in a corner of the garden where a vast bay tree now thrives.

The property was in the middle of a village of some 180 people, where we and a couple of Swiss and three Belgians were the only foreigners – apart from some Parisians. Although it was a small village, it was on the outskirts of two large towns. The initial asking price was £35,000 but we got it for £31,000. The pound crashed overnight, leaving us £3,000 short of the purchase price but, after some haggling on the part of a hungry estate agent, we managed to borrow the difference from the seller and so we became owners of a large but rather run-down part of a French village.

It was good to escape to a large house that was hot outside but cool inside in the summer and cold at nights outside but snug inside in the winter; warm winter sunshine reached our terrace at 9am. And just to have the locals say "*bonjour*" to us made it feel peaceful and secure.

It was totally different from the world we had lived in in the UK: there were just as many nice people but it was a smaller population, more content with their lives; our new house was in a village that was crime-free and had been for many years – a big and very important difference from where we had lived and worked in the UK. We once left the front door onto the street unlocked and when we went back three months later everything was as we left it.

From Stables To Château

We decided to take the plunge and move permanently to France in 1998 –to live where the grape pickers had lived. Brenda took the *TGV* to Paris and then to Nîmes and I drove a large lorry with all that we owned packed into the back. Her trip took six hours, mine took thirteen. It was one of the coldest days of the year – 1st February. The mistral was rattling the canal tiles when I got there and everything was frozen solid; the next day it snowed and it laid for the first time in fifty years – a good start to life in the warm and sunny south!

 people were kind and thoughtful; the big problem was what could we do for them. Not very much

There were no real problems settling into the French lifestyle. We came from a small community and we went to a small community. There were some people there who knew about the outside world only via their TV screen; some of the older ladies hadn't travelled further than the nearest large town in their lives, driving being restricted to men. When I first came to this part of France, the horse was just being replaced by the three-wheeled tractor in these vineyards; some of those tractors are still being used but there is often the latest BMW or Mercedes in the garage.

The men were and still are serious hunters; we were often given a wild boar's leg complete with hoof and fur. They often kill each other as well as the boars. On the doorstep sometimes were re-usable bottles full of local wine, and surplus melons found their way to us, as did asparagus and cherries. People were kind and thoughtful; the big problem was what could we do for them. Not very much.

We spent the first six months improving what we were living in and making a proper home with an eye to a future sale or rent. After this time the bank balance began to give us some concern and so we started seriously to look for work. Before we left the UK, we had looked through magazines for work in Europe and we had had an interview with a Swiss couple who were looking for somebody to look after their five children and teach them English whilst they travelled the world on business. We didn't get the job but, whilst following up past failures a year later, we found that they were again looking for a couple to work for them in their château some thirty kilometres away from us. I telephoned them and told them that we were available – and we had a job.

This got us into the French life system in every way: we became taxpayers and contributors to the social security budget as well as experts on the labyrinth of red tape and bureaucracy and the many hugely different aspects of daily French life.

We lived in a 1,500-year-old château that was in a constant state of being repaired by dozens of workers but was in fact a highly efficient, modern business producing wine that sold in the best markets in the world. The starting price for the wine was then around then €15 a bottle and the best was about €60 a bottle; a bonus was that according to French employment regulations we were entitled to three litres a day each free!

The château had two swimming pools, one dug in 730AD under the waterfall of the river that ran through the estate – all details of its construction fully recorded in the château ledgers – and the other a new pool three years old, also fully recorded. The downside was that we had to work. It was an 'on call' job that averaged out at around twelve hours a day and involved dealing with builders and their multitude of problems, and running a Versailles-type garden and dealing with the estate workers and their problems in Arabic, German, Spanish and French with some Afrikaans thrown in. The easy part was the teaching of and caring for five children between nine and sixteen, who could each already speak at least four languages fairly well. We learnt to adapt and compromise quickly but it was an interesting, demanding pastime, not a job for life.

The château was, as one would expect, complete with a castellated tower with a narrow winding staircase, assorted bedrooms, a vast garage for the various cars and an up-to-the-minute kitchen. When we left a private cinema was in the process of being installed. The walls were decorated with vast hand-painted murals taking the local countryside and wildlife as a theme. The main bathroom and corridors to the bedrooms were hung with erotic murals and pictures mainly based on Bacchus and others enjoying their life. The lady who produced these works of art came from Germany and spent several enjoyable weeks every year at the château.

Just before our arrival, work on the main bathroom was completed – at a cost of €115,000, excluding the 'interesting' murals – and an opening ceremony was called for. Everybody stood around watching the eight-person bath fill with water; a glass of champagne for everybody was in hand when it was noticed that the bath was sinking through the floor into the ballroom below. "Typical French builders," was heard to be muttered.

They, the builders, are either wonderful or awful; there is no in-between. They seem to be trained to a higher skill level than British builders and they only do the job that they are trained for; a painter paints, a plumber plumbs and a carpenter carps. They always arrive the two days late, making life difficult if you are trying to keep work progress smooth.

The local stonemason spends a good deal of his time each year carving vast marble statues for the grounds; these nearly always end up as fountains. He has two or three on the go at once, so he has two years' work at his fingertips.

The week after we started, our employers left for a six-week tour of their South African estates and we had a storm. The lightning destroyed everything electrical on the estate, from the wine processing equipment to the water pumping and communication systems, and blew a large hole in the roof over the recently re-finished bathroom, which was flooded. We modified the swimming pool water for domestic use and enjoyed life; the power got back to us ten days later. The modern way of sophisticated living is very fragile.

The owner worked and lived in a frenetic style. I would take him to Marseille airport at 6am to catch a plane to Frankfurt and then pick him up at Toulouse airport at 1am the next morning, in which time he would visit three other counties on business. He did this regularly, armed only with a briefcase and a strained look.

Strangely, we didn't find out what his occupation was until a fortnight before we left the château and only then by accident, when we had a visitor who told us about his new factory that was being constructed in Switzerland. Further details were revealed by *The Economist* magazine a year later; he is one of the wealthiest men in the western world.

Back To School

Exactly one year to the day we started at the château, we decided that we had had enough, gave our notice and returned to normal life – and visited the job centre in Nîmes. There were thousands of jobs – if you were an airline pilot, a doctor, a car mechanic or a floor sweeper. I know of an Englishman who, because of his naval experience, was offered a training course for work on the large canal boats that are to be found on the main waterways throughout France. He took it and is probably still busy working on the water.

The ANPE suggested that we have free French lessons to help us find work, which we did at the Langue Culture et Communication centre in Nîmes. The classes were full of Spanish-speaking people from all over the world; they could all understand each other but their accents and even the genders of nouns were different – fascinating.

 a major error I made was inadvertently asking a young lady in a builders' merchant's to perform a sexual favour

The communication problems we had (and still have) were mainly due to the mixture of four languages used in the area: French, Catalan, Spanish and Arabic. The people of different towns and villages, depending sometimes on the dominant religion, speak a different variant of French; e.g. a Catholic church has Spanish or Catalan overtones. In the large town of Alès 'proper' French is spoken, Nîmes has a strong Catalan influence and in Montpellier Arabic is widely heard. Much depends on where the canal diggers or various war refugees ended up. Just as the shape of church towers varies, a nail is a *clou* on one village but a *pointe* in the next. The winemaker at our local *cave coopérative* speaks German, Italian, and French but at home he speaks Catalan. We had big problems aligning our school French to these people; they just laugh and then correct us.

Never ask for a piece of pipe without looking it up in a comprehensive dictionary first. A major error I made was inadvertently asking a young lady in a builders' merchant's to perform a sexual favour. A *radio* is not a radio but an

X-ray; it took me a long time to work that out. The best way to learn a language is to mix with the locals and this is what we do; we aren't always sure of the conversation topic, but it's fun.

We took a month off and did a TEFL course. We did this in Lisbon, mainly because of the cost in the UK and France and the other two options, Prague and Budapest, were too many degrees below zero at the time of year we wanted to study. Hopefully we will soon start our own language school in one of the parts of the original barn that we have yet to renovate.

Local children are taught Spanish as their second tongue so they are reluctant learners of any other. The education system here appears to be chaotic and almost out of hand but the small local junior schools give an excellent basic learning process, the classes are small and the teachers know every child by name. The week's school meal menus are pinned up for inspection and it is obvious where the children learn to enjoy their food.

> *the vehicle registration departments are interesting, time consuming and a beehive of bureaucracy*

Secondary schools have a casual attitude to everything and it can be seen that large is not good and the system is rapidly becoming a disaster area, with a very high turnover in staff and a breakdown in discipline. Young French people are taught to respect their country and its culture to a greater extent than the British and very few of them really want to travel far. Until recently, national service was mandatory and surprisingly most of the young men we speak to enjoyed their time in the services as it showed them another side of life that had been hidden from them by the schools' demands for 'France first' in all matters.

Civil & Health Services

The legendary red tape quagmire proved to be frustrating but interesting. It depends if you want something from them or you have to pay them something; the latter is easy. Purchase a photocopier when you come to France – it will save you time and money.

Because we had worked for a vineyard, we found that we belonged to a mutual society called the MSA, which looked after all our paperwork for health contributions and benefits and the French old age pension that we now both receive. Some of the perks are quite remarkable: when Brenda went into hospital for her hysterectomy, we discovered that we could claim money for having our cat put into a cattery for the duration of her stay in hospital.

The LCC asked us why we didn't get in touch with our allotted social worker; we didn't know we had one. She guided us through many problems and we learnt that the French civil service works on the progress of a logical sequence of pieces of paper. The secret was to take every certificate, except our death certificate, all relevant letters and other documentation to the person we were going to see. That works fine until there is a change in the law made in Paris; the news filters slowly down to the south. One easy answer to difficult civil servants is to simply walk away and go back later, as there will be another person sitting in the chair on your next visit, who may be more forthcoming and helpful.

The *carte de séjour* caused us the most problems; the *préfecture* would only give us a card for one year instead of the customary five years – we never really found out why, so we had three in a row dated for just a year. A lot of the problems were due to the unhelpful attitude of one or two of the staff in the Nîmes Department of Immigration and their unwillingness to speak slowly and clearly and listen. The major stumbling block was the need to have a regular income: as ours was and still is very spasmodic we didn't qualify despite being financially on the limit. Eventually it was suggested that if we went to the Aide d'Immigration, another government department, we would be given some advice, and it was mainly due to their efforts that we had our last *carte de séjour* issued for five years.

Every February we get a large brown envelope from the tax office that has to be completed and returned before the end of the following month. The French government realised long ago that many people cannot understand these forms so they have provided a form filling service that is adjudged as fair as can be. (It also keeps the courts clear for real villains instead of tax dodgers.) We take all the paperwork to the tax office and join a queue, then complete bags of paperwork and, with our own entertainment and something to eat and drink, wait. The average waiting time for us is three hours. The tax thresholds are much higher here than in the UK, so we haven't paid any tax since we left the château but we have caught up on our reading.

The vehicle registration departments are interesting, time consuming and a beehive of bureaucracy; an early arrival is recommended – with a book. Some interesting people can be seen and heard there; this department also provides a soundless television to gaze at.

We have both made good use of the medical services here – both for accident repairs and for maintenance work as age takes its toll in aches and pains. Every large town has a free hospital and services for those who need medical treatment and don't have any means to pay for it; these are often an attachment to the private hospital as part of an agreement with the government. The medical and accident and emergency services are free and the response is immediate. The road ambulances aren't very well sprung but they are backed up by a large fleet of helicopters.

The local hospitals are excellent and are run on a business basis, so they regard you as an investment and their interest is in keeping you alive as long as possible. Sometimes wine appears on the meal menus. The local doctor is a phone call away and you, as a customer, are important. The MSA pays an average of seventy per cent of our medical bills and we pay for a small quarterly top-up insurance that covers everything we are ever likely to need, including the funeral if all else fails. A very good investment is the purchase of your burial plot from the local *mairie*; a double plot in the sun costs around €150.

Brenda needed a hysterectomy. From the first interview with the local doctor, via the X-rays to the keyhole surgery took three weeks and even then we had a choice of dates.

I had a kidney stone problem that required a hospital stay and then further treatment at a special nuclear unit in Montpellier, a town that has some of the best medical teaching and treatment facilities in the world. Kings, queens, presidents, Parisians and Americans go to the Montpellier area for their health needs.

A xenophobic Cockney couple in their mid-seventies bought a 300-year-old house, complete with five bedrooms and a sweeping marble staircase, in the next village seventeen years ago. They spend the summer in their French house but return to England for winter; between them they speak around ten words of French. One morning the husband came to us and said that his wife had severe stomach pains: what should she do? She had been having these pains for many months in the UK, where her local GP and hospital had put her on their waiting list, and they had suddenly got worse. It was assumed that it was her "womanworks" that were causing the problem.

We rang the doctor, who told us to bring her in immediately to the surgery, where she was examined and told that she should see a consultant gynaecologist as soon as possible. The doctor rang the consultant, who said that the patient couldn't be seen that day or the next due to pressure of work; would the following day, Saturday morning, be OK? We took her to the hospital and she saw the gynaecologist, who after an examination told her that the problem wasn't what had originally been thought but an infected colon, which should have been treated urgently in the UK. The doctor's bill was €18.50, the gynaecologist's fee came to €42, and the pills and potions cost another €30. Patient cured and Cockneys impressed: "Not bad for froggies!"

Making Friends & Influencing People

Entertainment is varied and, whereas in the UK we were really only workers and short-distance walkers, here we have branched out into canoeing, climbing and caving and we have become very good at just lying on the beach in the sun. The main reason for this is that most of the French still regard the weekend as theirs for the family and to enjoy themselves and so we join them. The other reason is that everything needed is here – from the snow-covered mountains in winter to the beach in both summer and winter –and apart from some equipment hire charges activities are free. We have started going to the cinema again. The French are one of Europe's largest groups of filmgoers; the cinema in Nîmes shows films from all over the world in the language in which they were made.

Three years ago we sold two parts of the property we originally purchased and bought a twelve-year-old bungalow in the next village set in two thousand square metres of olive grove, so we left one set of neighbours and found another lot. The French are careful in whom they chose to become friendly with; some accept you quickly and others take some time to say more than *"bonjour"*. We have made some very good friends in both the villages, as we go to the social functions, weddings and funerals. I often think the reason we were initially accepted was based on the fact that we both have had to work in the system to earn a living and learn the rudiments of the language, unlike most of the recent retired immigrants or holiday homeowners.

Very few of our neighbours have travelled abroad and we were initially something of a curiosity, but they could understand why we came to live here, as this part of France is regarded as the best place to live anywhere. It is now accepted that English cooking is good, we have introduced roast potatoes, parsnips, porridge, mint and horseradish sauce and Christmas pudding to the locals; all of these are to be found in the local supermarket but the French never buy them because they are foreign. Marie-Joe and Patrick, our neighbours, lived for a year in Glasgow whilst she was an exchange teacher and are solely responsible for the introduction of haggis to this part of the world. They also gave their children Scottish names and bemoan the lack of curry in the local diet.

in some of the small villages there is a very slowly building resentment towards the foreigners who are moving into the region

In some of the small villages there is a very slowly building resentment towards the foreigners who are moving *en masse* into the region, as the natives see the prices of property rising fast beyond the reach of the young, who are just looking for a place to live. A couple of villages near to us have as many as ten per cent of their houses owned by people from aboard (including Paris), and these are mainly used for holiday letting with the attendant problems of strangers in the village every week. Some of this frustration, I think, is due to hindsight as the French realise the value of their property and wonder why they didn't do as these foreigners are doing and make some apparently easy money by developing what they had to hand.

The French are a naturally jealous and covetous people and the arrogance of some of these visitors towards the local populace doesn't help. The average Frenchman deems it his right to double park in the main street and to ignore No Parking signs and speed limits but, when an Englishman or German does it, it is cause for aggression.

> *have some grasp of the French language and avoid the belief that the rest of your life will be a holiday if you live in France*

The other cause of discontent is the number of foreigners who work on the black and pay no taxes; this is another native right that is being eroded. One very French housewife told me that her husband has even stopped swearing at the English as he has realised that he is wasting his time and breath because they don't understand him. He has a village house next to an exclusive English-owned holiday home, which he is selling to Germans and he will shortly be moving to a house that he is building on the profit from the sale.

A downside of the British in France is that they assume nobody understands English. I listened to two British people talking about me whilst in a supermarket check-out queue and making a very downmarket appraisal of my appearance.

Why Are We Here?

We are here because the quality of life is so much better than in the UK. You can buy good reasonably priced wine in most places in Europe these days, and the sun shines in many places for as long as it does here, but despite being a flag-waving, 'proud to be English'man I want to live here. We are much healthier, as the environment is certainly less polluted. There is a vast area of open green space around us and the roads here aren't congested; the food we eat is normally grown or produced locally and is of very good quality – it is also reasonably priced. We eat out at least once a week and enjoy good food and service at an affordable restaurant. There are numerous sources of entertainment – from free jazz sessions in Nîmes to classical music on a Sunday afternoon in Alès. Our neighbours hold regular beach parties during the summer; we all take a picnic to the local beach and then eat, sing and play saxophones and a couple of guitars until midnight. There is ample employment for somebody who wants to work and the returns are often excellent, especially for any trade connected with the building repair and improvement industry.

Two Englishmen who came here less than fifteen years ago to two different towns are two of the main employers in our region. They became successful by providing the services that they advertise: it is simply a case of starting a job when they say they will and finishing it on schedule. The French have a justifiably bad reputation in this department.

The French motorist suffers the reputation of being the most dangerous in Europe. Our neighbouring department, Hérault, is regarded as having the number plate to steer clear of (34), as they have the most accidents per head of population in France, but they also have a great influx of drivers from other parts who arrive there after driving non-stop in the heat for many hours and therefore have many accidents.

We won't go back to live in the UK. We go back for two three-day sessions – in April and October. We once went fifteen months without visiting the UK and we felt as though we were in a foreign country. It seems very crowded, the roads are congested, the streets are dirty and everybody appears to be working overtime just to keep up with their way of life and debts. Although we are better off financially than we have ever been before, we certainly couldn't afford to buy a property in the UK that would compare with what we have now. Despite the fact that I am a devout anglophile, the UK depresses me; whenever I read an English newspaper, it is all doom and gloom and not the England that I knew, that I grew up and worked in. It was basically a happy country then, but I don't think it is that now.

My advice to anybody contemplating living permanently in France is to have some grasp of the French language and to avoid the belief and attitude that the rest of your life will be a holiday if you live in France. To live here without a good income from somewhere else means that you will have to work a lot harder to earn a living than you did in the UK, as we did and still do; unless you can speak excellent French, of course.

A lot of the initial paperwork involved in living here can be successfully completed before leaving England if you start the ball rolling six months prior to departure. The French embassy in London can even supply a *carte de séjour* if you are a pensioner and can prove that you own a property in France; most other relevant important information and documentation can be obtained and, of course, they speak good English.

Most of the French live very well indeed so it is good sense to join them in their way of life; they will laugh at you and your mistakes but, as it is nearly always in good humour, all you need is a good, open-minded sense of humour in return.

Norman Conquest

Harriet and Tim Seymour-Smith decided to make
their holiday house in Manche a permanent home.
Learning the language and finding work were just
two of the hurdles they faced.

I moved to France with my husband two years ago. We both worked in London and lived in Lindfield, West Sussex, which meant a long (two hours each way) commute each day. We decided in late 2001 that we had had enough of the daily commuter grind and, over quite a few late night glasses of wine one night, that we wanted to chuck it all in and live an idyll in our holiday home in northern France.

In the cold light of day, the idea still seemed attractive and we set about planning our escape. Fortunately we had moved to Lindfield three years previously and during that time the price of our house had risen dramatically. We therefore knew that we would be able to live in France for up to about eighteen months without paid work if the need arose.

It was, we knew, a major decision. Although we lived in a village in England, it was slightly different from the French village we had bought an old house in. Lindfield was right in the middle of the commuter belt, with a large community and regular trains to London from the nearest town, two miles away. Our French village consisted of fifty houses, no shops or local amenities, except a little hut that turned into a bar during the summer months and closed at 8pm.

D(og) Day

My husband, Tim, had bought the house, an old farmhouse near Ste Mère Eglise in Normandy over twelve years ago. His father had landed at Arromanches on 8th June 1944 and, having heard stories about it when he was young, Tim had become interested in the area and had therefore looked for a holiday home in Normandy. We used it for holidays and as a base for exploring other areas of France but we never had much time to do any real work on it. Consequently, although it was habitable, the decor, heating and plumbing left a lot to be desired. However, it was a lovely old house with stone walls, beams and four bedrooms with a large enclosed garden. We would never have been able to afford a house that size in England.

We decided to move over the following summer and, fortunately, had some friends who wanted to buy our house in Lindfield. This meant we could plan when to stop working, bearing in mind how long we would need to pack up and move over, and also to buy a dog and sort out all the formalities involved in exporting a pet. We had always wanted to have a dog but were unable to as we were both working and out all day when we lived in the UK.

We finished work two months before we wanted to move over to France. This was essential, as we needed to comply with the Pet Travel Scheme (PETS) so that Louis would be able to come back to England with us when we visited. At twelve weeks old, he had a microchip fitted, which was compulsory before he could be vaccinated against rabies. A week later he was vaccinated and thirty days later given a blood test. When this test came back clear (about five days later), the vet filled in a form, commonly known as a PETS passport.

> *we were surprised at the cost of DIY materials in France; paint was about forty per cent more expensive than in the UK*

We were now able to take the dog over with us, although he wouldn't be able to come back to the UK for six months after the blood test. After that time he could come back with us whenever we wanted to return to UK. However, each time we came back to the UK with the dog, we had to go to a vet in France and have a PETS re-entry certificate signed, injections against tapeworms and ticks carried out between one and two days before our journey, and sign a Declaration of Residence, which declared that we hadn't taken our dog outside any country that allowed dogs in on the passport scheme. The cost was quite high: about €50 at the vet's to have the documents signed and injections done and then €50 extra on the ferry ticket.

We decided to hire a van and take everything over in one go on the ferry. The good thing about living in our part of Normandy was that we were only forty minutes from Cherbourg. After staying at my parents' cottage for a couple of weeks to see friends and family, we set off at the beginning of June.

The Occupation

During our first couple of months in France, we took an extended holiday, apart from sorting out the furniture and having very basic work done on the house. This included sorting out the heating system; the hot water supply had been very dodgy due to a very old boiler. Judging from other people's experiences with plumbers, etc. we were very lucky.

We knew an English lady who lived in the next village, who recommended a plumber to us. He came round the day after we phoned him – he said he would come at 2pm and arrived at 2.02 – and replaced the thermostat, which we have managed with ever since. The charge seemed reasonable compared to what we would have paid in England. We also had our television wired up (by the plumber's brother!) so that we could receive British television from the Channel Islands; although we didn't need it much in the summer, we were to find it very useful in the long winter evenings ahead.

During that time we got to know some of our neighbours. As we had visited the house on and off for the past eight years, most of them knew the house was owned by a couple of *Anglais*. However, we did go and introduce ourselves to our nearest neighbours, which was well received.

We met some other neighbours by chance. On one occasion, one of our English friends broke down in their car. As she spoke no French and she had broken down only a few kilometres from where we live, she phoned Tim and asked him to help. He went out to where she had broken down and a few minutes later a car stopped and a Frenchman asked if they needed a hand. He said he had a tractor and went off to get it. He came back with a very antiquated machine, about forty years old, and Tim found out he was one of our near neighbours. After attaching the car to the tractor, they managed to tow it to a local garage. The upshot was that we were invited round for an aperitif in the evening and have been good friends with them ever since, although he and his wife speak no English. In fact, they have helped us with our French – and in return we try to teach them English. Generally, we have found everyone we have met very helpful and kind.

After a few months in our new home, the decor was starting to get us down and we decided to do something about it. The house didn't need any structural alterations, so decided to do all the work ourselves. This took a lot of time and energy but it was worth it in the end to see the house shape up. The main work was concentrated on the rooms we used most: dining room, living room, kitchen and our bedroom. It involved stripping the walls, putting lining paper up and then painting them. The woodwork also needed a fair bit of work, including treating the beams and sanding and repainting windows and doors.

going to local events was not only helpful for our French but also a good way of getting to know people

We were surprised at the cost of DIY materials in France; paint was about forty per cent more expensive in France than in the UK. In the end, Tim went back to the UK on a day trip and bought everything we needed in B&Q. Even with the cost of the ferry trip, we saved about thirty per cent. Also, items such as smoke alarms and lining paper were either much more expensive or unavailable in most French DIY stores, so we also brought these from the UK.

French Resistance

When we moved to France, our French was very basic. I had scraped through an O Level about sixteen years earlier and Tim knew very little, having stopped learning it at school as soon as he was able to. The first few months were fairly difficult, mainly due to the various legal matters we had to sort out with regard to living permanently in France.

These included obtaining a *carte grise* for the registration of our car in our department, applying for our *cartes de séjour* and *cartes vitales* (medical cards). We found that, if possible, it is best to be fairly patient when doing this. To obtain our *carte grise*, we first went to the Trésor Public (tax office) in our local town and obtained an import certificate. We then had a *contrôle technique* (equivalent to the MOT test) done on the car and took both these documents to the *préfecture*, thinking that we had all the relevant paperwork.

However, they then sent us to another town to the DRIRE office, where we had to obtain a declaration of conformity, saying that our car was safe to use on French roads. Finally we went back again to the *préfecture* and received our *carte grise* and new registration plates for the car.

Although our French wasn't that good, we worked out the questions we wanted to ask before we went to the appropriate office. This led to a much more receptive and helpful response. We found our dictionary very useful on these occasions and also used a French translation software programme on our computer, which, although it translated rather too literally, did give a general idea of what was required. We didn't find the internet that helpful – we found websites claiming to help if you paid an annual fee, which we steered well clear of.

We discovered our French gradually improving after the first few months for a variety of reasons. One of them was simply day-to-day living: talking to neighbours whilst out walking the dog and joining in local activities. We found that going to local events was not only helpful for our French but also a good way of getting to know people. I would recommend anyone moving to France and going to live in a small village to join in the local activities.

Most villages have various events throughout the year. The main one in our village is the annual *méchoui*. This is a lunch organised by the *mairie* (the local Mayor and committee), which the whole village is invited to. It costs about €20 per head. It is held in the local village hall, where everyone sits at long tables and is served a very good lunch, cooked on a barbecue if the weather is fine. For a small extra charge, you can buy local wines, Normandy cider and calvados. We found it a very good way of getting to know people in our village and enjoy a relaxed lunch at the same time.

Another reason our French became a lot better was that we started French lessons through the AVF (Accueil des Villes Françaises). After a few months of living in France, we looked into starting lessons and, to find out more about what was on offer, we went to our nearest town, Ste Mère Eglise, and asked at the town hall. They were very helpful and gave us the addresses and phone numbers of three organisations. The one we found best was the AVF. This is an organisation set up for people new to an area and open to all nationalities. It cost us €30 for two for a year's membership plus €15 each for a course in French. This was far cheaper than private French lessons.

We went along the first time with slight trepidation but were pleasantly surprised at the number of different nationalities there and also the friendliness of the staff. Initially, every person had to give a short presentation about himself in French, and based on this we were divided into three groups according to our level of French. Tim and I went into the intermediate group, for those who could hold a conversation but whose grammar and vocabulary still needed rather a lot of work!

Rather naively, we thought most of the other people wanting to learn French would be British, but surprisingly out of our group of about sixteen there was only one other British couple. The rest were Spanish, Chilean, Romanian and Russian. Many were fairly young women, whose husbands were engineers who had been sent on secondment to Cherbourg.

We very much enjoyed the class and have enrolled for a second year. We have a very good teacher and the classes are relaxed but help with grammar, pronunciation and general conversation. It is also a very good place to meet other people of different nationalities and I have made two very good friends, one Chilean and one Russian. Our common language is French, so this is another way to learn through speaking to other people with different languages. After our first two lessons we received an invitation to a *soirée* at the local town hall, at which the Mayor welcomed new AVF members. This was the first of many invitations, which have included picnics, trips to local places of interest and sporting events. We are both very impressed with the service the AVF provides and would highly recommend anyone moving to France to find out where their local AVF group is and join it. It is usually in a large town; our local group is in Cherbourg, the nearest large town to where we live.

Checking On The Natives

When we were renovating the house, we decided to set up as a small B&B (*chambres d'hôtes*). Running this is mainly my business, which I very much enjoy. We have received bookings by advertising on a website which lists B&Bs and hotels in all regions of France, and we have also designed our own brochure, which we have distributed to friends in England.

We have two bedrooms that we have redecorated and furnished in a simple French style, each with a private bathroom. We found out from Gîtes de France, the main Bed & Breakfast agency in France, that renting out fewer than three rooms has no major tax implications, as the income each year is fairly small. I fill in a tax return that I receive automatically from the local Trésor Public.

Running *chambres d'hôtes*, even one or two, is hard work but we have had very interesting people staying with us from Canada, America and England, who have all been very complimentary about the house and surrounding area. As it is very much a sideline, we do all the work ourselves and I also include a *table d'hôte* (evening meal) if requested.

After working a lot on the house, we decided to look for other work as well. We realised that, although we enjoyed running our *chambres d'hôtes*, this wouldn't earn us enough to carry on living in France indefinitely. We wrote to various companies in England involved in the tourist industry and have found employment with one of these companies.

We work as Regional Managers in Normandy and the lower Loire area, carrying out an annual inspection of *gîtes*, which involves ensuring that health and safety regulations are observed and checking the general condition of the properties. We also have an annual target for finding new *gîtes* for the company. This involves an initial inspection, taking photographs for the brochure, writing brochure descriptions and drawing up contracts.

> *take a course in French before moving so you at least have the rudiments of the language before you arrive*

As ninety per cent of the people we meet are French and cannot speak much English, this has greatly helped with our conversational French. Although it was rather daunting at first, we found that the more we had to speak French, the better we became at the language.

Although we work for a UK company, we have become what is known here as *agents commerciaux*. This is the equivalent of working freelance and means that we can work for a number of different companies within the same industry. We pay tax and national insurance in France and have been issued with a *Siret* number, which identifies us as registered with the appropriate authorities. Our tax rate is reasonable but we have found that National Insurance contributions are very high when working as an *agent commercial*.

Taking Advantage

One of the main reasons for leaving the UK was to have more quality time together. Although we are working again, we don't have the same rigid structure of nine-to-five work that we had before. Therefore, we can take advantage of where we live and use that opportunity to do a variety of things.

We have a much lower mortgage over here, which we will finish paying next year, and will also be able to pay off all our debts from the money from the sale of our house in the UK. Our work as Regional Managers, although freelance, gives us an adequate salary as our overheads are so much less than they were; the earnings from our *chambres d'hôtes* is our 'pin' money and usually put towards meals out, holidays and other 'luxuries'.

> **even if your French is very limited, try to introduce yourselves to your neighbours**

One of our major pastimes is cycling. We have discovered many cycling routes near where we live and try and go for a cycle ride once a week when the weather is good. We also both enjoy walking; as we have a dog, this is not only an enjoyable activity but essential as well. We never used to have the time to do this in England.

When we don't have guests for our *chambres d'hôtes*, we try to leave the weekends free so that we can explore further afield. We are lucky in that we live fairly near both Coutances and Bayeux and we very much enjoy visiting these towns as well as going further on to visit the *châteaux* in the Loire Valley.

We certainly don't intend to go back to the UK. Apart from the obvious things, such as the wine and cheese and the lower price of petrol, we like living in a village where everyone knows each other. We also like being able to explore the beautiful countryside on our doorstep. Most importantly, we have found work here so we can afford to stay.

I would thoroughly recommend the following to anyone who wants to live in France:

Take a course in French before moving so you at least have the rudiments of the language before you arrive. Once you have arrived in France, find out about local French lessons. I think the AVF is extremely good and it is also a very good opportunity to meet other people of different nationalities who may be in the same situation as you.

Even if your French is very limited, try to introduce yourselves to your neighbours. This is particularly important if you move to a small village, where everyone knows everybody. If you don't make the effort, some of the local people will think you are unfriendly. After all, it is their country you have moved to.

Join in local events. In France there seems to be a variety of activities going on in each village. Even if you don't have much time, try to go to the occasional musical evening or the local *méchoui* or equivalent.

We were very lucky in finding work over here. If you need to work in France, try to set something up before you come over. If you are thinking of running *chambres d'hôtes*, remember that there are major regulatory and tax implications to letting more than three rooms. Also, if you want to join Gîtes de France, either as a *gîte* or as *chambres d'hôtes*, write and get their list of requirements; they are quite strict!

One thing one misses in the UK is family and friends, although, as we live near Cherbourg, we can always go back 'home' to visit our family and friends. Also we now have a large house, so our family and friends can come to us. Nevertheless, I have found having email very useful for keeping in touch and also a lot cheaper than long telephone calls.

If you are a stressed or nervous type of person, I wouldn't recommend living in an isolated area. Everything takes a long time and one just has to be patient.

Finally, remember why you have come to France. Most British people come to France to enjoy a more relaxed way of life and afford a better home that they could buy in the UK. Don't forget this when you are weighed down by French bureaucracy!

On Another Planet

Kelly Amorim left her home in Sao Paulo to live with a Frenchman in Rouen, believing that life would be better there. Eight years later, she has her feet firmly in France, but her heart is still very, very far away.

Before came to France I lived in Sao Paulo, Brazil. From 1992 till 1996 I worked for a big American hotel in the reservations department and I shared a four-room apartment with a Brazilian girl (Monica), an Englishman (David), a Swedish guy (Bertil) and a handsome Danish boy (Sören), who was my fiancé at that time.

I had met Sören during his training courses in Brazil. He was studying at a French school of commerce and we managed to see each other during our holidays. We thought it would be a good idea if I could take some French lessons and go to France, so I did.

After a while, however, it seemed that something was going on between my French teacher (Olivier) and me. I was so confused that I decided to stop the classes and take a flight to Denmark, to meet my future 'family-in-law'.

Unfortunately, after two months there and in despite of loving Sören's family and friends with all my heart, I knew that something had changed and I realised I didn't want to be engaged to him any more, so I went back to Brazil and moved in with Olivier. But he couldn't get a job in his field (he is an engineer) in Brazil and had to return to France.

> *we had only few neighbours*
> *and, as far as I could see, they*
> *didn't seem to appreciate*
> *foreign people there*

After living with him for a year, I took the hardest decision of my life: to quit my job and come to France . . . with Olivier.

Arrival

I arrived in northern France in November 1996 (it was damned cold!). At the beginning, we were forced to live with his parents for a while. Olivier's family is very traditional (*conservatrice*) and they wanted us to get married "like everybody else in the family". It was too early for me to talk about marriage after what had happened with Sören, and Olivier was very understanding on this point. But things got complicated when I realised that I was pregnant.

We moved from his parents' house to a small apartment in the middle of Rouen to avoid "persecution" and, once in our home, we established a *contrat de concubinage* (co-habitation contract) at the *hôtel de ville* in Rouen and we were ready to announce the news to his family.

Today I think we took the right decision, because I know now how complicated is to get divorced when you have small children.

After my second child, we bought a small old farm (*une fermette*) with 6,000 square metres of land, which needed a lot of work doing to it before we could even think of living there, and I realised for the first time in my life what the words 'hard work' meant!

In order to save money, we lived in a small caravan for four months – until the house was ready. At the same time, we tried to *élever* some ducks, hens and rabbits. We had a goat too, later . . . The garden was completely neglected; it was very far from what the French call a *jardin anglais*. I didn't have enough time to take gardening lessons or read the right magazines with all the work we had to do, but I dreamed about a beautiful garden . . . I tried to grow some flowers and make *massifs* (beds) but the ground was so dry and unsuitable that I worked hard for about six months – for nothing.

Anyway, what else could I do in such small village – barely a hundred people and none of them interested in me? We had only few neighbours and, as far as I could see, they didn't seem to appreciate foreign people there.

Once the house was ready we invited our two nearest neighbours to have a drink, and guess what? Right: no one came! I was so mad about that that I bought two bottles of good whisky and I knocked at their door and said: "Sorry, but since you weren't available that time, Olivier and I insist that you drink a toast to our new house; I hope you enjoy it!" So I left them the bottles and left their house.

After that I was entitled to some "good mornings" and even to some fruit and vegetables from their garden (I really appreciated that) but no invitation: the coldness was there to stay.

Today Olivier and I are separated and I live in an small apartment with my two kids in a village of about two hundred people. There is a school but no bakery or bank or shops (which is quite common in France). I still have problems with my neighbours, but this time it is because they are very old and really don't like foreign people in their country. You guessed right: I am looking for another apartment!

A Serious Foreign Person

The first three years were very difficult for me: I had no car and Olivier used to travel a lot during the week so I was alone with two small kids in the middle of nowhere and, of course, "down" almost all the time. I missed my country, my friends, and my family. And I had the feeling that I was living not in another country but on another planet!

At that time, I used to talk to Katia, my best friend (and a real chicken soup for my soul), who has lived in the USA since 1998, to find out her reactions to the country, and they were far from similar to mine! Although Americans and Brazilians are very different, it had taken only few months for her to adapt and now she felt at home. Continent Complicity?

In the past five years, Katia has come to France three times to see me and, in spite of loving the country (she has travelled throughout the north and the south), she still has the same feeling that I did at the beginning, about the cultural differences between the French and the Brazilians.

I must insist on the fact that we (Brazilian people) are really warm and love foreigners. We do our best to welcome them and make them feel happy in our country. So I was expecting the same, I guess.

French people are special and so is their language! In Brazil, when I was younger, I took English classes and had Spanish and German lessons, but when I started to learn French I had the feeling that I would never be able to open my mouth and speak French with the same *aisance* that I do with the other languages. Although I had had some French classes in Brazil, I realised that I didn't speak it at all when I arrived here. And it isn't because it is more complicated but because of its peculiarities!

For example, I couldn't understand why we were supposed to say "no" when we mean "yes" (*n'est-ce pas*), or how to use the word *plus* properly (*plus de sucre, moi non plus, il ne reviendra plus*), or why we say "tiol" when it is written *tilleul*, "des oe " when it is written *oeufs* . . . And then there are all those *terminaisons* that sound the same: -*au, -aux, -aud, -ault, -ot* . . .

When I arrived here I was very happy to have English lessons, even if it was rare to find someone to speak English to. In the first months, I only spoke English and Portuguese with no special effort to speak French, but after a while I was sick and tired of miming every time I went to the baker's and I decided to learn French on my own: I bought all the French books that I had previously read in Portuguese (Balzac, Molière, etc.) and with the help of a good dictionary and the patience of Olivier I started to be a serious foreign person.

At the same time I repeated every single phrase that I heard even if I didn't have a clue of its meaning (and it was at this time that the first rude words appeared in my vocabulary!).

Attitudes At Work

I started speaking good French and I had an opportunity to work as a secretary for a few months. I took some classes at a Hotel and Catering school and things (and days) changed for the better. After going to the school I didn't have any particular problem finding a job, as I applied for those which required language skills. I worked for three high-class hotels, for about four and a half years.

she said: 'OK, you want to stay here because you are pregnant... but how can we be sure that the baby will be French?'

After discovering neighbours I discovered colleagues, and once more I was disappointed in the differences between them and me. In Brazil we don't make any difference between a friend, a neighbour and a colleague: we treat them exactly the same way, with a lot of courtesy and help. In France everyone is 'on their own', especially in the workplace. We are supposed to do our job and not pay attention (or give a hand) to the colleague at the next desk.

In Brazil it is quite common to go for a drink after work, to talk about ourselves, our hobbies, our kids and so on; here all that is seen as a *manque de savoir vivre* and they prefer to keep their distance. OK, I know: familiarity breeds contempt! But wouldn't it be pleasant to say hello in the morning and really mean it? Should we live like foreigners when we spend eight hours a day together? Wouldn't it be nice to work knowing that we are appreciated for our personality and friendly attitude? Maybe I am too philosophical to accept this kind of life.

I also had a boss who is a typical example of what I really don't like in a human being: he is a racist but "not with good-looking Brazilians like me". He owns a smart hotel and thinks that his hotel is "too nice for Arabs"; even if there were rooms available, for them we were always full.

Once I heard an amazing discussion between him and his chef, who is from Algeria. After complaining about the good situation Arabs have in "his" country, he finished the discussion by saying: "But of course this doesn't apply to you because you've been in France for so long now that in your heart I'm sure you're French and can understand me" . . .

The State Of France

The bureaucracy is crazy in this country! I had a visa for three months and at the end of the second month I requested a new one but, since I wasn't married, the administration refused it. A few weeks later, Olivier and I went to visit Bruges, in Belgium, and on the way back, an amazing thing occurred: when I came to the Belgian frontier to re-enter France, I was given a three-month visa, without even asking for it!

These three months passed and I went to the *préfecture* to request a *carte de séjour* because by this time I was pregnant and planning to live in France: after I had waited about three hours to get the papers to *officialiser* my request, they called my ticket number. The lady at the desk looked me very attentively and said: "OK, you want to stay here because you are pregnant . . . but how can we be sure that the baby will be French?"

I was so surprised that I answered: "Well, the reason I am asking to stay is because the baby's father is French and I want to have it in his country. But look, if it's really important to you, maybe I could send you a tape of his first words and you will be sure then!"

She didn't appreciate my sarcasm and asked me to fill out the papers as soon as possible, which I did.

A few moths later I had my baby, but it wasn't until a year and a half later that I received my *carte de résident*, valid for ten years. It was very difficult it and took me a lot of patience to obtain it. Today I understand the system better and I think that, in spite of the bureaucracy, France has a very good heath and social protection system.

My kids are both at a French school (Luc, 6, at *Maternelle* et and Paul, 5 in *CP*). I don't think the education system is bad if I compare it with the Brazilian one. One thing I find amazing: in Brazil we don't have access to language classes, although we can pay for them; here in France, children start English/Spanish classes very early and have them for years but once they are teenagers or adults they can barely communicate . . . They are so lazy!

there is no violence and, despite their coldness and natural réserve, French people are very polite

In a sense, France has lived 'up' to my expectations. I didn't know much about the country but when we were in Brazil my fiancé told me: "If your life is nice and comfortable here, in this third-world country, try to imagine what it will be like in Europe!"

I tried. But I was far from imagining that it wouldn't be so easy.

Today I really appreciate being here, with my French kids and a few friends. There is no violence and, despite their coldness and natural *réserve*, French people are very polite. I love to travel and discover all the treasures that this old country can hide . . . I love to read about its kings and its history. It is so fascinating!

I do *Capoeira*: a Brazilian activity that mixes dance and Martial Art. It was introduced to Brazil by the slaves, who, being afraid of their masters, were forced to do it in secret – to train in order to prepare their revolution. Today *Capoeira* is practised in almost every country and in France is very 'in'.

Unfortunately, I don't speak Portuguese with my kids; I don't have any explanation for that. But I do tell them a lot of stories, explaining the way of life there, and I show them pictures and films, cook a lot of Brazilian food, etc. And I really intend to do something for them: even though Brazil is not so old, I want them to discover its history as I did and, even if life there is completely different in many ways, I think it is a part of them and they shouldn't miss it.

I try to teach them that it is a real opportunity to be able to travel and see how other people live, to taste other dishes, eat other fruits, smell other perfumes . . . And I certainly preach respect for others! They are very curious and ask me a thousand questions about Brazil and other countries. I get the feeling that they will have a real passion for travelling!

I may say that I was really proud when one day I heard Paul say to one of his school friends: "You know I'm very lucky because I can have, at the same time, my feet here and my heart very, very far way, just like mum!"

I am working hard in order to be able to take them to visit Brazil very soon. I am doing my best to live a good life with them here but, once I am retired, I will definitely move back home.

CAR REGISTRATION DOSSIER

Meant To Be

The Ainsby family moved to Nord virtually on the spur of the moment and rented the first house they looked at – it all seemed fated. But they soon discovered that not everything in France is straightforward.

Since moving here in 1995, I have always believed that we were meant to be in France – call it 'fate' or whatever – and the way it happened and what has happened since just confirm that belief.

Our family consists of David, my husband, who works as an international transport driver, our two daughters, Tara and Lorna (who were seven and four when we moved here) and me, Linda, 'housewife'.

In the summer of 1995, we went on a week's holiday in Vendée. We had a lovely time by the sea, *en famille*. David had often had family holidays in France and when we got married we toured the country for two weeks by motorbike.

On our way home from Vendée, David had arranged for us to stay with a work colleague, Eric, and his wife, Norah, who live in a small village just outside Cambrai in Nord (department 59) in northern France. He and Eric worked for the same company and were both based at Beauvais at the Massey Fergusson tractor factory, delivering tractors and machinery throughout France.

Unbeknown to me, David and Eric had been talking about our moving to France and David was convinced that it was what we should do – the only problem being to persuade me! When we were shown their home, we began to realise what we could buy over here. It also made us realise that, being only two hours from Beauvais, David would be able to get home a lot more often (his job meant that we had little family time together and we never knew when he would be home).

Taking The Plunge

The following day we visited most of the *notaires* in Cambrai. We were looking to rent first, rather than buy. We got details of a house for rent, which was being renovated at that time. Norah knew the village and we found it easily. We looked around the house and knew we could live there – no work needed and an affordable rent (less than we were paying in England). Our lease in England was also coming up for renewal, so there would be no problem with a moving date.

The house was opposite the village school, a *garderie* and the *mairie*. Although the school was closed, one of the teachers was there, and she spoke a little English. We introduced ourselves and explained why we were there. We informed her that our girls couldn't speak French and asked if she thought this would be a problem? Her answer was: "They will learn." I don't know if Madame Fontaine ever realised that her reply helped us to make the decision to move to France.

We returned to the agent's, got a copy of the rental agreement, and went back to our friends, armed with a dictionary. The next day we signed the agreement, paid our deposit and headed back to England. We lived at Whitfield, just outside Dover, so didn't have a long journey home.

> " *driving over here is particularly bad (I often say that the French should be banned from their roads!)* "

The next few months went too quickly. We had one more visit before moving over to complete paperwork, sort out insurance (which you must have before moving in). Eric and Norah were able to introduce us to many people, including an insurance agent, a doctor and a dentist. I would say we were also lucky – our French was as good as Del Boy's, and we took a chance with using a dictionary instead of a translator.

Les Rues Des Vignes

At the beginning of December 1995, we moved to Les Rues des Vignes. We organised removal people to move us out, travelled to France the next day and stayed with Norah, then moved into our house on the third day. The removal people had no problem finding us and everything went very smoothly. (I should say that this was our seventh move in twelve years, so we were well practised.) Mind you, I nearly returned to England on the day we came to France because David, who had said he would be there, then told me that he wouldn't be able to and that meant I had to deal with everything myself.

The village has about 2,000 inhabitants. It has three cafes, a school, a church (whose bell rings on the hour and again a minute after), a *boulangerie*, a large village hall, a *mairie*, a large dog/cat food factory and lots of little businesses. The region is extremely agricultural and the scenery changes every month according to what crops are growing.

Looking back on our first year in France, it really could have gone either way. We enjoyed the challenge of moving to a foreign land and getting to know the customs and people. School fete evenings playing Lotto are brilliant for learning your numbers! However, moving to the country, where people are not used to foreigners, can also be hard. People were kind, but as soon as I opened my mouth, a look of fear descended. However, they soon got used to my accent and my *franglais*.

One thing I found out quite early on was the French love of paperwork. When dealing with any thing such as sorting out a bank account, health cover or insurance, a *dossier* has to be opened. Birth certificates, marriage certificate, passports, salary slips, all need to be photocopied. We were fortunate that no one ever asked for a translation of these documents. At the *mairie*, it did take some time to organise our *carte de séjour* because they had never done this before. Formalities were made easier because David was in employment and able to show his salary slips. Once we had our the *carte*, we were able to get registered at the local Caisse Primaire d'Assurance Maladie.

We bought a car in Holland and had to go through the formalities of getting it French registered. We visited the local DRIRE office and got the necessary paperwork. We got the car through a *contrôle technique* (equivalent to the MOT test), visited the local Hôtel des Impôts for a tax declaration, and obtained a 'certificate of conformity' from the manufacturer. Then back to the DRIRE to confirm that all the paperwork had been completed satisfactory. Finally to the *sous-préfecture* for a *carte grise*. I had a happy smile on my face when I finally got French number plates!

> *if you support the school (e.g. parent evenings and school fetes) the teachers will do everything they can to support you*

Driving over here is particularly bad (I often say that the French should be banned from their roads!). There is a rule, particularly in villages, that you have to give priority to traffic coming from the right (even if you are on a main road and the one on the right is a little side road). I think this is crazy!

The Three Rs

The school was brilliant (as we had hoped it would be after meeting Madame Fontaine). The first day was traumatic for all of us and, when we walked over with the girls, Tara turned round and said, "I can't do this mum." Walking away without her was one of the hardest things I have had to do. However, after twenty minutes David and I looked out of our window and saw her playing happily with her new friends. Even if they don't understand each other, children will always be able to communicate and play.

The teachers gave us a lot of help. I went over at the end of each day, and together with the girls would listen whilst a teacher recorded into a cassette the lesson for the following day. For six months, I had to look up every word that was used in each lesson. It did help that Tara could read in English and had been at school for three years, but Lorna found it easier learning and writing French (probably because she was just starting school and was younger). Learning a new language isn't easy but after seven becomes much harder.

During holidays, we were invited round to teachers' homes and got more help then. It was very kind of them to invite us to their homes and make us feel so welcome. I can't help wondering if we would have got this kind of help in England.

The standard of education, I believe, it far better. The three 'R's method is still used and I am sure it helps – repeating times tables and learning poems off by heart does improve the memory. It did seem strange going to school on a Saturday morning (but they did get Wednesdays off).

Now, eight years later, both the girls speak French like the natives. Tara started *lycée* this year and, although finding it hard, has made many friends and is happy. She has a long day, getting up at 6am, catching the bus at 6.45 and sometimes not finishing until 6pm. Lorna is in *5ème* at *collège*. Again, we have had a lot of help from the school. She got in with the wrong crowd and I was asked in for a meeting. The English teacher had also been asked to be there in case I had any problems with translation. I have found that if you support the school (e.g. turn up for parent/teacher evenings and school fetes) the teachers will do everything they can to support you. I would imagine that this would not be the case if parents didn't bother.

Norah and I started going to French lessons in Cambrai. We originally had to pay but sometimes we did get a term free. Unfortunately, we found that our teacher was more interested in talking to us in English. I actually learned more through helping the girls with their homework, but it was good to get out and meet people. I realise now that you really have to speak French every day, and preferably to French people in order to improve.

Police & Doctors

We did have some incidents during our time at Les Rues des Vignes. During our first year there, in order to save money, the street lighting was turned off after 11pm. One night (at about 4am) I heard a noise. We had to park our car across the road and the noise was a group of three men trying to break into it. Luckily, because we woke up and put on lights, opened the window and shouted at them, they drove off (in their car, not ours). We rang the *gendarmes*, who arrived, had a look around and said they would come back in the morning. They next day two of them arrived, with their portable typewriter and typed a statement there and then. Within days of our incident, the mayor's office got broken into at night and ransacked. After this, the street lighting was left on permanently!

Again, during our first year, I got a phone call to say that David had been rushed to hospital with a suspected heart attack. Obviously worried, I managed to get the girls looked after and rushed down to Beauvais. Norah came with me. We found him in a room on his own, wired up with all the latest equipment. It was difficult to find out what was wrong with him, as there no one seemed to speak English. However, everyone was very kind and he was constantly monitored. After ten days he was released. Although the symptoms were like a heart problem, he had actually overdosed on caffeine (he doesn't drink coffee in France any more!).

Tara had a problem with her jaw/face. In England we had been told that treatment would not be started until she was at least fourteen; here we were informed that we had almost left it too late. She has been having treatment since 1997, which culminated in an operation last year. We had been recommended a specialist at this hospital and within fourteen days had been to see him and fixed the operation date.

She had to go to Lille (an hour's drive) and stay in for four days. As she was just under fifteen, I had to be with her. We had a room to ourselves, which had a television, telephone and bathroom. We saw the specialist three times a day and could always get hold of a nurse if needed. English was only spoken when a student doctor visited and wanted to practise.

Because we wanted this specialist to carry out the operation and also to choose the date so that Tara could have it during the summer holidays and not have to have time off school, we opted out of the state system and paid for private treatment. Our *mutuelle* (complementary insurance company) queried this and we had to increase our cover to qualify for more than a small reimbursement. In the end, out of €2,000 we were reimbursed around €1,600. It was worth every cent.

Buying A Barn

We rented for five years. We had decided to buy after the first year, but it took us four more years to find a house. We wanted to stay in the village, but house prices seemed to be too high, or properties were not what we were looking for. We had decided to buy a property with a view to having my parents, Val and Ted, living with us. We wanted something that would have an outbuilding that could be converted into a house for them.

We found our house after going out for a drive one Sunday afternoon. David immediately said, "Arrange a viewing," because he saw this big barn. He wasn't interested in the house, just the barn! Originally a farm, the property was built after the First World War and was in a U-shape. The house was next to a stable, which was next to the barn, which was next to a cow shed.

It was in a village called Honnecourt-sur-Escaut, only ten kilometres away, which meant that the girls wouldn't have to change schools – even though I would have to take them and pick them up each day. The layout of this village was completely different – on either side of a canal – and it was slightly smaller. We found out that the house had been empty for about ten years. There was an awful lot of junk throughout. The previous owner had started renovating it but stopped – I can't even say midway through – so we knew there would be a lot to do. However, the *écurie* would make a lovely cottage for my parents, and the barn was in a good state, including the roof.

Mum and Dad came over that week to see it (they were living in Cornwall at the time and were retired). We fixed another viewing and they agreed with me that the property would be ideal for everyone. Perhaps if they had known that it would take eighteen months to complete their house, they might not have come over. But then again, they did say that they had always wanted to do something like this!

By this time David was away, and he hadn't seen the property. However, he trusted our judgement and told us to make an offer. We had already discussed at the *notaire*'s what the house was really worth and we went straight in with that offer (not the original asking price, but a realistic one). The next day we were told that it had been accepted. I organised the signing of *compromis de vente* and David actually signed before seeing the property! (He was happy enough getting his barn – and we had also taken lots of photos.)

> *we took them over to the house and immediately saw Francine's face – it had a look of horror on it. She thought we were mad*

The *notaire* we used was extremely helpful and gave us copies of the *compromis* and the actual contract before signing. Yet again, with the help of a dictionary (and translation package on a computer), we were able to understand what we were signing. We were confident of what we were doing because we now had an understanding of French and we had been in France for five years. Anything I didn't understand, I would write down and ask at the *notaire*'s.

A visit to our bank secured the loan. We would, in fact, be paying just a few francs more than our rent. Paperwork was sent out, and everything seemed to go through without any problem.

The day of actually signing for the house was my fortieth birthday, at the end of 2000. We had been told that it is a big occasion in France and so we dressed up smartly. The whole thing took about an hour – making sure we understood each page of the contract, then initialling all of them and then a final signature. We were handed the keys, departed and went straight over to the house to have another look. We didn't stay long, as there was no heating and we were in the middle of winter! There was central heating in the house, however, and once we had got a delivery of heating fuel we discovered that it worked beautifully.

Conversion

We had decided that we would keep the rented house for four months, and that Mum and Dad would move in with us. Overall this worked well, although there were one or two 'flare-ups' – only normal! After New Year, Mum, Dad and I started to go over daily and begin work.

We had originally planned to get a builder in to convert the cow shed into a beautiful little cottage. However, when we got people in to give us a *devis* (quotation) and we mentioned our budget, either we were laughed at or we never heard from them again. So we decided to do it ourselves. We did get people in to do windows, doors and a new roof. The roofers did a great job. We weren't so lucky with the window people (the masonry work was terrible).

We soon realised that what we needed was power tools (the more the better!). Also we got a trailer and a cement mixer. Mum and Dad had sold their car and bought a van (which they also used to move over with). This was ideal because we were able to buy plasterboard, wood, rolls of insulation, stairs, cement, sand, etc. We got to know all the DIY stores in the area and read all the free publicity each week to see what was on special offer.

We had some French friends, Nestor and Francine, who had given us a lot of help when we first arrived in France. We took them over to the house and immediately saw Francine's face – it had a look of horror on it. She thought we were mad! However, when Mum and Dad's place was finished, she actually wanted to move in herself.

 if you try to fit in and do things the French way (even if you don't agree with the way they are done) you should get on

One mistake we did make was doing our own electrical installation. We unfortunately used British cable and, although it is CE approved, the people carrying out the inspection for our certificate of conformity didn't care for it and we failed our first inspection. We had to replace most of it. I ended up sending many letters, together with photographs, explaining what we had done. Finally we sent back the form, which listed the problems that had been fixed, and we received our certificate by return of post.

Our part of the house is still not finished. With only one salary coming in, we don't have the money to finish it. But we can live with this because the house only cost £35,000 and we took out a mortgage for ten years (three down, seven to go!).

Life In France

We often ask the girls whether they liked being here and the answer is always the same (particularly after we have just returned from a visit to England): "Yes." Lorna has mentioned that she will probably take French citizenship; Tara's not sure. They have a great group of friends and what has pleased me most is that they were able to have a childhood. In England I have found there is so much pressure on children to grow up too quickly. It is not the case here in France.

Life in France is slower. There is a sense of community. Once, when something was broken at Lorna's school, her class was taken into the Mayor's office and told that it wasn't acceptable to damage school equipment – they didn't do it again! On another occasion her whole class went skiing; financial help was given by the village to those families who weren't able to afford it.

I have now started looking for employment and have signed on with the government agencies. However, as my French has not really improved (because we always speak English at home), and with unemployment in the north being particularly bad, I don't hold out much hope of finding a job.

David now has a job (with the same company) which enables him to get home every weekend. We bought ourselves a Land Rover and often go out 'green laning'. The French don't seem to mind this and, as long as you keep to the lanes and respect the countryside, there isn't a problem.

There are three English families near us and we all try to help each other out when needed. We are also close friends with several French families and we always try to speak French when they come to visit or we go to them (this is always much easier after a glass or wine or two!). I think it must seem funny for our neighbours to hear us speaking English but they don't seem to mind.

Life has its ups and downs, no matter where you are. Overall I think there are more pluses to living in France than minuses. We often (during the summer) sit outside in our courtyard at about 5pm and have our 'happy hour'.

we were meant to be here . . .
it has been hard but it has been
worth it. Bonne chance to
anyone who is thinking of
taking the plunge

We look down the hill onto the canal, watching the barges going up and down, and reflect on what has been done that day and what needs to be done the next.

We are of the opinion that if you try to fit in and do things the French way (even if you don't agree with the way they are done) you should get on. I'm not sure that we would be able to adjust to going back to England. There are just too many people and cars and not enough space.

So, looking back on what I have written, I still say, "We were meant to be here." Yes, it has been hard but it has been worth it. *Bonne chance* to anyone who is thinking of taking the plunge!

A Will To Succeed

Eager to escape the rat race in south-east
England, Audrey and Charles Fleming moved to
Dordogne in 1992 – after vowing not to live there.
Their 'rural idyll' cost them hard work, near
bankruptcy and linguistic ridicule.

In our mid-thirties with good careers, no children and a large mortgage on a house in Wokingham, Berkshire, we wanted to escape the 'rat race' in south-east England, work for ourselves and own a property that would contribute to its own running costs. We couldn't afford anything large enough in the UK so decided to look further afield.

We resigned from our jobs, sold the house, put the contents into storage and took off travelling – overland on a motorbike to South Africa. Of course, the travelling didn't have much to do with house-hunting but we couldn't miss the 'opportunity' of being temporarily mortgage-free.

A year later we were back in the UK and, with good memories of many holidays in France, we decided to see if we could make a life there. France wasn't too far from 'home' and family and we knew that lots of English people were making the move, so we thought we would take advantage of the cheaper property prices too.

We trawled through *French Property News* and made a series of appointments with French agents through the British agents who were advertising. We decided not to look further than a day's drive from the ferry ports and started in an area we had enjoyed on holiday. We were fairly determined not to move to Dordogne, although we had never been there. This was probably **because** we had never been there and therefore had preconceived ideas about the place and because we knew that there were a lot of English people already there. In the event we chose Dordogne because it offered the environment we liked – on the edge of a village in rolling countryside and forest – and the house was the one where we felt we could make a home.

Laying The Foundations

The house we had chosen was old and in need of modernisation but we felt it needed no more than 'updating' and decorating. As it had, at some point, been two houses it was clear that we could quickly create a *gîte* to let; and there were barns for future expansion.

Buying the property was fairly straightforward. We had an English-speaking agent who was helpful and we didn't have any real problems, but that was more through luck than any particular knowledge or effort on our part.

Once we had signed the initial paperwork, we went back to England to sort out the details of moving. It was at about this time that I discovered I was pregnant and it seemed a good time to get married. We said our farewells, loaded a few camping essentials, plus an Aga and our long-suffering cat, on to our van and drove south. We arrived in the village, signed the papers and took possession of our new home in July 1992 – a fortnight after the wedding and with me three months' pregnant.

As we settled in we arranged for our furniture to come out of storage to France. The village has only about 600 residents and is much smaller than anywhere I had ever lived, but we coped fairly well with the change in our lives, partly because we had already sold our house, resigned our jobs and spent a year overseas travelling. In that sense we had already made the break from our old life. We also had some money in the bank as a 'cushion', a strong relationship and a will to succeed.

The money we came with ran out very quickly and we (i.e. Charles) had to find work. This delayed work on our house, although it led, eventually, to our starting our own building business, which now employs other English tradesmen. We are still, twelve years on, renovating our house, although we have created three self-catering *gîtes*, in outbuildings, in the meantime. Our own house has always had to be a lower priority than making the *gîtes*, building the business and, therefore, providing an income.

I explained that we wanted the thing like a beach to go with the cement

Creating the first *gîte* was a larger, more expensive task than we could have known. There were layers and layers of wallpaper bonded to the plaster and, whilst the wallpaper only came off in postage stamp-size pieces, the plaster seemed to fall off and crash to the floor with alarming regularity. The upstairs boasted a bedroom but the ceiling was mostly on the floor and the wallpaper firmly grafted to the walls. Battleship grey and mustard yellow seemed to be the only colours the previous owner liked.

The 'kitchen' was black with soot from the cooking fire and there were strange, decaying things lurking in glass bottles and stone jars in the cupboards. The cupboard shelves were covered in layers of newspaper and oil and grease and I spent many hours with wire wool, paint stripper and a chisel trying to salvage them to save money on replacements. Every corner of every room was home to some large creepy-crawly.

In the early weeks, we went off to the local DIY supermarket to buy sand and cement. We found an assistant and he understood 'Portland cement'. Next we wanted the sand but I could only remember the word for a beach so I explained that we wanted the thing like a beach to go with the cement. The assistant looked confused but after several of my attempts his face lit up and he marched us off through the shop to show us . . . beach mats!

Birth & Business

In January 1993 our son, Thomas, was born and that really changed our lives. After many, many hours' labour the midwife asked me how I was feeling. I tried to make light of it and translated the English phrase 'piece of cake' into French. She paused for some thirty seconds and then asked if I was hungry.

Both our children were born in France, although we contacted the British Embassy for birth certificates and to make sure they were registered in the UK records. We hadn't really considered the practicalities of having children in France but the timing of our move made it happen that way. Although I don't know how it would have been in the UK, I believe it was better here. I enjoyed excellent ante-natal care and the births were in modern hospitals where I had a private room with telephone and TV and en-suite facilities.

Thomas had to go back into hospital for a minor infection at about a month old and I had every confidence that he was getting good, timely treatment in modern, well equipped surroundings – even if we didn't exactly understand all the medical words.

> *we quickly discovered that the French didn't speak O Level French*

Eleanor was born two years later and made our family complete. I had always wanted a boy and then a girl and, as she was born on Christmas Day (the perfect present), I was very smug – and still am. But Eleanor had a convulsion soon after we left hospital and so she, too, had to return to the postnatal unit. Eleanor's problem was more serious and long-term but, again, she had excellent care and treatment in a modern, well equipped hospital. Her ongoing care and various therapies have always been prompt, professional and dedicated to her needs at any time.

We have always worked for ourselves in France: running our building business and managing three *gîtes*. It has been difficult to employ French people to work in the building business because they have different working practices and hours to us – a cultural difference. They, of course, expect no less than two hours for lunch but don't need endless tea-breaks to make it through the day.

The clients of our building business are all British and seem to expect an all-year, all-encompassing service and we have bought cars for them, made dental appointments and even gone to the chemist with them to explain very personal matters requiring medication! The *gîte* guests are British, American or Canadian and the few French enquiries we get usually fall by the wayside.

Building the businesses has been a mixed experience. Booking the *gîtes* for the summer season has usually been pretty straightforward and, although we thought it would be our main income, it soon became clear that it would fall very short of our needs.

Charles looked for work as an electrician and quickly found that English second home-owners needed heating and plumbing and any number of other things, so he became multi-skilled and learnt, quickly, as he went along. Charles did the week's course at the *Chambre de Métiers* to become registered to work and then found that work was very thin on the ground. The minimum payments to the state for self-employed tradesmen are very high (much greater than those in the UK) and meeting these was a big commitment.

We spent a very worrying year trying to earn enough and, when we fell behind in making our payments, we found ourselves in real difficulties with 'the system' – which we didn't understand. We found a French accountant, who helped us sort things out but, even so, it took another two years and a lot of money to clear up the financial mess. Fortunately, business took off at this time, which allowed us to dig ourselves out of it.

A Sticky Situation

Before moving to France Charles had spent a lot of time overseas on business but neither of us had lived overseas. We only had O Level French and quickly discovered that the French didn't speak O Level French. Once we realised that every word of French we had ever learnt wasn't going to be enough, we found someone to help us learn more. We had 'lessons' for a couple of years but it wasn't very formal and it was always difficult to concentrate after a day's work and with two small children interrupting us.

Eventually, we gave up our lessons and Charles decided he was content with the level he had attained, feeling that he could communicate as well as he needed to. I was more frustrated at not being able to communicate fully and properly and, when an English girlfriend invited me to join her in formal lessons with a local teacher, I jumped at the chance and put a lot of time into doing my homework. I am still not as good as I would like to be but I now accept that I probably never will be.

Nevertheless, language itself (or lack of it) has never stopped us achieving anything but our early accounting difficulties were nearly disastrous because we didn't understand the different way things are done here. French tradesmen make the same payments and experience the same difficulties, I am sure, so the system wasn't 'picking on us'. Similarly, French tradesmen work alongside our business: we have our British clients and they have their French clients. We know that their clients are unlikely to employ a British company and that they are reluctant to work for absent, British second home-owners.

We have had a lot of help over the years and we have been lucky, and worked hard, to overcome difficulties and problems. Generally, we take one step at a time with something new or unknown and try to remain polite and friendly. We don't complain to the French if we disagree with their rules or systems, and we try to get them on our side.

It hasn't all been plain sailing, though.

Apart from the difficulties with the business, we nearly had a disaster on our hands again in 2000. We had the opportunity to buy some barns and land adjoining our property that belonged to the same family who had sold us the house. This, however, was not as straightforward as the first purchase.

There was a farmer renting the barn but we didn't know of any rights or lease agreement. At the time, we were also renting a part of the barn, from the same owner, and we had no lease or paperwork. The *notaire* in the village knew that the farmer was renting the barn so we, **stupidly**, didn't raise the matter. The contract we signed said that the buildings and land were being sold free of any leases, rights, etc. so we assumed that was the case. But, when we asked the farmer to leave, we discovered his rights – which were formidable.

Simply, he had the right to stay as long as he liked. We weren't farmers and we had only been able to buy the land because he (as an occupying farmer) didn't want to buy it. The previous owner lived forty kilometres away and employed the Gallic shrug, suggesting that, as the farmer had been there when she inherited the barn, she had nothing formal regarding his occupation.

Fortunately, the *notaire* arbitrated between us and the farmer and he agreed to leave – in 2004. So, for four years we were unable to use the buildings and land we had bought. The *notaire* denied that any of this was his 'fault' and the previous owner continued to shrug.

Whilst this has not been disastrous for us, it could have been. It seems that the *notaire*'s statements in the contract of sale were meaningless and, if we buy property in future, we will employ our own solicitor and ask more questions.

The situation caused ill-feeling between us, our neighbour (on the side of the farmer), the *notaire* and the farmer and, if he hadn't agreed to waive his rights, he could have decided to stay there for ever.

Village Life

The children are now in school in France and we are very pleased with their schooling. The teachers never saw lack of French as a difficulty and both children only started to learn French when they started school. We still speak English exclusively in the house but their 'outside' life is entirely French. Some words and phrases will probably always be in English or French and they do make silly grammatical mistakes in English (by using the French grammar rules) but they are bilingual – something we will never be!

> *the biggest difference in our lives is probably having the children rather than living in France*

They probably think of themselves as British and, although we are still referred to as *'les Anglais'*, we have never encountered prejudice. There must be some people in the village who don't accept us but we have never been aware of any obvious hostility and the children are probably seen as being French.

Our village school is small but well equipped and well run. The teachers are professional and committed and approachable. Eleanor is now nine years old and experiencing learning difficulties (associated with her original illness and its aftermath) and the teaching staff throughout the school are supportive and flexible in their approach to her different needs. The commune and school are very much a partnership and the level of education and extra-curricular, social activities offered to pupils is, I believe, exceptional for such a small school.

My only criticism of their education would be disappointment at the lack of 'creative' work. The curriculum allows very little, if any, time for music or art and the children are never asked to write creatively. There is no disputing, however, the solid grounding they have in the three 'R's.

Thomas is now eleven and is becoming useful when I want to use a particular phrase or explain something in French. I have managed very well up to now but it is good to have someone on hand to spot silly mistakes. Helping them with their homework has been useful to me but some of the French grammar Thomas now brings home is pulling away from my limited knowledge. I have struggled with his maths homework for years and he now knows to "ask daddy".

When the children were pre-school, our neighbour called in with her, grown-up, daughter and her daughter's new puppy to show it off to our young children. I knew the word for puppy was *chiot* but didn't realise the T is silent. I enthused about how pretty the *chiot* was and how we would love one for our children because children really should have a *chiot*, etc. They both looked slightly stunned but eventually the daughter broke in and explained that *chiot* (silent T) means 'puppy' but *chiotte* (with the Ts sounded) is the French for 'shithouse'. Hopefully, I can avoid such pitfalls in the future.

When we came to France, we thought we would have more leisure time and that was one of the principal aims. Certainly we do have leisure time: relaxing with food, wine, friends and the children. In the UK our spare time was spent eating out, exercising and taking short breaks to reward ourselves because we had worked hard. I am sure we have less spare time here but that may be because we run businesses here as opposed to being employed, as we were in the UK. The biggest difference in our lives is probably having the children rather than living in France!

Our spare time now often involves the children and their activities. Our holidays tend to be spent visiting family in the UK and trying to give the children a sense of their roots, their heritage. This might sound a bit grand, but we believe it is important to keep their horizons as broad as possible. So many of the locals don't, or won't, travel outside France (or even Dordogne) and, although we feel comfortable in a small village, we had travelled and experienced more before we settled here. We would be happy for the children to stay here but we really feel that they should see some more of the world before they make their choice.

We get on well with our neighbours and the villagers but none of them have become close friends, although we socialise occasionally with the parents of the children's friends. Social events tend to show up our language deficiency in that it is very difficult to follow relaxed, fast conversations in a noisy room where several people may be talking at once, the subject matter changes quickly and a lot of local slang is used.

> *the French seem to think it
> entirely natural that we
> should want to live in their
> wonderful country*

There are still, definitely, cultural differences too in that we may have opposing views to political or national issues. This doesn't mean, of course, that we can't remain friends with someone but there has to be common ground and we often find that our different backgrounds, interests and views are at odds. It is often best to stick to the local gossip, the children and what we did in the holidays.

Looking Foolish

Friends in the UK tended to be people we used to work with or who lived close by. In France our closer friends are other British people with children of a similar age. We don't shop much in the UK when we are there now, as we have found that most of the goodies and treats are available, at a price, in the larger hypermarkets here. Our English visitors still come with a few tins of baked beans, precious teabags or Marmite but there is no point importing electrical goods, fitted kitchens, paint, tiles, plasterboard, etc. (and people do!). We use the local shops and suppliers and services and, if something is incomplete, faulty or breaks, we can sort out the problem locally and quickly with the minimum frustration.

We haven't encountered any animosity here from the locals but I am sure not everyone is truly welcoming. Most seem to accept foreigners and prefer the British to, say, the Germans or Dutch. We have bought a house the French didn't seem to want, use the local shops, have children in the local school, pay our taxes and try to 'contribute' to the community. The French seem to think it entirely natural that we should want to live in their wonderful country but don't understand how we could leave the extended family in the UK.

Our quality of life here is better than in the UK. The pace is slower, we have a cleaner environment in a small community and a larger house in a location we couldn't afford in England. I feel that the children are safer and receiving a better education. My experiences of health care are better and, as a couple, we spend more time together.

There is no doubt that the better climate and being able to enjoy summer evenings and the rural life at a slower pace contributes to my feel-good factors. I like the affordable wine and good food and I quite like being known in the village and a little further afield.

The minus is being away from family, friends and not being as good at the French language as I would like to be, but that is something I could sort out if I really applied myself. The fact that I can't communicate well enough is my problem, not their fault. I often tell myself that I would be more involved with the school and contribute to the community more if I spoke better French but I am not sure that is really true; it may be the excuse I use here in place of the excuse I used in England that "I'm too busy". Charles is very content with his language skills and his level of involvement locally but I often feel frustrated and that I am missing out on something, but I should sort it out – not complain.

We didn't have great visions of what France would offer: it wasn't the 'dream' everyone talks about and we were basically happy in the UK. We weren't running away from the UK nor looking to hide or 'drop out' in France. France was just going to be something different and, hopefully, better. I think not having 'the dream' has led to our being happier here, warts 'n' all, and neither of us would go back. Even in times of trouble with Eleanor's health and the uncertainty of the business we never felt we would stop being here – we just had to get through the difficulties and make it work, somehow.

In fact, we can't imagine going back to England – I don't know what circumstances would force that upon us. We couldn't duplicate our lifestyle now in the UK: couldn't afford the size of house in a similar location and certainly wouldn't like the hustle and bustle and the traffic, and the prices. Even if we could go back in time, knowing what we know now, we would still move to France, but bring more money and a bigger dictionary!

After twelve years here, I try not to give advice to people thinking of re-locating to France – we have seen so many come and go, for all sorts of reasons. But I do feel strongly that not enough people think or plan, realistically, about how they are going to make a real living here. If you aren't retiring with a pension or have an income, you will need a job and you shouldn't expect the French to employ you. Even if you speak very good French, you have to have some very special skills they can't find locally to be considered for employment. Similarly, there aren't that many British companies in a position to offer employment. And can you really make a proper living from a few B&B rooms or a *gîte*?

It is also as well to realise that you will have to register your business or yourself and make tax, medical and pension payments – just as you would in the UK. Even the minimum payments are significant, so don't underestimate how much work you will have to do to keep up. It has become increasingly difficult for anyone to work 'on the black' and it is illegal. In any case the French don't like it – nor do the British who are already here. You can't expect to make a new life in a new country and not 'pay your way'.

It should be fundamental to learn the language and always use what you have. Don't believe the fallacy that 'they all speak English'. English may be the international language of business but it won't go far in the local bread shop and it wasn't much use to us at the builders' merchant's.

Only recently I took Eleanor to a birthday party and the host mother asked me if I minded Eleanor "having fossils". That's how it sounded, anyway. I said I was happy for Eleanor to do whatever the party theme was and left them to it, thinking that, as the house was set in large, wooded grounds, there must be some sort of 'fossil-hunt' planned. When I returned to collect Eleanor I hardly recognised her, or the others who came running to greet me. Each little girl was beautifully, carefully made up with a flawless complexion, sparkling eyelids and glittering fingernails and perfect, rose-bud lips. The *pièce de résistance* was the 'fossils': *faux-cils* – false eyelashes!

*we expected to make mistakes
and look foolish occasionally
and aren't particularly self-
conscious about being 'different'*

It is worth remembering that we all stick out like sore thumbs (however good our language skills) and that we are in a foreign country and should always try to be a good ambassador. Be polite and keep a smile on your face. If you don't like something, don't complain; go home. And NEVER tell the French what the English do, or how it's done in the UK: they aren't interested, unless they ask. Wherever you choose to live in France and whatever you do, the everyday chores and stresses of life will come here with you – you can't leave it all behind.

We expected to make mistakes and look foolish occasionally (perhaps not quite as often as we must have) and aren't particularly self-conscious about being 'different' in what we do and the way we live. In fact, I think we probably quite like it.

Another Angle

In 2001, Christian Mieschendahl took advantage of a company transfer to move from his native Germany to Normandy. Life in France wouldn't be so different, he thought – just another language to pick up. But it wasn't quite that simple.

It was at the end of August 2001 that I moved from Germany to beautiful Normandy, France. At that time I lived in Düsseldorf, near Cologne, and had the chance to change my place of work within the company. I was thirty, nearly thirty-one, and for nearly ten years had enjoyed a bank holiday on my birthday; it would be the first time I had to work on 3rd October – the French were never that fond of integration with Germany.

I was never particularly Francophile; in fact, some years ago I rather fell in love with Spanish culture. However, at that time, going to France represented my only realistic chance to move abroad, my only opportunity to change the daily rhythm of my life and to have a different experience – I was prepared to just go for it.

An Optimistic Move

In terms of my expectations about life in France, I was very relaxed: I didn't expect anything in particular apart from having to pick up a new language. Moreover, I wasn't particularly worried about any potential culture shock. For me, the differences between France and Germany were possibly limited to thorough '*Vive la France*' patriots vs. green environmentalists collecting and separating tons of waste in their houses, but certainly nothing of tremendous importance. I didn't feel pressurised into taking a decision for life but knew that I could change or quit whenever I felt like doing so.

As I was being sent by my company, I already knew my work environment; I had even worked with my French colleagues for a couple of years. All in all, I was very optimistic and was looking forward to experiencing everything I was destined to experience.

be aware that in France – at least outside Paris – you rarely find English-speaking individuals

I had chosen to live close to my job, in a small town of approximately 5,000 inhabitants. Adapting to a rural lifestyle is a personal thing. When I say 'rural', I should tell you that throughout my life I had been used to living in big towns – with populations ranging from at least 250,000 people up to ten million. Anyway, 'rural' is always relative and the nearest motorway junction was only five minutes' drive away.

In the end I adapted, probably because men are designed to do so. There are two sides to everything in life. Such a decision obviously has an effect on your life, as you have to cope with rural 'particularities'. Such a change can be already quite a challenge in your home country, but it is probably even more of one if you move to a small village where there is also a language barrier. On the other hand, it may also allow you a quicker insight into a foreign culture as you are forced to improvise and consequently make contact with local people more rapidly. In a rural area, the country's traditions are better preserved and less mixed up by international influences.

Administrative Hurdles

Although my move was assisted by the company, clearing all the administrative hurdles was a bit of a hassle – not because the French authorities were extremely difficult to handle but simply because of my inability to communicate in French. I had had two years of French at school, but there was really nothing left of it when I came over. Just before my move I had one week of intensive preparatory lessons.

I had to organise my *carte de séjour*, which should by now have been abandoned for citizens of the European Union, insurance policies, car registration, flat rental, etc. Without the help of friendly colleagues at work, it would probably have been a bit of a troublesome undertaking. This, I guess, is not a specially French thing. But be aware that in France – at least outside Paris – you rarely find English-speaking individuals.

Don't be too afraid, however: I never (well, rarely!) encountered impolite or impatient civil servants. And something else which is probably true for all countries, especially where there is a language problem: accept that not everything will run smoothly. There will be misunderstandings, delays, even penalties because you have missed a deadline. However, in my experience authorities tend to be quite understanding if you try to cooperate. Try to anticipate official administrative processes by not waiting till the last moment and to check whether what you are doing is right. If the language hurdle appears too high, it is best to meet the person concerned, even though this takes time. You gain self-confidence and, when you see the person, you get it sorted out.

Although ready for France, I was a bit sceptical about living in the countryside. My office was roughly thirty-five kilometres south of Rouen, known as 'the city of a hundred steeples', where William the Conqueror was crowned. I had chosen to live very close to the office – approximately three kilometres away – instead of wasting my time in the rush hour, day after day, morning after morning and paying the *péage* (2.11 francs at that time) by commuting from Rouen to my workplace in Val-de-Reuil.

I had chosen to rent a flat. I wasn't spoilt for choice: the flats I had seen in Rouen were *n'importe quoi* (not worth considering) and opportunities around Val-de-Reuil, which in any case I considered inappropriate for reasons of safety and comfort, were quite limited.

I learned that in France you tend to be more season-dependent. As well as normal market mechanisms such as supply and demand, you have the French summer, when many companies reduce activities to half or even zero, at least for a couple of weeks. This is the best time for job changes. Associated with this is the search for accommodation, so the best time to look for flats is before June, when people cancel their rental agreements in order to allow for the notice period, which is normally three months. From September onwards it tends to get more difficult. For houses, which are usually owned, it may well be different, as buying is a more long-term decision and may be a bit less dependent on work-life rhythms.

My flat-hunting was handled by an agency, first because most landlords seem to deal only with agencies, and second simply for reasons of efficiency: I had to organise viewings so that they coincided with my business trips to France.

In the end I was very lucky: I found an idyllic island, not far from my workplace, with a nice apartment on two floors, with a large balcony and a fantastic view over the river Eure, something rare I suppose, if you are only renting a flat. I probably could have insisted on more support from the French side of my company in finding something, but I didn't and I never regretted it, having ended up on my island, though Rouen is a very charming town indeed. But for the reasons I have explained, I preferred just to go there at weekends from time to time.

Language Barrier

It was my first serious experience on French territory. Countless holiday experiences had only temporarily enabled me to assure a constant *baguette* supply in the early morning hours. It probably goes without saying that, if you don't already have a good command of French, it is time to learn it. In France, particularly outside Paris, you rarely find people who (want to) talk to you in anything other than French.

As I have mentioned, my level was basically zero when I moved to France. I was only able to carry out my job because I was with an American company and the business language was supposed to be English. It was supposed to be, but the reality was very different.

I found it quite difficult to pick up French and it takes time, as for most languages – at least if you don't speak another foreign language, ideally a Romance language such as Italian or Spanish, which helps a lot. The first year I had intensive classes, comprising four-hour sessions once a week, at the *Alliance Française*. I never really found the time to devote myself to studying vocabulary and grammar or doing substantial reading at home – nor even to do the homework given to me during my language course. Again, it goes without saying that, if you don't, you limit your progress. But it is hard when you are working full time.

> *I remember moments when I was p***** off because nobody seemed to make an effort to let me participate in the conversation*

I followed the philosophy that in time I would manage. I watched TV, I met people and soon had a French partner. After one year, everybody told me how well I spoke and that I was really fluent. However, you yourself know your level and limits. Real integration and understanding of people does only happen through the language. The more you invest in picking it up, the better. It pays off and I should have done much more, in retrospect. This is only to encourage you!

The French love their language. On the one hand, they have every reason to do so; it is a very nice language, with plenty of idioms, and it allows you to express yourself in a flowery and yet precise way. However, this aspect of the language was less interesting to me as, firstly, the German language easily keeps up in this respect and, secondly, I have never reached that level. On the other hand, it makes it more difficult for foreigners to communicate, at least until they have improved their level.

For me, there has been only one frustrating aspect of being in France: I remember moments when I was pissed off because nobody, but nobody, seemed to make an effort to let me participate in the conversation, particularly as I wasn't used to this in Germany, where people make more of an effort. On the other hand, what is the point in getting annoyed about a situation you cannot change? You must exploit it and benefit from it, i.e. by learning French.

I know many English people who have a damned hard time learning German because Germans don't give them a chance. I would certainly not claim that Germans are most cosmopolitan people in the world because I have also seen the other side of the coin, when my girlfriend and I visit Germany and she struggles to understand and make herself understood.

I believe that my level of frustration was amplified by my work circumstances: I was ready to face the challenge of speaking French in daily life, but at first I wasn't ready to accept that in business people speak in their mother tongue, simply ignoring the fact that one person at the table doesn't understand (bearing in mind that the official business language was English). It was OK for the canteen – after all we were in France and in France you speak French. But not for work. I was driven nuts and it took me quite a while to accept the situation. And I basically came here in order to learn French; what must it be like for people who move to France for work reasons but not particularly for the culture?

> " *I had serious problems in convincing my Human Resources manager to grant me any holiday* "

I don't know what it is like for native English-speakers, but the language is pretty much the first thing that comes to mind for someone from the German-speaking world: the French speak French. Of course they do. Today, I view at it from a slightly different angle. After all, German-speaking people are reluctant to communicate in anything other than German beyond a "Hi, how's life?"

But you don't do the French justice if you refer only to the language problem; there are plenty of positive aspects to living in France, which can easily be undermined by this.

Finally, I would like to pay tribute to my girlfriend's father, who always, from the very beginning, made an enormous effort to talk to me, to repeat, to explain . . . I appreciated that a lot. And this is the only way you can learn.

I realise that I have dedicated by far the longest part of my story to the language. As you can see, this was one of my major preoccupations while living in France!

No Holiday

I haven't a lot to say about work, which is just as well, as I have to catch up after the last section! Finding a job was unnecessary (initially), as I was sent by my company. As you know, I work for an American company and, although I had some troublesome meetings, plenty of information was nevertheless communicated in English.

Administration and labour law may of course be different from what you know from home. I remember that I had serious problems in convincing my Human Resources manager to grant me any holiday, simply because in France, by law, during the first year of a work contract you aren't entitled to take even a day off but you get paid in lieu once you leave the company!

But this sort of thing is hardly life-threatening. Overall, the employee is extremely well protected against unfair practices by his employer, which is remarkable. As in other European countries, it is more and more common, in times of high unemployment, for French employers to exploit job-seekers by offering only limited contracts ranging from six to eighteen months. Bearing in mind the odd holiday rules, if you are unlucky, you will have to survive for years without a proper holiday.

A few years ago, the French government scored an own goal by introducing the thirty-five hour week. Companies couldn't manage the workload, so they found a compromise whereby working hours stayed the same for all employees but, as a compensation (after all, the law is the law), they granted between twelve and twenty-four extra days off per year. This is convenient in a country where the best way to spend your leisure time is to travel!

After a year and a half, I started looking around for a new job. The job market was difficult. In France, companies don't tend to pay your travel expenses. Even for phone interviews they sometimes ask you to phone them. You have to ask for reimbursement! This is why many companies don't organise appointments very well: they aren't paying, they don't have to do the travelling, so why should they bother? It is up to you to make the point that you cannot come over four or five times to see them and to gently persuade them to meet **your** agenda.

As far as the working culture is concerned, I wouldn't want to criticise the French. I strongly believe that your work environment is mostly characterised and shaped by the management the company is led by. Admittedly, the cultural background has its influence too, but the resulting environment is undoubtedly caused by many factors.

During work, however, I rarely felt fully integrated, except perhaps in my own department. This was mostly due to language problems. Some people wouldn't talk to me and I therefore found it difficult to approach them in a casual way. This became better with language progress. As I have said before, integration only happens through the language.

You start to realise how much information is actually communicated between the lines. And if the language isn't your mother tongue, you realise how much you aren't getting and are probably well advised to have good rapport with one or two colleagues, who can fill you in afterwards. This is very important as regards company politics.

You also experience what it means to be in the minority. You feel more vulnerable, even if other people don't intend to make you feel that way; you are more sensitive to allusions, as you cannot help constantly referring to your national background. On the other hand, you learn to take things less personally and you are very well advised to do so, simply because people don't mean it. It is you who is the foreigner; everyone else, the locals, makes less of a calculation as to whether what they say may be taken as an insult or not. Of course, sometimes it is, but to stay literally 'cool' is the best strategy.

I am deliberately making this remark in the context of work, as your behaviour is somewhat less natural in a working environment; you cannot always act as you would like to. In private life, you can make your point more bluntly, without of course causing offence. Nobody wants to feed prejudices but to dispel them. In this way, you also learn a lot about yourself, which is a precious experience.

Tax & Insurance

From my limited experience and exposure in this field, I dare say that French administration and bureaucracy is pretty similar to what most Western Europeans are used to. I guess re-registering my car in France was most the work-intensive procedure, but even this went smoothly in the end.

The income tax system may be different from what you have experienced in your home country. Income tax isn't deduced from wages by the company you work for, but you must declare your previous year's income (normally in March) and approximately the following September you pay the bill to the tax office.

As a tenant you pay an accommodation tax at the beginning of each year, calculated according to the monthly rent you have to pay. When moving flats, people try to avoid paying accommodation tax by scheduling their move before end of December and not moving into a new flat until mid-January (that is when you normally get assessed) and thereby not being officially registered. In the interim, they stay with their parents or at a friend's place. As the owner of a flat or a house, you have to pay another tax, which is far from inconsiderable. It is therefore worthwhile to get some advice before investing in property.

With respect to money, if your home country is part of 'Euroland', adapting is very easy, although the vast majority of French people still calculate in French francs – some even in old francs! My girlfriend's father still does so and I have given up threatening not to listen to him any longer! It is a good way of keeping the mathematical corner of your brain fit.

At the beginning of my stay, I had an account at BNP Paribas, but the service was so unpleasant (I may have been the only unlucky one) that I changed to La Poste. As with most European post office accounts, you get good offers and often pay no charges. Standing orders, however, are quite customer-unfriendly, and it is best to use internet banking.

If you aren't used to having a private supplementary health insurance, you should consider having one in France, as state insurance covers only basic expenses and rarely a hundred per cent of the cost of medicines. Most big companies offer their employees a *mutuelle*, as it is called.

Depending where you are from and what you are used to, you may be pleasantly surprised by the overall service and the benefits offered. However, the health system in France, like most others in Europe, is living beyond its means and this will be reflected in higher contribution rates sooner or later.

Skating & Skiing

France is a beautiful country. It is perfect for travelling, as you can combine cultural aspects (France is full of history and ancient monuments) with the basic elements you need in order to relax from daily stress, i.e. beaches, sports, hiking, hanging around in bars, etc.

As far as the cultural aspects are concerned, in bigger towns you will find everything you need, as there are cinemas (some even showing films in their original language), theatres, etc. As France is a centralised country, however, most major cultural events take place in Paris.

I was disappointed to find that cycling and roller skating are virtually impossible. Simply because France lacks proper asphalt tracks (indispensable for skating) which aren't also used by cars. I decided to store my skates in the attic rather than ending up in a ditch – French drivers don't seem to really care, although the Tour de France is very popular. I guess that French communities are coming round to the idea that separate tracks significantly increase the quality of (leisure-)life, as they are starting to build them. There are times, though, when roads are closed – for a mild summer evening, mostly on Fridays – and you can safely skate.

 amazingly, there hasn't been a single person that I have met by myself and made friends with

As I live in a small village, my cultural exposure has been a bit limited compared to what I had before when living in bigger towns, but this is partly due to my own inactivity.

I have never had close contact with my neighbours – not for specific reasons, simply because there is no time in my daily schedule. But I have normal relations, I say *bonjour* and borrow an egg now and then . . .

Amazingly, there hasn't been a single person that I have met by myself and made friends with. This is probably due to the fact that I was with my girlfriend and I was fully occupied with her social environment, so there was no time left to meet other people. I met people at work, of course, but I kept work contacts out of my private life; I preferred it that way. On the one hand, this facilitated my rapid integration into my French environment: I had immediate contact with all my girlfriend's friends and family – an ideal way to get the feeling of the French lifestyle. On the other hand, I missed the experience of finding people on my own. But this is up to each person; I don't believe it isn't possible.

French people are very polite. I remember when we went skiing with the UCPA (if you like sports, I can highly recommend this organisation) in Tignes. Due to the different levels of ability in the group of friends I travelled with, I found myself on my own in a skiing class, solely with French people. I had no problem getting to know them and engaging in small-talk – sometimes more – but after the class, I was bound again to the group of people I travelled with.

> *a fellow countryman joking*
> *about the French offends*
> *you less than when the boot*
> *is the other foot.*

As I keep saying, everything depends on your language skills, because the French normally prefer to speak French!

Stereotypes & Prejudices

I am not at all a lover of stereotypes and, when you are abroad, the first thing you should do is to overcome prejudices. True, many of them have some reason behind them. But you give yourself a hard time if you think in generalisations. Moreover, you don't do justice to the single person in front of you. In any case, isn't it because you find yourself in the minority that you feel insulted? Obviously, a fellow countryman joking about the French offends you less than when the boot is on the other foot. It is always the personal touch that counts, so stay away from generalising about the French just because you have had a bad experience (which you will have) and thereby spoiling your overall quality of life in France.

I am not a saint and I also have lots of prejudices, even though I try to keep them out of my head. It is a human characteristic to want to distinguish oneself from others. But if you want to pin me down to some generalisations, OK, here goes. The French are pretty proud of their '*Grande Nation*', probably like any people in Europe – apart from the Germans, who still confuse sensitivity to what happened in recent history with a normal level of patriotism. The French have their resentments towards the British (nothing serious, and most of them cannot even explain why). The French believe that Bavaria is Germany and that Germans are very rough and rigid people (the French are not alone here). Nevertheless, I managed to convince a French girl to think differently! In any case, such prejudices are of no importance; you will learn to laugh about them.

I have found the French very polite. That is why they probably don't always express what they think. For instance, I have never heard anything bad said about Germany. In contrast, my German friends make remarks about France and the French which offend my girlfriend. It is a cultural thing. My friends never intended to insult anybody but Germans tend to be more direct – there is nothing wrong with that; it all depends on what you are used to. I realised this because I had the chance to look at myself from another angle.

Although many aspects of my story refer to France, they aren't necessarily France-specific, as you will gain similar experience (with a different angle) wherever you are abroad. Also, the Frenchman in the north differs significantly from the Frenchman in the south!

Au Revoir

For work reasons I am about to leave France after two and a half years here. But I am prepared to return if circumstances allow (provided I am allowed to work in English and I can convince potential future employers to grant me time off in my first year of employment!).

It hasn't always been easy but I have good memories of my time in France. The French love food and don't mind spending a significant amount of their income on it. I come from a country where people are willing to spend twenty thousand euros on a nice kitchen but don't want to spend thirty cents on a kiwi fruit. I have the impression that the French have the gift of enjoying life more than others and that they add a pinch of ease to their daily soup.

When I was frustrated or felt offended (the latter rarely), I would overcome my anger by reassuring myself that I had had an additional experience compared with those who stay only in their own country (like most of the French).

France isn't a dangerous country; you don't have to get advice on health hazards or anything like that. But if you really want to make the most of your time here, you should get some sound advice before moving. You would do the same in your own country if you wanted to buy a castle, for example – to find out what the financial implications were, etc. And the better your level of French, the easier daily life will be. Logical, isn't it. But you can also make it work without good French. It's up to you.

Have a pleasant stay in the land of Louis XIV; it will certainly be on the sunny side.

Culture Clash

Fresh out of college, Ann Koepke moved from Washington state to Upper Normandy to work as a language assistant for six months. Four years later, she was still there . . . but not for long.

I moved from Woodinville, Washington (about a half hour from Seattle), USA to Rouen, Upper Normandy in September, 2000 to work as a language assistant. My French professor at my university told me about an 'assistant' program. Native speakers work in French primary and secondary schools teaching their language for a period of six months. As I was fresh out of college and not too sure of what I wanted to do with my French degree, I thought this was a great opportunity. The salary was quite good: around €800 a month for twelve hours a week of work –certainly enough to live on. And with such a relaxed schedule, I knew I would have lots of time to enjoy the experience of living in France.

I had previously lived in Caen in 1997–1998 as part of a university exchange program and had enjoyed living in the Normandy region. Rouen was my first choice out of three possible cities and I was fortunate enough to be posted here. The city is about an hour from Paris and has about half a million inhabitants.

I planned on staying in France for just six months, but that has turned into four years! I was able to renew my contract as an assistant for another school year, and then was hired as a university assistant at an engineering institute, INSA (L'Institut National des Sciences Appliqués). I found my university position through word of mouth. Here I do basically the same sort of work I did as an assistant, but the pay is better (€1,100 a month for the same number of hours) and I must say the work is more interesting, as the students have a higher level of English. I mostly speak English, although my French comes in handy when I need to explain difficult concepts.

> **the first thing that really shocked me was the way people stare at you as you walk down the street**

As an assistant, I sometimes felt like I was babysitting the students; there were a lot of discipline problems and a lot of time was wasted just maintaining order in the classroom. At the university, the students are for the most part highly motivated and very curious about English and the United States. I also feel I am more respected by my colleagues; my colleagues at the *lycée* weren't particularly supportive. I often felt that they just threw their students at us for an hour and didn't care what we did with them! At INSA, there is a much more pronounced feeling of partnership and team spirit among the faculty.

Adjusting To French Ways

Having already lived in France, I was prepared for some of the cultural differences. The biggest challenge was adjusting to 'city life', as I have always lived in semi-rural areas. The initial exhilaration of living in a foreign country wipes away a lot of the culture shock; I have found that, if you are prepared for some real cultural differences, the surprises are easier to handle.

French and American society resemble each other in a lot of ways, which is deceptive. I really wasn't prepared for discovering how different our respective mentalities are.

The first thing that really shocked me was the way people (men and women, but especially men) stare at you as you walk down the street. French women will literally look you up and down (with no effort at subtlety whatsoever) as you pass by them. And French men turn their heads and stare. This was quite unnerving at first. Americans tend to be quite friendly, even with strangers, and it isn't unusual to make eye contact and smile and even say hello as you pass someone in the street. It really is quite automatic for me, and I brought this habit to France. I either got stony face stares from people or had men following me and inviting me to *"prendre un verre"* because I was so *"charmante"*! There is just not the same social ease among strangers over here.

This alternating unwanted attention and snubbing really took a toll on me the first year I lived in France. But you do get used to it. I used to feel very rude when I simply ignored the advances of random men on the street; now I know that by just walking by them with my horse blinders on, I am saving myself a lot of hassle. And the staring bothers me less now. I read that you should take it as a compliment: people are only looking at you because they find you interesting. If they thought you were boring, they wouldn't bother.

What most bothers me about the French mentality is their lack of civic duty. You cannot walk down a sidewalk without dodging dog poop. You will invariably see someone throw their *croissant* wrapper on the ground when there is a garbage can a meter away. People park their cars in the middle of a busy street so they can hop out to get cigarettes. And don't even get me started on the smoking! The 'No smoking' signs that are posted in all public places might as well not be there.

I suspect that this lack of respect for the rules bothers a lot of French people, too, but I think they don't feel there is much they can do about it. A friend once told me that the French highly value "personal liberty" and that each person feels they have the right to decide for themselves whether a rule is just or not. If you go up to someone and say, "Hey, clean up after your dog!" or "But there's a garbage can right in front of you!" the offender will feel aggressed, as if you were infringing on his personal freedom. To me, this is nonsense. I think most citizens of democratic nations highly value their personal freedom but they also see the value of rules. With French logic, rules don't really serve a purpose as everyone just interprets them as they see fit.

I do wish the French would stand up and say something when someone does something rude. I have often said that Americans wouldn't stand for someone smoking in a non-smoking part of a building, but to be honest, I have never proved that statement as I have never seen anyone at home smoke where they aren't supposed to. I wonder whether, if one French person took a stand against someone littering/smoking/letting their dog do his business wherever he likes, other likeminded citizens would back him up.

I can't speak for all situations, but the other day I was on the train and there was a group of thirty-something men sitting in front of me. One of them had a laptop computer and was playing movies on it for everyone around them to hear. No headphones! I finally couldn't stand it and told him that I didn't appreciate having to listen to it. He refused to turn it off and told me that I should move, as I was clearly the only person in the train bothered by it. I couldn't believe it. I was stammering my disbelief when suddenly other voices around me said, "Yeah, we agree with her!" "Right, turn it off; it's annoying!" The embarrassed men were then obliged to turn it off but not without a lot of show at how unreasonable I was being. But I really was pleased to see that it just takes one person to stand up and the rest will follow.

Something else that continues to bother me is the lack of customer service in most places. Here the rule is not 'the customer is always right' but 'the customer is usually wrong'. Going to the supermarket can be quite an ordeal. The cashiers take their time ringing up your items and often intersperse their tasks with conversations with colleagues – apparently, talking and working cannot be done simultaneously. You can't go into a store expecting to be entitled to good service; you have to work for it. I always put on my friendliest smile and try to charm the cashier/waiter/shopkeeper into giving me one in return. It has become a kind of game for me: Ann the American against Isabelle the surly salesgirl. Will Ann manage to melt Isabelle's frosty, unwilling-to-lift-a-finger-to-help-you exterior? Uh oh: Ann needs to return a purchase; she doesn't have the receipt! Stay tuned, folks . . .

Do remember that none of this behavior is due to the fact that you are a foreigner. I was recently having lunch with a friend at a *brasserie* and the waiter was rude and indifferent, giving off an attitude of "How dare you interrupt my day and require me to **work**!" Both of us are pretty accustomed to this sort of thing, so this guy just made us giggle. (Seeing the whole thing as funny is a great coping mechanism in many a stressful situation.) A Frenchman next to us was lunching with his friend and saw the situation. After the waiter walked away, he leaned over and said, "Don't worry; he wasn't that way because you're foreign. He was rude to us, too!" So, French service industry employees aren't just rude to a limited number of people; they are rude to everyone. Hm, should this make us feel better or worse?

 French employees aren't often motivated and excited when it comes to their jobs . . . they are just trying to get through their day

It is true: in America, customer service is usually pretty exceptional and I have probably been spoiled by this into thinking that everywhere else in the world should be the same. But I still can't get over the attitude of tradespeople in this country.

I will never forget what happened when I went to the bank to pick up my debit card. I had received a letter in the mail saying that my card was ready for me and I could come to my local branch any time to pick it up. So, I traipsed into the bank, all eager to be equipped with my new French spending equipment. I beamed as I presented the letter to the teller and told her why I was there. She didn't even look at the letter; she just said, "It's not here." Huh? "What do you mean it's not here?" I said. "You haven't even looked." With a huff, she lugged herself out of her chair, slammed open a filing cabinet and returned with my card. She thrust it at me. The whole transaction took less than two minutes.

I still can't understand why she didn't want to give me my card; maybe she was having a bad day, maybe her feet were tired and she didn't want to get up, who knows? But it taught me a lesson: French employees aren't often motivated and excited when it comes to their jobs. Forget pleasing the customer, they are just trying to get through their day. Don't expect them to make an effort to make yours easier and more pleasant; they don't consider that part of their job requirement.

The cultural differences can be difficult to get accustomed to. My year in Caen during the exchange program was exciting, tumultuous and sometimes very difficult. There was many a time when I would call my parents in tears, saying, "You don't know what it's like over here! It's horrible!" And of course they would respond by telling me how lucky I was to be living there and how many people would love to have that opportunity. Of course, I came to realize they were right. And as soon as I left France the first time, I was itching to come back. So, it isn't always an easy transition, but it is a worthwhile one.

Coping With Landlords

Moving is often stressful, and can be especially so in an unfamiliar environment. When you are trying to adjust to so many new things, it would be nice to not have to worry about the 'small' matter of finding a place to live and just throw all of your energy into trying to mentally adapt. But, of course, one needs to find a home.

> *landlords are landlords throughout the world, and they will try to make money off you if they can*

My move over to France was relatively easy, as I was only planning on staying one year. Now that I have been here for four, the move back to the States will be another story! I didn't move any furniture, as I planned to buy everything in France. I didn't bring a pet over from the States, but know from good friends who did that it is quite easy to bring a cat in: there is no quarantine between France and the US. To bring your pet back to the States, you just need a certificate from a French veterinarian stating that the cat is in good health.

I rented a property, which was relatively straightforward. However, I encountered some unexpected and unfamiliar procedures, which I found very frustrating. For example, renters' insurance is obligatory in France, unlike in the US. Your landlord can demand to see an *attestation* proving that you are indeed insured.

After living in my apartment for a year, I suddenly found an ominous, official-looking envelope in my mailbox. The *taxe d'habitation* had arrived! This is a yearly tax renters pay on their apartment, which is calculated on the property's value. It is usually a little more than one month's rent. This is a very unwelcome surprise. Fortunately, depending on your income, you can have it substantially reduced. If you earn too little to be taxed, you will end up paying only a fraction of the initial fee. Of course, you have to read the fine print before you even know about this possibility!

My landlords recently sprung the concept of *charges récuperables* on me. Every month, renters pay maintenance fees for the building based on the landlord's estimate of what the bill will be. At the end of the year, the landlord gets the actual bill for maintenance fees. If what the landlord actually has to pay is more than the monthly sum the renter has been paying, the renter needs to pay him the difference. So, you might get a letter from the landlord at the end of the year saying, "Oh yeah, by the way, I messed up, so you owe me €250." And then they can raise your monthly fees for the following year!

Be sure to do a thorough walk-through (*état des lieux*). Landlords are landlords throughout the world, and they will try to make money off you if they can. My toilet made a funny sound when I moved in, but I didn't want to bother my landlords with it as they seemed so nice. It was only after a couple years that it started to seriously leak and I had to have a plumber come in and spend a couple hours on it. I had to pay the bill and I kicked myself for not saying something when I moved in.

If you live in the provinces, you shouldn't have much trouble finding a place. To find my first studio apartment, I went to a youth center and looked on the notice board. I took the first place I visited, and was very lucky with my landlords; they were great. For the second apartment, a friend told me about it, as he knew that the person was moving out.

I currently live in a one-bedroom apartment in downtown Rouen. It is exhilarating living in the city center; you really feel you are at the heart of things. And your surroundings soon start to feel like home as you find your favorite café, the best *boulangerie* to buy your bread in and the nicest place to eat your lunch when it is sunny out.

Learning The Language

Living abroad is filled with challenges and rewards. Naturally, to make the most of your experience, you need to make an effort. An essential factor in ensuring that your experience is a positive one is to learn the language. Even with a bachelor's degree in French, my spoken French upon arrival was pretty mediocre but is now fluent. My French didn't improve very much the first year, as I spent most of my time with fellow Anglophones.

It is very easy to stay cocooned with your Anglophone friends when you arrive; speaking English is so easy and familiar. You have tons of other things that are new and sometimes scary and sticking with your countrymen seems like a good idea at first. But if you want to improve your French and have a more rewarding, authentic experience, you need to venture out into the Francophone world. It is scary at first but once you start, your confidence grows and it just gets easier and easier.

After just a few months of really making an effort (which means not worrying about your accent or whether you are making a fool of yourself) my French noticeably approved. It was only after I forced myself to speak French as much as possible that I improved by leaps and bounds. No one ever used to comment on my spoken French; now people are always saying how good it is! That really is gratifying; those initial moments of anxious effort have really paid off. Buying a TV can also be very helpful: not only will you pick up some everyday expressions, you will also feel more 'tuned in' with what is going on in the country.

Most French people are very understanding of your language limitations, provided you make an effort! I have found that the majority of French people will try to talk to you in English. They are as keen to practice their English as we are to practice our French. However, it does get annoying when the minute you say, *"Bonjour"* they start trying to speak to you in English!

Getting A Carte De Séjour

To stay in this magnificent country, you will need a residence paper, called a *carte de séjour*. The process of getting this little square of paper is by far the most frustrating thing about living in France! Though it is a struggle obtaining it, once you have got your *carte de séjour*, everything else becomes possible and you have more or less the same rights as a French citizen. But, be prepared: bureaucracy takes on a whole new meaning over here!

First you have to get a visa from the French consulate in America. If you have all your papers, that is pretty simple. When you arrive in France, you have to go to the *préfecture* and sit in a room for a couple of hours just to get a list of documents you need to be issued your *carte de séjour*. You will be given an appointment for a month later. You can choose to not make an appointment and try your luck arriving just before the office opens. If you do this, you will endure a human smush something akin to the Shanghai bank rush as people try to cram through the gates. If you are lucky enough to get a ticket, count on waiting about five hours before being seen.

People hoping to get state housing subsidies cannot do so until they get a *carte de séjour*. For non-Europeans, this takes about three to four months! Also, to subscribe for health benefits you need to have your papers in order. There is a lot riding on getting this little piece of paper!

So, once you have assembled your stacks of documents, you go back to the *préfecture*. Often you will be told that you need another document not mentioned on the list! "But it wasn't on the list," you exclaim helplessly. " Not my problem," shrugs the bureaucrat. You must make another appointment in a month.

Once you finally obtain your temporary *carte de séjour*, if you are a non-European, you must go to Paris for a medical exam. Well, the exam center isn't actually in Paris; it is on the outskirts of Paris. I was dreading this, but it is actually not too bad. You get cattle-herded through the motions but in an efficient manner, Once you have been given your health certificate, you make **another** appointment at the *préfecture* and, if all goes well, this time you should have your *carte de séjour*.

I have found that when it comes to ease of procedure, it really depends on who you see. For example, if you have a *carte de séjour* for one year, technically after it expires, you need to go back to the US to get your visa renewed before you can apply for a new work permit. I was fortunate to have a *préfecture* employee who kindly chose to overlook this and just issued me a new one (after I had assembled my documents anew and gone back for another medical exam!).

A Right To An Education

By now, you have determined that there are quite a few differences between the French and Anglo-Saxon cultures. But why are we so different? I have many theories about this, and most of them are rooted in the way we are brought up and educated.

 the fundamental difference I see is that American students see university as a privilege, French students see it as a right

I have no children of my own but, having taught in a school and a university, I naturally have an insight into the education system – which needs to be seriously reformed. Students pay practically nothing to go to university, so they don't appreciate how lucky they are. Discipline (or the lack of it) is unfortunately a major issue in primary and secondary schools, as well as in universities!

Maybe I am just getting old and crotchety, but when I was in high school, I really don't remember hearing a constant chatter of students when the teacher was trying to talk. It was a constant battle in the *lycée* where I taught. It is even the case to a lesser degree at the university.

At first I thought it was just me; surely they weren't like this with the veteran, more seasoned teachers. After sitting in on a colleague's class, I found out that it wasn't just me. It is next to impossible to get students to sit quietly for sixty seconds. I can understand this to a point in a *lycée* – they are kids after all. But at college? This didn't happen at my university, especially not in small seminars. This is why I say that students don't realize how lucky they are to get a virtually free education.

Of course, American parents do often pay the tuition of their kids. But that is a constant debt kids have hanging over their heads and I think that most of them want to get the most out of it. If a son or daughter starts slacking off in a subject, most parents are delighted to remind them just how much money they are paying so that they can have an education! And many students aren't so fortunate to have their schooling paid for and must take part-time jobs to pay for tuition; this **really** makes you appreciate what you are paying for! The fundamental difference I see is that American students see university as a privilege, French students see it as a right.

When it comes to the secondary school system, I think too much is spent on the academic side of things. I realize this sounds a bit ridiculous; after all, children do go to school to get an education! But I think there is nothing wrong with encouraging students to have a life outside of books: I would love to see sports, part-time jobs and other extra curricular activities integrated into the French student's life. Not only would they be more well-rounded and fulfilled, but it would give them some vital perspective. The world will **not** come to an end if you fail your physics exam.

France vs America

I realize that I may sound a bit over-critical of France. I think that when you are away from your home country, it is much easier to forget about its shortcomings and instead focus on the problems of your new country. I always find myself defending France and the French as soon as I am back in the States. While France may have its problems, there are certain aspects of life that are superior to that in the States.

Coming from a country with no national health service, I have found life with *la Sécu* (*la Sécurité Sociale*, the national health service) terrific! I had my gall bladder taken out here and, scary as it was, everything went fine and I paid next to nothing. I know that at home, even with a health insurance policy, I would have been worrying about how much the bill would be.

In America, health insurance is a personal choice. You get to keep all of your paycheck and are responsible for sorting out your own health coverage. But frankly, I like having this sort of thing decided for me!

life can be stressful, in France as in any other country . . . there are plenty of options to unwind, some which are familiar to you and some that might be a bit new

There are lots of people in the US who think, "It will never happen to me," and then go bankrupt when they fall ill. I love knowing that I can see a doctor when I need to. I can get my teeth cleaned twice a year here, which is seen almost as a luxury in the States. Unfortunately, the 'Etat Providence' (welfare state) that we have in France is often subject to abuse and the generous system I know today might not exist tomorrow. But I definitely think it is a good idea to oblige your citizens to have health care; they may grumble about paying for it every month, but it is for their own good!

Life can be stressful, in France as in any other country. Over here, there are plenty of options to unwind, some which are familiar to you and some that might be a bit new. I often go out for a drink with English friends (Rouen has quite a large English community; Americans are harder to find); most of my French friends aren't into the 'pub crawl' thing. Long, lingering dinners are something I have come to appreciate. My all-time favorite activity is sitting in a café with my *café noir*, reading and people-watching. I feel like a real Frenchwoman when I do this!

"So how will I make friends to do these fun activities with?" the anxious newcomer often asks. Well, you will make them as you would at home. I get on well with my neighbors and some of them have become close friends. I get on very well with my work colleagues, but I wouldn't say we are exceptionally close. They are all much older than me and I never see them socially. At work, they are great and I really enjoy talking with them both on a professional level and on a personal level. When I worked at the *lycée*, it was a bit easier because some of them were roughly my age, and I did become friends with some of them and see them out of work on a fairly regular basis.

Most of my French friends I have met through other friends. My closest friends I have met through my neighbor. I go to the same café every day so I have gotten to know the staff; I wouldn't exactly call them friends but having a local spot does make you feel more like you belong.

And don't forget, as a foreigner, you have an instant 'interesting quotient'. People will be immediately curious about where you are from and why you have chosen to live in France. If you are feeling shy, remember that most French people would love to find out about your country, which very well might be one they have always dreamed of visiting.

That said, I have usually had to make the first move in initiating a friendship (asking for someone's phone number and then calling them to invite them out for a coffee or to the movies). I sort of expected people to make all the effort since I was new in this country but you can't always count on people to know you want to be their friend. Once I made the first phone call to a potential friend, the rest was easy! The French friends I have made are fabulous and having them in my life has really made my stay in France rewarding.

I think one of the most important things I have learned here is that people are people. My French friends aren't any different from my American or British friends: they are hospitable, caring and fun!

Along with the 'interesting quotient' gift you get as a foreigner, you also become an un-official spokesperson for your country. People will probably want to know your views on hot political events. As an American, I have had some unpleasant experiences. There is a real anti-American sentiment over here. I have found that French people are extremely curious about what I think about my government, but they have their minds made up already! They certainly have opinions about Americans but most have never even been to the US.

I think the anti-American feelings were always there but they certainly weren't as acute as they are since the war in Iraq. I think the French have always been a bit jealous and resentful of America: of its wealth, power and influence. I think this is why the French are so proud of their country. They say, "Well, America may be richer and have a bigger army, but our food, cathedrals and culture are the best in the world" (which is funny, because they think Americans are overly proud of **their** country!). I think many countries have a hard time coming to grips with the fact that the US has achieved so much in such a short time.

A lot of these misunderstandings can perhaps be explained by our different histories. Everyone can tell you when the US came to be: 1776. But when did France become France? In the time of Charlemagne? Louis XIV? The Revolution of 1789? Or maybe back in the time of the Gauls? French history is older and perhaps more complex. They have known war and occupation and true humiliation. The US has never been occupied; we have only been fortunate enough to be the liberators. Perhaps the French resent the fact that this two hundred year-old child of a country liberated them. I think they have tried very hard to compensate for past difficulties and are very defensive of their own country. But they love to criticize the US. And they would also love to visit the US. Do they love us or hate us? It is definitely a little of both.

I can't get over the fact that such an overwhelming majority of the French oppose the current American government. It isn't the fact that some of the French don't like the present administration that shocks me but the fact that this disapproval is so homogenous. I really have started to wonder if the French have been conditioned by their own media into being anti-American. Diplomatic relations between France and the US have been pretty frosty since the second war in Iraq began, but you don't see an anti-French sentiment in the US equal to the anti-American feeling in France. This might be because of the two countries' respective influence in the world: France, although powerful, doesn't rival the US in terms of global might. I think French people think that what America does in the world has an effect on them personally whereas most American people don't worry at all about the decisions France makes.

Anti-American statements used to really bother me; things people said just seemed so ignorant and naïve. Examples: "Americans are all obese and stupid"; "everybody owns a gun over there"; "they are trying to colonize the world"; "they only do bad things". People have even said that our own government is the real world terrorist. But now I try to just take a deep breath and let these things go. I am not going to change opinions that have been formed by a lifetime of media influence.

Yes, it does annoy me when a French person thinks they know the entire political and cultural history of the US because they have read one book by Michael Moore but I hope that someday they will take the time and energy to really examine the situation or even go to the country they claim to know so much about and form a real opinion.

A Defining Experience

Living and working in France has been a defining, dynamic time in my life, a great opportunity to further explore cultural diversity. There are things I have disliked, but many others that I have loved. Some of the negative aspects about France that I have found are the lack of community connection (*le lien social*), the 'every man for himself' attitude, the disrespect for rules, the reluctance to take responsibility (and apologize!) for a negative situation. A **short** list of the positive aspects are the long, leisurely dinners, the mind-blowing cultural heritage (cathedrals, castles, museums, Roman ruins), the fact that people never seem rushed to do anything (this can be both positive and negative, depending on my mood!) and the realization one makes that deep down, people are people, wherever you are.

> *it hasn't always been easy but great experiences rarely are ... every day feels like an adventure and new possibilities seem so accessible*

It can be frustrating to live here, but the good experiences outweigh the bad. The culture is truly different from what I have previously known. If, five years ago,

I had to make the decision to move to France, with the considerations I have developed now, I would definitely do it! Yes, it hasn't always been easy but great experiences rarely are. Here, every day feels like an adventure and new possibilities seem so accessible.

One of the most important pieces of advice I would give to people coming to France is to be open-minded. Don't expect things to be as they are back home – wherever that is. Things will be much easier to deal with if you realize that the mentality of the French is unique. And don't take things personally: behavior that you consider shocking and inappropriate isn't strange for French people, and as you have chosen to live there, you have got to adapt. And take heart, you will!

However, much as I love living here, after four years, I am ready to go back 'home' for a while. My quality of life probably won't be the same, and I know I will miss France, but home for me is still the US. Of course I miss my family and the American way of life. But to be honest, I am really thinking about my future and what I would like to do professionally. I enjoy teaching, but don't think I want to do it for the rest of my life. I am not sure what else I would be entitled to do to make a living in France. So, I am primarily going home for career reasons.

> *I know I am incredibly lucky having the chance to experience another culture. And I believe that living here has shaped me*

If I could come back to live in France, working in a job I loved, I think I would do it. I do believe I could live here permanently. After all, I have lived in the US for twenty-two years and in France for only five, cumulatively. Perhaps after more time living in France I could truly get used to and maybe even adopt the French mentality. But for the moment, I am looking forward to living in the US again. I think that the US will probably always remain home for me. The familiarity that results from being born and raised in a country breeds a beautiful affection and admiration.

I will always marvel at the chance I have had to live in France. So many Americans dream about just visiting this country, let alone living here. I have really tried not to take it for granted when I walk by a thousand-year old cathedral on my way home or when I jaunt off to Paris for the weekend. I know I am incredibly lucky having the chance to experience another culture. And I believe that living here has shaped me: I am more resourceful, patient and culturally enriched. I can now say I know a culture, language and way of life other than that of my native country. I like to think that when I go back to America, I will be able to bring back a part of the French Ann to share with people.

How wonderful it would be if the world could become united using all of the positive aspects of each country. We could finally realize that our cultural differences have the potential to make us stronger, more peaceful and happier.

ORDER FORM 1

Qty.	Title	Price (incl. p&p)*			Total
		UK	Europe	World	
	The Alien's Guide to Britain	£6.95	£8.95	£12.45	
	The Alien's Guide to France	£6.95	£8.95	£12.45	
	The Best Places to Buy a Home in France	£13.95	£15.95	£19.45	
	The Best Places to Buy a Home in Spain	£13.95	£15.95	£19.45	
	Buying a Home Abroad	£13.95	£15.95	£19.45	
	Buying a Home in Florida	£13.95	£15.95	£19.45	
	Buying a Home in France	£13.95	£15.95	£19.45	
	Buying a Home in Greece & Cyprus	£13.95	£15.95	£19.45	
	Buying a Home in Ireland	£11.95	£13.95	£17.45	
	Buying a Home in Italy	£13.95	£15.95	£19.45	
	Buying a Home in Portugal	£13.95	£15.95	£19.45	
	Buying a Home in Spain	£13.95	£15.95	£19.45	
	Buying, Letting & Selling Property	£11.95	£13.95	£17.45	
	Foreigners in France: Triumphs & Disasters	£11.95	£13.95	£17.45	
	Foreigners in Spain: Triumphs & Disasters	£11.95	£13.95	£17.45	
	How to Avoid Holiday & Travel Disasters	£13.95	£15.95	£19.45	
	Costa del Sol Lifeline	£11.95	£13.95	£17.45	
	Dordogne/Lot Lifeline	£11.95	£13.95	£17.45	
	Poitou-Charentes Lifeline	£11.95	£13.95	£17.45	
				Total	

Order your copies today by phone, fax, mail or e-mail from: Survival Books, PO Box 146, Wetherby, West Yorks. LS23 6XZ, UK (☎/▤ +44 (0)1937-843523, ✉ orders@ survivalbooks.net, 🖥 www.survivalbooks.net). If you aren't entirely satisfied, simply return them to us within 14 days for a full and unconditional refund.

Cheque enclosed/please charge my Amex/Delta/MasterCard/Switch/Visa* card

Card No.   _ _ _ _   _ _ _ _   _ _ _ _   _ _ _ _

Expiry date _____   Issue number (Switch only) _____

Signature _____   Tel. No. _____

NAME   _____

ADDRESS   _____

_____

_____

* Delete as applicable (price includes postage – airmail for Europe/world).

ORDER FORM 2

Qty.	Title	Price (incl. p&p)*			Total
		UK	Europe	World	
	Living & Working Abroad	£14.95	£16.95	£20.45	
	Living & Working in America	£14.95	£16.95	£20.45	
	Living & Working in Australia	£14.95	£16.95	£20.45	
	Living & Working in Britain	£14.95	£16.95	£20.45	
	Living & Working in Canada	£16.95	£18.95	£22.45	
	Living & Working in the European Union	£16.95	£18.95	£22.45	
	Living & Working in the Far East	£16.95	£18.95	£22.45	
	Living & Working in France	£14.95	£16.95	£20.45	
	Living & Working in Germany	£16.95	£18.95	£22.45	
	L&W in the Gulf States & Saudi Arabia	£16.95	£18.95	£22.45	
	L&W in Holland, Belgium & Luxembourg	£14.95	£16.95	£20.45	
	Living & Working in Ireland	£14.95	£16.95	£20.45	
	Living & Working in Italy	£16.95	£18.95	£22.45	
	Living & Working in London	£13.95	£15.95	£19.45	
	Living & Working in New Zealand	£14.95	£16.95	£20.45	
	Living & Working in Spain	£14.95	£16.95	£20.45	
	Living & Working in Switzerland	£16.95	£18.95	£22.45	
	Renovating & Maintaining Your French Home	£16.95	£18.95	£22.45	
	Retiring Abroad	£14.95	£16.95	£20.45	
	Rioja and its Wines	£11.95	£13.95	£17.45	
	The Wines of Spain	£13.95	£15.95	£19.45	
				Total	

Order your copies today by phone, fax, mail or e-mail from: Survival Books, PO Box 146, Wetherby, West Yorks. LS23 6XZ, UK (☎/▤ +44 (0)1937-843523, ✉ orders@ survivalbooks.net, 🖳 www.survivalbooks.net). If you aren't entirely satisfied, simply return them to us within 14 days for a full and unconditional refund.

Cheque enclosed/please charge my Amex/Delta/MasterCard/Switch/Visa* card

Card No. __ __ __ __   __ __ __ __   __ __ __ __   __ __ __ __

Expiry date _____   Issue number (Switch only) _____

Signature _____   Tel. No. _____

NAME _____

ADDRESS _____

_____

_____

* Delete as applicable (price includes postage – airmail for Europe/world).

SURVIVAL BOOKS ON FRANCE

Buying a Home in France is essential reading for anyone planning to purchase property in France and is designed to guide you through the property jungle and make it a pleasant and enjoyable experience. Most importantly, it's packed with vital information to help you **avoid the sort of disasters that can turn your dream home into a nightmare!**

Living and Working in France is essential reading for anyone planning to live or work in France, including retirees, visitors, business people, migrants and students. It's packed with important and useful information designed to help you **avoid costly mistakes and save both time and money.**

The Alien's Guide to France provides an 'alternative' look at life in the 'Hexagon' and will help you to appreciate the peculiarities (in both senses) of its inhabitants.

The Best Places to Buy a Home in France is the most comprehensive and up-to-date homebuying guide to France, containing detailed regional guides to help you choose the ideal location for your home.

Lifelines books are essential guides to specific regions of France, containing everything you need to know about local life. Titles in the series currently include Dordogne/Lot, and Poitou-Charentes.

Renovating & Maintaining Your French Home is the ultimate guide to renovating and maintaining your dream home in France, including practical advice and time- and money-saving tips.

Foreigners in France: Triumphs & Disasters is a collection of real-life experiences of people who have emigrated to France, providing a 'warts and all' picture of everyday life in all parts of the country.

Order your copies today by phone, fax, mail or e-mail from: Survival Books, PO Box 146, Wetherby, West Yorks. LS23 6XZ, United Kingdom (☎/▤ +44 (0)1937-843523, ✉ orders@ survivalbooks.net, 💻 www.survivalbooks.net).